Agents of Change

Agents of Change

Studies on the Policy Environment
for Small Enterprise
in Africa

Edited by
Philip English
and
Georges Hénault

INTERNATIONAL DEVELOPMENT RESEARCH CENTRE
in association with
INTERMEDIATE TECHNOLOGY PUBLICATIONS

Published in Canada
by the International Development Research Centre
PO Box 8500, Ottawa, ON, Canada K1G 3H9

and

Published in the United Kingdom
by Intermediate Technology Publications Ltd
103-105 Southampton Row, London WC1B 4HH, UK

English, P
Hénault, G.

Agents of change : studies on the policy environment for small enterprise in Africa. Ottawa, ON, IDRC, 1995. xx + 353 p. : ill.

/Small enterprises/, /national policy/, /Africa/ — /policy making/, /private sector/, /fiscal policy/, /regulations/, /financial administration/, /financial institutions/, /innovations/, /competitiveness/, /case studies/, /conference reports/, references.

A CIP record for this book is available from the British Library.

UDC: 334.746.4(6)

A microfiche edition is available.

The paper used in this book is recycled as well as recyclable. All inks and coatings are vegetable-based products.

ISBN: 0-88936-726-4 (IDRC)
ISBN: 1 85339 272 3 (IT Publications)

CONTENTS

Part III. Regulatory Reform

Part IV. Financial Services

Part V. Innovations for Increasing Competitiveness

Part VI. Conclusion

FOREWORD

Donor collaboration, cynics sometimes say, is an oxymoron. There is, however, one example of donor collaboration that is still going strong after about 15 years — the Committee of Donor Agencies for Small Enterprise Development. Initiated by the World Bank in 1979, this committee now includes 17 bilateral agencies, 15 multilateral institutions, and 2 other international development organizations.

As befits a group focused on small enterprise, it is informal, with no legal status. But the committee seems to serve a need, as donor representatives keep coming back. The committee's objective is to promote small enterprise in developing countries by

- exchanging information on the programs of participating agencies;
- sharing experiences and lessons learned in project implementation; and
- coordinating efforts in this field.

The committee has been particularly active in the first two areas. There have been regular annual meetings, nine conferences have been organized, and the *Journal of Small Enterprise Development* was launched in 1990. Attempts at better coordination at the country level are somewhat more problematic because they depend a lot on the initiative of individual field officers. But, as one of our members said at the close of the most recent conference, one of the principal ways in which donors can serve as a catalyst in small-enterprise promotion is through the transmission of ideas. In this respect, the committee has undoubtedly been a success.

Our second conference was held in Abidjan, Côte d'Ivoire, in 1983, and had a regional focus on Africa. After various, more thematic conferences, we again turned our attention to this troubled continent when we met in The Hague in 1991. This meeting was seen as an exploratory step on the way to a larger conference to be held, once again, in Africa in 1993. In each case, the emphasis was on the policy environment because of its crucial importance and past neglect. The best papers from the conference in The Hague were published in *Small Enterprise and Changing Policies: Structural Adjustment, Financial Policy and Assistance Programmes in Africa*, edited by Helmsing and Kolstee (1993).

That conference was especially notable for involving a large number of African speakers. As Helmsing and Kolstee (1993, p. 6) emphasize, "it has become painfully clear that there can be no major progress in tackling Africa's development dilemmas without strong and clear participation by African policymakers, practitioners and researchers." Encouraged by its success in The Hague in 1991, the Committee chose to extend this approach in Abidjan in 1993 by moving the conference back to Africa and by further limiting the role and number of non-Africans.

At least two other modifications were adopted for 1993. First, it was agreed that there should be a greater diversity of participants. Whereas the conference in The Hague in 1991 was dominated by researchers, this one would have a greater share of speakers and listeners from governments, banks, nongovernmental organizations, and private enterprise itself. In this way, it would be firmly anchored in the reality of current experience and, hopefully, would also include some genuine agents of change.

Another significant modification adopted for 1993 was a change in focus — away from the definition of appropriate policy and toward the process of designing and implementing such policy. It was felt that at least the basic principles were fairly well understood, but somehow they were not finding their way into policy reform. The conference proposed to explore the ways in which some countries manage to galvanize the necessary political will and what obstacles continue to block the path for others.

The conference was a truly collaborative effort. Its agenda and objectives were initially discussed in the committee's annual meeting in 1992. A subcommittee was formed, and it met again in March 1993. From then, the Canadian International Development Agency (CIDA) and the International Development Research Centre (IDRC) took the lead, with the assistance of Georges Hénault and other members of the subcommittee. Eighteen donors contributed to the financing and helped in almost as many different ways. The list of invited delegates was put together through a collaborative process. Even the title was chosen by committee (and it probably shows it).

Yet, somehow it all came together in Abidjan in late November 1993. Some late arrivals were moved to other hotels because another conference got some of our rooms. And there was a danger that the whole country would be closed down with the imminent death of its long-standing president, Félix Houphouet-Boigny. But at the close of the conference, everyone seemed to agree that it had met its objectives.

Perhaps policy and program design dominated the discussion, more so than process, but it became clear that many of the basic principles of policy and program design are still being debated by practitioners. Problems tended to figure more prominently than success stories, but this is part of the challenge facing Africa.

The discussion was led by Africans, the debate was lively, information was shared, and new contacts were made. And there were certainly some agents of change in the room. We hope that as a result of the publication of these proceedings, those who were unable to attend will agree with us that sometimes donor collaboration does work.

Philip English, IDRC
Gilles Lessard, CIDA

PREFACE

Before discussing the objectives, structure, approach, and content of these proceedings, I would like to place this work in the context of the issues surrounding African development.

The issue of the small-enterprise sector in African development

Social and economic development on the continent of Africa occurs through the private sector (anything that is not public), whether this involves cooperatives in the areas of production, marketing, and credit, traditional associations, or even micro-enterprises, small and medium-size enterprises (SMEs), large-scale enterprises, and multinationals.

Historical overview: development policies that tend to exclude small enterprises

For more than 25 years, African countries, as well as large international agencies, have emphasized the vitality of economic agents and their spirit of initiative and entrepreneurship. The decade 1980–1990 was declared the Industrial Development Decade for Africa. In 1980, the heads of African states adopted the Monrovia Declaration, which was the basis for the Lagos Action Plan (OAU 1980). The 1981 World Bank report, *Accelerated Development in Sub-Saharan Africa: Indicative Action Plan* (Berg 1981), emphasized human resources and productive sectors in a regional and macroeconomic context. The report defined industry as the motor of development and had only a brief, half-page discussion of entrepreneurial spirit. The contribution of SMEs to the economic vitality of Africa was not accorded any special significance. This is puzzling, because it seems that the economic growth of Western countries, especially after the Second World War, has been due to the work of the SME sector. Another 8 years passed before the World Bank

(1989a) said, in one of its long-term prospective studies, that there was a need to foster entrepreneurship to ensure sustainable growth in sub-Saharan Africa. The significance of small enterprises was finally recognized in the examples in Chapter 6 of the study, particularly the cases of Kenya and Côte d'Ivoire.

This reluctance to explicitly encourage the SME sector could undoubtedly be explained by a certain ideological unwillingness to support the private sector with public funds. For reasons of efficiency, management training has been aimed at officials of cooperatives, nongovernmental organizations (NGOs), and even state-owned corporations. From funding large projects managed by large-scale enterprises we have moved on to microprojects driven by the momentum of the informal sector.

Structural adjustment programs that reinvent the relevance of the small-enterprise sector

International cooperation policies started to promote small enterprises during a time of profound change in the role of the state in African economies. The calls for "more government" in the 1970s and "less government" the 1980s were replaced by calls for "better government" in the 1990s. Structural adjustments and the trend toward privatization pushed the bloated public service in African countries (which acted in a somewhat reactionary and defensive manner) to downsize and to create enterprises to give their departing members employment. There now appears to be a consensus on the validity of actively fostering business as a source of economic growth. Has business not gained its credentials by stimulating African economies?

The pluralism of Africa

With these changes in the role of the state in the economy, people became more acutely aware of the disparities between African countries. Although most African nations had clearly defined developmental objectives by the end of the decade, a number of differences still remained in the way policies affecting entrepreneurship were implemented (Commonwealth Secretariat 1991). To this we might add that African countries are very heterogeneous to begin with.

Without dwelling on the linguistic differences between English- and French-speaking countries in Africa, one may recall that, in the view of Helmsing and Kolstee (1993), some countries, such as Angola, Malawi, and Mozambique, have a small industrial base, whereas others, such as Côte d'Ivoire, Mauritius, and Zimbabwe, have a substantial industrial base to draw on.

A more integrated and holistic approach to small-business development has been adopted as a result of the growing awareness of the importance of the private sector in Africa and in recognition of the diversity of the continent. As evidence of this, I need only mention the creation in the past few years of a number of networks linking African organizations devoted to small-business development; between August 1993 and January 1994 there were also some seminars and conferences on the problems of the small-enterprise sector.

Small business: from the periphery to the centre of African development policies

States and international organizations now agree on giving priority to the needs of the private sector.

Also, enterprises are organizing into networks, taking control of their own destiny. The number of meetings, conferences, symposiums, and other seminars is increasing, allowing for a dialogue among the continent's economic partners to identify common solutions.

Two examples of networks created to exchange information on increasing the efficiency of African enterprises eloquently illustrate the dynamism of the private sector on the African continent:

- The West Africa Business Network is an association of business people in the subregion; it publishes a bulletin under the aegis of the African Development Bank (ADB 1993).

- The entrepreneurship network of the Université des réseaux d'expression française (UREF) brings together researchers and representatives of the private sector to improve their knowledge of the problems facing African enterprise, particularly in the French-speaking countries. The proceedings of two of UREF's conferences have been published (Hénault and M'Rabet 1990; Ponson and Schaan 1992). The proceedings of another of its conferences are in press.

I can mention a few recent conferences and workshops to illustrate the spirit of the times. These conferences and workshops helped us define the objectives of our meeting in Abidjan in December 1993.

- In August 1993, a technical conference was held in Nairobi, Kenya, on the importance of capital markets in Africa (Mensah 1994). In fact, the channeling of the local economy and investment funding constitutes a major challenge that the 10 stock markets in Africa must face.

- In October 1993, the Sahel Club of the Organisation for Economic Co-operation and Development (OECD) organized workshops in Accra, Ghana, and these were attended by representatives of the private sector. The workshops focused on four major themes concerning business development in West Africa: (1) financial restructuring, (2) the development of an entrepreneurial class, (3) competitiveness among businesses, and (4) improved dialogue with the state (OECD 1994).

- In January 1994, the International Labour Office (ILO) and its section for the development of businesses and cooperatives organized the eighth regional African conference in Mauritius. The theme of the conference was Entrepreneurship and Small Business Development in African Urban and Rural Sectors (ILO 1993).

Diagnosis and common solutions by members of the Committee of Donor Agencies for Small Business Development

In recent decades, regulatory policies and frameworks unfavourable to business development impeded efforts to assist SMEs. More recently, researchers and entrepreneurs have stressed the importance of suitable policies for assisting small enterprises. The elements of this type of policy are well known. What is lacking is the know-how to develop and implement strategies in cooperation with all concerned.

Many African decision-makers would like to know how the private sector, particularly SMEs, could play a greater role in the economic development of their countries. In many cases, liberalization has created a free-market environment, more favourable to the private sector. There are fears, however, that without support and access to ample resources during the adjustment period, the SMEs will be unable to succeed. The choice of Africa as a location and focus of this conference is justified by the extent of the changes occurring on this continent and by the need to strengthen institutions supporting small enterprises in Africa.

As the headquarters of the ADB is in Abidjan, this was the most logical choice for our conference, for the same reason as it was 10 years earlier, in 1983, for the ADB-hosted symposium on small-enterprise development (organized by our committee). During the opening session, A.O. Sangowawa, Vice-President of ADB, was pleased to mention "the historical importance" and contemporary relevance of this theme. Ten years later, he presented a very interesting diagnosis of the difficulties facing SMEs in Africa:

> ...small enterprises have to be fostered because of their great potential and value in creating employment, achieving equitable income distribution, alleviating poverty, building up local technological base, promoting participation of vulnerable groups, particularly women, in the development process, providing training ground for entrepreneurial and managerial skills, providing opportunities for use of own capital resources, and acting as ancillaries to large-scale enterprises. Although many African governments have realized the importance of small enterprises and the need to develop them few have launched comprehensive and effective policies to promote them. The lack of an appropriate institutional framework and of adequate infrastructures, inadequate financing schemes and inefficient information systems are some of the important obstacles which still hamper the organized development of small enterprises in Africa.

Members of the Committee of Donor Agencies for Small Enterprise Development believe that the governments, entrepreneurs, chambers of industry and commerce, NGOs, financial intermediaries, and other key participants (the donors) could do more to promote SMEs. To find the criteria for success and avoid any problems, an effort must be made to exchange knowledge and to learn from experience.

Objectives of the conference and of the proceedings

The conference organizing committee identified the following four categories of objectives:

1. Share know-how on developing and carrying out policies and programs for financing SMEs.

2. Stress the role of the public and private sectors in creating an environment to foster the emergence and blossoming of small business.

3. Help coordinate the implementation of action programs for small-enterprise development in several countries.

4. Create a forum for sharing the experiences of English-speaking and French-speaking African countries.

The objectives of the conference proceedings are obviously those of the conference. However, it would have been difficult to fit the great variety of texts presented by some 200 participants from 24 African countries into a single book. Constraints on the size of the published proceedings made it necessary to limit the number of presentations included. This required a difficult and stringent selection process, obviously based on quality but also on the need for a thematic, regional, and linguistic balance. This was the reason why, for example, the selection committee had to decide, with regret, not to include papers on experiences in other major regions of the world.

The selection committee attempted to identify not only the most revealing experiences, but also those that would be useful to any country or region of Africa.

Structure and content of the proceedings

The proceedings follow the same plan as the conference. Its main theme — expressing the contribution to many debates on the problems facing SMEs — is the role of agents of change in developing and implementing policies.

Part I is the introduction, bringing together viewpoints from the private sector, the public service, and international organizations.

Part II discusses the process of designing and implementing national policies that make SMEs one of the priorities of African development.

Part III stresses regulatory reforms in this context, notably the way in which the legal, regulatory, and fiscal framework affects the dynamics of business growth.

Part IV deals with the agents of change in financial services. Whether from formal or informal financial systems, working and investment funds for African small enterprises are essential to ensuring balanced growth.

Part V discusses innovations to improve the competitive potential of small enterprises. These innovations are in the areas of technology, the grouping of small enterprises into export consortia or corporate associations, and, finally, the training of entrepreneurs.

Part VI is the conclusion. It presents a summary of the presentations that could not be included (because of the constraints previously mentioned) and the debates and discussions following the various presentations.

Although I am aware of the limitations of this type of work and the fact that much remains to be done, I hope that these proceedings accurately reflect the richness and variety of the ideas discussed during three intensive days in 1993. I am convinced that this conference will raise many questions and offer some answers to the problems of SMEs on the African continent.

Georges Hénault, *University of Ottawa*

ACKNOWLEDGMENTS

One cannot acknowledge those who have contributed to this publication without expressing gratitude to those who helped make the conference a success. The list is long.

It begins with the co-chair of the conference-organizing subcommittee, Gilles Lessard of the Canadian International Development Agency (CIDA), who took the lead in coordinating this conference and maintained his remarkable cool throughout the many ups and downs. Next is the co-chair of the Committee of Donor Agencies for Small Enterprise Development, Biff Steel (World Bank), who framed the initial conference proposal and delivered the keynote address. The list continues with the members of the subcommittee who helped us plan the conference: Marilyn Carr (UNIFEM), Michael Farbman (United States Agency for International Development), Bert Helmsing (Institute of Social Studies, The Hague), Franz van Rijn (Dutch Ministry of Foreign Affairs), Leila Webster (World Bank), and David Wright (Overseas Development Administration, United Kingdom).

In Ottawa–Hull, Daniel Lussier and Jean-Baptiste Sawadogo provided critical organizational support at CIDA; Marleny Tanaka and Margaret Langill, at the International Development Research Centre (IDRC), were very helpful, particularly in making travel arrangements for participants. In Abidjan, the Canadian embassy was a great help. Its greatest contribution was in identifying Victor Luboyeski, who, with a team of assistants, may just have saved the day by supervising all the logistical arrangements for the conference.

We thank all those who prepared and presented papers at the conference. In addition, we appreciated the willingness of some of these same people and others to act as chairpersons and rapporteurs at the various sessions. Their names are listed, along with those of the participants, in Appendix 1. Jake Levitsky, the former chair of our donor committee, contributed in many ways: providing an oral summary of the conference at its close and a written version soon after, as well as advice in the editing of this volume.

We wish to acknowledge the assistance of Bill Carman and his colleagues at IDRC in preparing these proceedings for publication.

Finally, the list would be incomplete without the donor agencies that financed the conference (see Appendix 2). ✻

Part 1

Introduction

OPENING ADDRESS

Ferdinand Kacou Angora
Minister of Industry and Trade,
Côte d'Ivoire

Ministers, ambassadors, representatives of international development institutions, Mr Chairman of the Committee of Donor Agencies for the Development of Small Enterprises, representatives of the donor agencies, conference participants, honoured guests, ladies and gentlemen, I want to take this opportunity, on behalf of my government, to extend the warmest welcome of Côte d'Ivoire to all the distinguished participants in this high-level conference on the development of small and medium-size enterprises (SMEs) and to thank the donor agencies who organized the event in cooperation with the African Development Bank (ADB).

Let me say to the Chairman of the Committee of Donor Agencies for the Development of Small Enterprises what a pleasure it is that the committee chose Côte d'Ivoire to host the work of this conference and what an honour it is to have such high-calibre participants gathered here from all corners of the world to discuss this complex and timely topic.

Mr Chairman, I want to thank the committee on behalf of my government for this significant show of confidence and friendship at a time when Africa's political and economic systems are under such strain.

Our meeting, our discussions, and our thoughts are going to revolve around the theme "Agents of Change in the Design and Implementation of Policies for SMEs in Africa." For Côte d'Ivoire and for most African countries south of the Sahara, one could not choose a better topic to mobilize business leaders to assist in developing Africa. This choice of topic is an eloquent testimony to the importance we all attach to the role of SMEs in the development of our economies.

How can one speak of growth of any kind without enterprise? How can one imagine development without enterprise? Ladies and gentlemen, dear guests, we all recognize that enterprise is the very solution to the problems of economic and social development.

Yet we must remember that the development of our economies is a task beyond meeting the requirements for growth: it is also necessary to meet basic human needs for food, health, and education and to overcome the inequalities, unemployment, and poverty that have caused our countries such concern during this decade.

When we think about adapting our economic policies to the realities of today's world, in this era of political and economic liberalism, we must recognize that the only way to grapple effectively with the problems of development is by harnessing private initiative as the engine of growth. If we look at the development process as a straight line into the future, we can see that the small enterprise of today, whether in the formal or the informal economy, can become the medium-scale firm or the big business of tomorrow.

This linear idea of progress may seem simplistic to some, but small business is the seed from which economic progress can grow and spread out to all sectors of society. No one doubts any more the role that small business can play in developing economies like ours — creating an industrial fabric, providing employment and engaging our people in productive activity, slowing the exodus from the countryside, and promoting rural development.

To be more specific, experience has shown us that small business has the following characteristics:

- Small business is more open to imagination, which is the key to inventiveness.
- Small business helps integrate research policies into an overall business strategy by promoting the spread of knowledge to the various pillars of enterprise.
- Small business fosters creative intuition to make up for its lack of resources.

I am afraid that in some political and academic circles, there are those who still believe in the discredited Schumpeter theory, that only big business can produce innovation.

Of course, it is true that big firms still do the bulk of spending on research and development (R&D), but no one can point to any direct correlation between the size of a firm and its research activity. Indeed, studies in Great Britain, Sweden, and France show that the small firms are the innovators. After all, in regions of dynamic growth like Silicon Valley and Southeast Asia, the SMEs do the best research.

Private initiative, innovation, and imagination are the keys to development, and the encouragement of SMEs is one way to get those keys. It is high time we admitted that in most of our countries, our efforts to encourage SMEs have fallen far short of their mark.

In this connection, ladies and gentlemen, allow me to say a few words about the efforts that Côte d'Ivoire has made to encourage small business during the last few decades. The two decades after independence saw a series of efforts to create a technical-support infrastructure for the development of SMEs. In 1968, the Office for the Promotion of Côte d'Ivoire Enterprise (l'Office de promotion de l'enterprise ivoirienne [OPEI]) was created, which operated like an industrial and commercial Crown corporation. In 1982, this became to the National Enterprise Promotion Assistance Centre (Centre d'assistance à la promotion de l'enterprise nationale [CAPEN]), an administrative agency.

The year 1968 also saw the creation of the Credit Guarantee Fund for Côte d'Ivoire Enterprises (Fonds de garantie des crédits aux enterprises ivoiriennes [FGCEI]), which was intended to help SMEs obtain short-, medium-, and long-term bank credit. Two years later, in 1970, a special fund for SMEs was created to supplement the proprietor's initial investment by 15%. The FGCEI and the special fund were subsequently dissolved — the FGCEI, in 1981; the special fund, in 1982. From 1968 to 1982, though, about 300 SMEs were created, with an investment of about 7 billion XOF (in 1994, 570 CFA francs [XOF] = 1 United States dollar [USD]).

I should also mention the major role played by the development banks created by the government. The banks, which have since been dissolved, were crucial to the creation of SMEs in Côte d'Ivoire.

CAPEN was the last agency created by the government to promote SMEs, and it was dissolved in 1992. With its mandate to carry out assistance policies for SMEs, it promoted the creation of 46 small businesses in Abidjan alone between 1982 and 1989, for a total investment of 1.7 billion XOF.

To create a sound business climate, the government has set up industrial and handicraft zones for SMEs and has given them tax and customs privileges under the investment code. The government has also taken special steps to help the marketing efforts of small enterprises.

The government is now paying particular attention to the artisan and handicrafts sector and recently set up six regional technical training centres for artisans and for entrepreneurs in the informal sector.

The government also conducts many programs and pilot projects jointly with various bilateral and multilateral aid agencies. One example is the National Marketing Assistance Program (le Programme national d'assistance aux commerçants ivoriens [PNCI]) set up with the help of the Aid and Cooperation Fund (Fonds d'aide et de coopération). Another is the Trades Enterprise Promotion project carried out with the help of the United Nations Development Programme (UNDP) and the International Labour Office (ILO). This project has led to the creation of more than 30 regional firms in the forestry, construction, and agro-industrial sectors. Yet another example is the PDU3 project, supported by the World Bank and supervised by the French Association of Volunteers for Progress (Association française des volontaires du progrès [AFVP], an NGO). The purpose of this project was to measure the effects of credit on development in the nonstructured sector.

So, ladies and gentlemen, there you have a brief overview of the efforts the government of Côte d'Ivoire has made to encourage small business. Côte d'Ivoire has been tirelessly pursuing these efforts. Yet now, we are determined to replace the models we used during the first two decades to assist small business. Now we favour a participatory approach, where the government, instead of acting alone, will be a partner to the private sector while continuing to meet its responsibilities for designing sectoral policies and creating the proper fiscal, legal, and institutional framework for private initiative to flourish.

The participatory approach is well under way in Côte d'Ivoire. A good example is the public-sector–private-sector liaison committee that Côte d'Ivoire created as an instrument for real dialogue and cooperation on all questions affecting business.

One of the concrete things this committee has already done is to present proposals to the government for dealing with the problem of fraud. ✻

Views from the Private Sector

Alain Bambara
President, Cosmivoire, Abidjan,
Côte d'Ivoire

The entrepreneurial spirit is more or less developed in all human societies. In Africa, the significant role played by our artisans bears witness to the fact that this spirit exists among us too. However, consumption patterns, the absence of a money-based economy, and colonization have fostered the development of a race of consumer agents, to the detriment of the entrepreneurial spirit. It was, therefore, natural that all entrepreneurial initiatives were taken exclusively by expatriates, whether these expatriates were from Europe, the Middle East, or even the Sahel. The needs are so tremendous, however, that there is and always will be room for initiative.

I started in a heavily dominated sector in my own society and was forced to strengthen my national base with the aim of conquering the regional and, in part, the international market. In fact, we must now acknowledge that the economy is being globalized and that development is likewise being globalized.

From the dawn of independence, the leaders of Côte d'Ivoire decided to promote private enterprise by establishing offices for this purpose. Today, we are forced to conclude that all these structures failed, and we have a right to ask how this happened. Some people have questioned our culture, that is, African culture. They believe that a purported absence of individual and collective personal standards could provide the beginning of an explanation. Others, who are more pessimistic, think that living and climatic conditions make it difficult to produce lasting results. We can list all the national, regional, and continental structures that have now disappeared, such as the Industrial Development Bank of Côte d'Ivoire, the Credit

Bank of Côte d'Ivoire, the Côte d'Ivoire Enterprise Credit Guarantee Fund, the Fund for Loan Rebates to Small and Medium-Sized Enterprises, the National Agricultural Development Bank, BICT, UAM and its special structures, CAMO and its special structures, and so on.

Do the funding structures blame their demise on SMES that do not honour their commitments? The list of donors is very long. In view of all the global structures created to foster development of the private sector in Africa, why is there a discrepancy between the means available and the slim results obtained?

Putting Africans to work is a considerable investment. Because these funds are not available on easy terms, African states have chosen to become economic operators themselves. African states are turning to the private sector and transferring this heavy responsibility to it, and this is going on at a time when the private sector, in its national make-up, is nonexistent and when the return on foreign investment is no longer as high as it was at the dawn of independence. All this presents a sizeable challenge.

To learn the criteria for success, that is, for profit and enrichment, and to create an environment that promotes the emergence and expansion of the private sector are noble endeavours. It is a problem of culture. In fact, according to Babacar N'diaye, the President of the African Development Bank, the problem of culture arises as soon as people are asked to follow strategies and policies for the economic and social development of their country. In our enterprises, we are experiencing some difficulties in communicating the need for preventive maintenance to safeguard the means of production, and occasionally it seems that the concept of amortization is a difficult one to understand.

The World Bank claims that Africa, more than any other continent, has placed its fortunes in foreign investments. In Africa, unlike in Mauritius, everybody believes in the principle that a project started by an individual will fail. All the pitfalls and difficulties are presented to the individual as insurmountable. Individuals are told that the sector they wish to start their business in is dominated by expatriates and that they do not have a chance. They are advised to go and look for more profitable sectors, as if such sectors existed and had been overlooked by the expatriates.

Many of our administrative officials lack the mentality to encourage others to venture into entrepreneurship. The officials even start to smother enterprise by the way in which they exercise their authority. Such behaviour quickly discourages less assertive spirits. Other people better placed to describe this than I am will talk about financial and regulatory harassment.

I can only say that such harassment is part of the enterprise environment in Africa and that the entrepreneur must cope with it and find a way out. For some time, of course, our governments, in their attempts to disengage themselves from the productive sector, have been taking measures to improve competitiveness and to make the institutional and regulatory framework less restrictive. If such measures can be improved, the conditions for starting up and expanding SMEs will also be improved.

Insufficient capital and security are often mentioned as a problem for SMEs. It is a fact. I remember once applying for credit at the National Agricultural Development Bank for my pineapple plantation. At that time, this bank asked me to put up my house in town as equity for my plantation. Often, the real estate of the promoter does not constitute adequate security.

Furthermore, I have just applied to the International Finance Corporation of the World Bank for credit and received it. The investment agreement is an 82-page document with 36 pages of conditions to be met to obtain the loan. You can easily imagine the difficulties that an SME would experience if it found itself in my position.

It is generally agreed that investment in Africa is more costly than elsewhere. Soap-making equipment ordered from an Italian supplier by a small French enterprise is 30% cheaper than the freight-on-board factory price for the same equipment ordered on the same day from the same supplier by Cosmivoire for Africa. Consequently, the cost of creating employment in African countries is exorbitant.

Family pressure and cultural values in Africa have been described by great thinkers, such as Henri Bourgoin and Daniel Etounga Manguele, as having negative and restrictive effects on entrepreneurship.

I believe that others are better qualified to speak on this subject than I. I will only stress that the all-powerful state's practice of placing orders with SMEs that are in debt and cash-starved and then failing to pay them is working toward the disappearance of a sector that the state itself wishes to promote.

Finally, some people have emphasized the lack of entrepreneurship; I take this to mean formal and organized entrepreneurship because the informal sector is growing rapidly and many Africans seem to find satisfaction in it. I believe that the informal sector results from the development of the formal urban sector. I also believe that the informal sector is the reservoir for future promoters of the formal sector. I notice that women as heads of enterprises are predominant in the informal sector. Women represent more than half the population, and this should permit them to contribute more to economic and social development than they have in the past. I, therefore, hope that the informal sector will no longer be regarded as the way all the evils of the formal sector reach us. ❋

Keynote Address

William F. Steel
Principal Industrial Economist, Africa Technical Department,
World Bank, Washington, DC, USA

Private enterprise in many Asian countries has contributed to growth rates in the order of 6% per annum, giving rise to the "Asian miracle." The conditions facing private entrepreneurs in many African countries, however, make simply surviving a miracle. The challenge before us is to turn the miracle of survival into the miracle of growth by investigating how government policymakers and regulators, financial systems, and other agencies can themselves become the agents of change to support small entrepreneurs in transforming the economies of Africa.

Hence, the underlying rationale for this conference is that Africa's entrepreneurs **can** be agents of change and growth, but they cannot do it alone. We need to learn lessons from successful cases of change — from Asia and Latin America, as well as from Africa — not just what has been accomplished, but who did it, how, and why. The focus should be on the **process**: what conditions stimulate and empower people to make changes that help small enterprises fulfill their potential contribution to employment and income generation? This overview discusses the rationale for the specific subtopics of the conference and how they fit into the framework of enterprise development.

The matrix of INs

The conference title is "Agents of Change in Policy Development and Implementation for Small Enterprises." So there is a policy axis, and there is an implementation axis. Within these axes, the forces of change can be found in six areas, what I will call the "six INs" of small enterprise development: INvestors,

ENterprises, INcentives, INputs, ENvironment, and INstitutions. As shown in Fig. 1, the INs may be grouped into a matrix with three dimensions:

- The central dimension is the **enterprise** itself, and it depends first and foremost on the investor.
- The second dimension is the **markets** in which a firm operates. Factors of this dimension are the incentives that determine costs and benefits (profits); and the inputs needed for the production process.
- The third dimension is the **support system** that is available to help an enterprise solve problems and to facilitate the working of markets. Factors of this dimension are the business environment and a wide range of institutions.

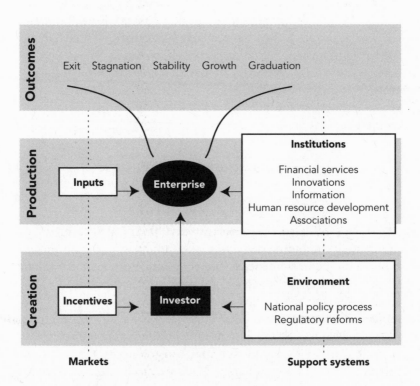

Figure 1. Agents of change in small-scale enterprise development.

The third dimension — support systems — is the principal focus of this conference. The policy axis cuts across the lower half of Fig. 1, affecting investment in the creation of enterprises through incentives and the business environment. The implementation axis cuts across the centre, affecting firms' ability to produce competitively through access to needed inputs, finance, technology, information, skills, and other business services.

The result of these forces determines the outcome for the enterprise. Outcomes can range from stagnation or exit to stability, growth, or even "graduation" to a new level of size or technology (top of Fig. 1). The conference focuses on the process of change in the institutional and policy environment — in particular, who can make such changes and how — that leads to increase in the rates of enterprise creation, survival, growth, and graduation.

What follows are some "stylized facts" for each of the six INs in terms of the changes that have already occurred and the present status of small enterprises in Africa. These characterizations refer broadly to countries that have already embarked on an economic reform or structural adjustment program; however, the specifics vary greatly from country to country.

The market dimension

Incentives

Incentives refer to the determinants of the profitability of investment, including demand for output, prices of outputs and inputs, and taxes. In general, the economic policy environment in the post-independence period was not favourable to small enterprises. Incentives favoured large state and foreign investments over small private ones. Large import-substitution industries received protection, and pricing policies were unfavourable to agriculture. Because most small enterprises and microenterprises are located in rural areas, policies that restrained agricultural incomes limited the demand base for small, off-farm employment activities.

Inputs

Imported inputs have historically been licenced or directly allocated by governments, and finance has been heavily controlled. Small-scale enterprises (SSEs) typically lack access, whereas large enterprises have often received preferential access. Besides finance and foreign exchange, input controls have often covered commodities such as sugar, flour, and wood.

There have already been substantial changes that allow market forces to more freely determine prices and access to inputs. Structural adjustment programs, however, have had both positive and negative effects on the small private sector (Helmsing and Kolstee 1993). On the positive side, they have opened up new opportunities, particularly for exports, and removed the dominance of the state — both as a direct competitor and in determining the allocation of resources. In particular, liberalization of input markets gives SSEs greater access to resources. And greater attention to agriculture is helping to restore the rural demand base for goods and services supplied by small enterprises. Many small enterprises have been able to adapt and even flourish, especially in countries with growing economies, which have made it easy for smaller firms to export.

On the other hand, growing competition has made it harder for other small enterprises to survive and grow. This is largely a function of the rapid growth in the number of new labour-force entrants, accelerated by downsizing of the public sector. Competition is especially a problem for microenterprises, where barriers to entry are low. There is also competition from imports as restrictions are lifted and a country's foreign-exchange earnings or aid receipts grow to allow low-cost imports of competing finished products, not only inputs. (This has been less of a problem in countries that have used their exchange rates to provide extra protection for domestic value added.)

In sum, the playing field has been leveled considerably. Yet many observers feel that small private enterprises are not adequately equipped to play and are still at a disadvantage in the game of producing competitively. Small enterprises exist in an environment of economic change — whether there are structural adjustment reforms or not — and our goal is to enable small enterprises to adapt to and benefit from these changes as much as possible. Let us look more closely at the agents of those changes.

The enterprise dimension (part I)

Investors

The central agents of change are the investors or entrepreneurs themselves — risk-takers who are able to identify and manage profitable investments and who provide employment, both to themselves and, if successful, to growing numbers of other workers.

At one time it was often said that Africa lacked entrepreneurs. That myth has been laid to rest: for example, studies under the Growth and Equity Through Microenterprise Investments and Institutions (GEMINI) program, sponsored by the United States Agency for International Development (USAID), and studies under the Regional Program on Enterprise Development (RPED), sponsored by the World Bank and a number of the donor agencies that are also responsible for this conference, show that many people are willing to invest their own savings to go into business. Whether these entrepreneurs can mobilize sufficient capital and skills to establish large industries is another story, but the entrepreneurial spirit is certainly there and documented. Now, how can we best bring it out and nurture it? Before completing the discussion of the enterprise dimension, let us first examine the support systems that can either nurture or constrain entrepreneurs.

The support system dimension

Business environment

Political and social attitudes toward profit-seeking in private businesses can determine whether those with entrepreneurial potential will come forward. If profit-making endeavours are not rewarded and respected, assistance in entrepreneurship development will not get very far. Broader policy measures to change attitudes will be needed. Hence, the second agents of change, besides the investors themselves, are the national leaders and politicians, who set the tone. That is why this conference begins by examining ways in which national leaders have incorporated or can incorporate small business into the policy agenda.

Negative attitudes are often manifested in a restrictive regulatory environment — the second specific issue examined at the conference. Indeed, the high cost of complying with regulatory policies may constitute a powerful barrier to the growth and graduation of formal SMEs, encouraging firms to stay very small and informal to avoid the regulations.

Note that administrative officials in the agencies charged with implementing policies can be agents who resist change, especially liberalization measures that take them out of the picture. Creating a "one-stop shop" doesn't do much good if the people who mind the shop lack the power or incentive to make final decisions. Thus, it is important to go beyond broad issues of national policy formulation and regulatory reform and propose practical implementation methods that actually change the behaviour of the administrators.

Institutions

The term "institutions" covers a broad range of implementing agencies. It is useful to distinguish facilitating institutions, which influence how well markets work to provide inputs, from assistance institutions, which support entrepreneurs usually on a one-to-one basis or through interest groups.

In designing institutional development programs, it is important that we take a systems approach — that is, recognize that it is insufficient to develop one aspect, such as credit, in isolation without considering the functioning of the system within which it operates. The issues are complex, and actions in one area may have unintended consequences in another. For this reason, policy changes that address fundamental problems are often preferable to direct interventions that introduce new distortions.

Financial system

The financial system is one of the most important facilitating institutions. A responsive financial system is widely regarded as critical for expansion of the small-enterprise sector. However, because banks in developing countries generally have little interest in or experience providing term loans to small enterprises, a key question is whether it is more effective to encourage greater interest by banks in SSE clients or to facilitate the emergence of alternative institutions and instruments that would be more responsive to the needs of SSEs.

Liberalizing financially repressive financial policies — controlled interest rates and directed credit — has not in practice proven sufficient to substantially improve the access of SSEs to formal financial institutions. (Where financial policies such as fixed or subsidized interest rates reduce the incentive to lend to small firms, policy reforms are the first priority.) The failure of banking systems to act as agents of change with respect to small enterprises in Africa can be attributed to several factors:

- their historical orientation toward the import trade, large clients, and the government;
- the restructuring that they are going through to clean up their portfolios;
- tight money policies that limit the volume of credit;
- government borrowing that crowds out the private sector; and
- the failure to introduce technologies that would reduce high transaction costs and risks in small loans and substitute for the absence of collateral.

Fortunately, as well as innovative, specialized banks, many other institutions are experimenting with SSE finance. Such institutions include NGOs; informal savings collectors and lenders; self-help organizations; nonbanking financial institutions; donor agencies; and suppliers and others who provide trade credit.

One important conclusion of those who have taken a systems approach to financial development is that there has been too much emphasis on credit — saving is an equally important part of the system. Especially for would-be microentrepreneurs, the availability of appropriate savings mechanisms may have a wider impact than credit programs and should at least go hand-in-hand with credit.

Information plus innovation

Besides finance, other facilitating institutions contribute directly to the normal process of production and sales. In particular, small businesses find it difficult to obtain critical information on markets, inputs, and technology. Key agents of change are often those who enable firms to fill a profitable market niche or to introduce a cost-saving innovation.

Who can provide such information? In more developed countries, it is often the private-sector suppliers and buyers themselves: equipment suppliers come to sell the latest technology; buyers specify what they need to satisfy current demand. These agents have certainly been important in the newly industrializing countries of Asia.

These international buyers have recently begun coming to Africa. For example, major US department stores and importers are competing vigorously for African products — first of all for "Afrocentric" products (handicrafts and specialty clothing) but, more important, for standardized garments, especially those for which quotas make Asian suppliers relatively expensive (World Bank 1993). Supplying just 1% of the US market alone would yield 275 million USD of garment exports a year — more than 10 times what the major sub-Saharan countries are now exporting. Thus, there is a gap between this demand and what Africa is currently able to supply. Besides financing, SMEs will need both market information and innovation to meet quality and quantity requirements. Hence the need to examine what catalytic agents can help them to fill that gap.

Intermediaries that may facilitate the process include government agencies, NGOs, donors, and private foreign investors. In most African countries, intermediary agencies have a relatively important role to play in initiating change, opening up markets, and spreading information. They may have to begin as assistance agencies, with the ultimate objective of developing permanent, self-sustaining facilitating institutions that provide marketable business services.

Human resources

Assistance institutions can fill gaps, help firms cope with policy changes in transitional periods, provide services that are costly for individual firms, and build capabilities for sustained development. Perhaps the most important assistance institutions are those that build up the human resource base, especially by providing education and training. A policy-level issue is whether education and training are designed to enhance not only the capability of the workforce but also the supply of entrepreneurs and managers. The influence of culture can come in here, for example, as it influences the ability of women to enter and succeed in business.

Survey evidence shows a consistent correlation between entrepreneurs' general level of education and their success. The education system itself, therefore, is an important potential agent of change. But the evidence is not so clear on training programs, especially those driven by the perceptions of the agencies that supply them. Assistance programs in this area usually try to instill in people the particular attitudes or skills that are presumed to be lacking. A critical question is how to ensure that such programs actually respond to entrepreneurs' demands and overcome constraints.

Associations

Business associations are an important form of mutual assistance through which the entrepreneurs themselves can lobby more effectively for changes in policies, regulations, and the business environment. In the past, some governments have tended to see independent associations in an adversarial light; some countries control the dialogue through state-sponsored chambers of commerce and industry. With increasing democratization and a decreasing role for the state in the economy, associations may be better able to build a partnership with government to create a more suitable climate for private-led growth.

The enterprise dimension (part II)

Enterprise

The enterprise is the visible form through which we observe the effects of all the other forces and agents of change. Many types of enterprises can be broadly considered small: self-employment, family firms, cottage industries, artisans, microenterprises, and SMEs. Although the precise definition may vary by study, program and country, when we are designing programs we must make sure the definition is suitable for the particular operational objectives and for the likely outcome for the type of enterprise (see the range of outcomes at the top of Fig. 1).

For example, survey data show that the vast majority of microenterprises will remain micro and that many people have a business primarily for supplementary household income than for a full-time occupation. For many women who are fitting business activities around household and child-rearing responsibilities, graduation to a larger business outside the home may not suit their business plan. In such cases, the primary objective for the enterprise is to help ensure survival and security of income. Interventions geared entirely to the growth of the enterprise may fail. Nevertheless, some improvements in management techniques might improve profits without necessarily changing the scale and location of the enterprise.

On the other end of the scale, graduation to new levels of production and technology is an important part of the development process, whether for individual firms or for the overall production structure. In some Asian countries, graduation of SMEs has generated as much employment growth as the entry of very large enterprises. The questions are whether support systems are conducive to this type of dynamic growth and what types of interventions might help overcome obstacles. ❈

Part II

The
National
Policy
Process

FORMULATING A NATIONAL POLICY FOR SMALL ENTERPRISE: THE KENYAN EXPERIENCE

Isaya A. Onyango
Strategy and Policy Analysis Division, Office of the Vice-President and Ministry of Planning and National Development, Nairobi, Kenya

James Tomecko
Kenya Industrial Estates, Informal Sector Programme, Nairobi, Kenya

Introduction

Kenya's small-enterprise sector is defined as being all of those businesses that employ 1–50 people. It is estimated that 2.1 million of Kenya's workforce are employed in the sector's 912 000 enterprises. The sector is growing at an impressive rate. In 1993, for example, it grew 20%; the large-enterprise sector, on the other hand, recorded a rather sluggish 2.3% growth in the same year. The implication of these growth rates, if they continue at their present levels, is that in the foreseeable future small enterprises will employ three out of every four people looking for a job in the nonagricultural sector of the economy. In addition to its importance in job creation, the small-enterprise sector contributes 33% of the value added in manufacturing and the retail trade in Kenya. These are compelling reasons for the Government of Kenya to take an active interest in the continued growth and expansion of small businesses.

Policy formulation in the
post-independence period

Immediately after independence the Government of Kenya, like the governments of many other newly emerging nations at that time, directed a great deal of support toward the industrial and commercial sectors of the economy. Government policies and strategies were centrally planned and clearly oriented toward import substitution and the development of large-scale industrial and commercial enterprises. Punitive regulations discouraged foreign ownership. This type of policy environment led to protectionism, the increased use of subsidies to foster locally manufactured content, massive public ownership of enterprise, the establishment of a regulatory framework to control the private sector, and enterprise development policies favouring the few and large. Because larger enterprises always perform better than small ones in a highly regulated environment, most small-enterprise support programs were designed to compensate for this imbalance.

The central actor in the promotion of small industries was the government, which in fashioning its policies and measures drew heavily on the Indian model sometimes called the "integrated approach." The model was based on the premise that for small businesses to start and expand, a whole range of subsidized services is needed:

- preconstructed commercial sheds;
- extension services that prepare feasibility studies and give advice on technology choices;
- management and technical training;
- supplies of raw materials; and
- subsidized credit.

It was not until the late 1970s and early 1980s that this approach was largely discredited as being too expensive and inappropriate for developing entrepreneurship. By the middle of the 1980s the government was searching for a new model that was more in keeping with an open-market economy and a more liberalized business environment. Kenyan entrepreneurs were more plentiful and capable, and they were beginning to articulate how the regulations introduced in the 1970s were hampering their expansion.

The need for a fresh approach
to policy formulation

By 1986 the ever-increasing employment problem was also beginning to manifest itself, and with it came a heightened awareness of the growing contribution that small businesses make to employment. All of this was stressed in a government publication entitled *Economic Management for Renewed Growth* (Kenya 1986). The document, which went before Parliament as Sessional Paper No. 1, clearly pointed out that modern wage and rural farm employment were growing much too slowly to absorb a labour force that was projected to expand by 6 million entrants between 1986 and the end of the century. The only area of the economy that appeared to be growing at an accelerated rate of 11–12% at that time was the informal, or small-enterprise, sector. The government, therefore, began to examine the impact of its interventionist strategies. It became clear, for example, that

- the industrial estates in both urban and rural areas had not stimulated the kind of growth that had been expected from them;

- the extension services, for all of their costs, had not proved popular with the entrepreneurs; and

- the disbursement of subsidized credit to the sector had been minimal, and recovery rates were poor.

By 1986, however, the country's institutional infrastructure had developed considerably. Aside from parastatals such as Kenya Industrial Estates (KIE) and the Industrial and Commercial Development Corporation (ICDC), which had spearheaded the government's programs in the 1970s, many NGOs had entered the field of small-enterprise development. The Kenya Rural Enterprise Program (K-REP), the Partnership for Productivity, the Undugu Society of Kenya, and the National Council of Churches of Kenya (NCCK) were only some of the NGOs that were experimenting with grass-roots methods for reaching smaller enterprises.

Because of this dramatic increase in small-enterprise promotion, projects were starting to move in different directions and inconsistencies were beginning to emerge. Whereas some foreign donors and NGOs were supporting banks that gave repayable loans to entrepreneurs to start and run maize mills, others, with the sole objective of promoting employment, gave away maize mills to women's groups. Church organizations entered the lending business, providing subsidized loans, but other NGOs, trying to achieve sustainable incomes, charged market interest rates. Mistakes were being repeated in the areas of infrastructure and supplies of raw material. There was a clear need for some consistency in the approach to the sector.

To spearhead a new initiative, the Government of Kenya took two important steps: it created a special unit in the Ministry of Planning and National Development to coordinate inputs for the 1989–1993 national development plan (Kenya 1989a); and it established a task force in the Ministry of Industry to prepare a set of recommendations for government action. The task force, for all its good intentions, lacked the human and material resources needed to collect even the most primary information. The results of its deliberations were, therefore, unimpressive. At this point, the government asked the United Nations Development Programme (UNDP) to help it begin to formulate a strategy. After agreeing on a broad budget and time frame, the government and UNDP began to consider the preparation of a national strategy and an investment program for small-enterprise development. The joint project was known as the Creation of Enterprise and Promotion of Entrepreneurship (CENTRE) Project (Malkamaki et al. 1991).

Three approaches to formulating a national strategy

In choosing an approach to formulating a national strategy, the government considered three distinct methods:

- the "external experts" approach, in which several foreign consultants are brought in to analyze the situation and prepare a report;
- the "task force" method, in which a select group of local experts, usually civil servants, is appointed for a short time to prepare a report; and
- the "participative planning" method, in which predominantly local experts interact over an extended period with selected external experts to generate recommendations on which there is a wide local consensus.

The first method had already been used in Kenya by the
ILO when it prepared a world employment report on the informal sector (ILO 1972). The method resulted in a document of
high quality. Where it fell short, however, according to the team
leader of the mission, Hans Singer of the Institute of Development Studies of the University of Sussex, was that there was
very little Kenyan ownership of the recommendations. Consequently, implementation of the proposals was very difficult.
Although the proposals of this report had indeed been relevant
and many of them were reflected in a subsequent sessional
paper, the execution of the plans never took root within the government or the private sector.

The second method had also been tried. The previously
mentioned task force, which had been appointed after Sessional
Paper No. 1 of 1986, had met several times but had failed to
come up with a meaningful action program that was well
researched and capable of standing up to the standards
demanded for the next 5-year plan. The members of the task
force had been primarily institutional representatives rather
than interested and competent individuals. In addition to the
poor composition of its membership, the task force lacked a
budget to sustain its operations.

The third method, backed up by adequate human and
material resources, seemed to offer the best prospects for building both a strong local consensus and a capability for follow-up
in the next stages of implementation. The team consisted of
local experts from the public and private sectors who were
assigned by their employers to the task of strategy formulation
on a part-time basis for an initial period of 3–4 months. Such
experts included investment bankers from public and private
banks, extension or promotional officers from the government,
senior civil servants from the relevant ministries, heads of relevant NGOs, private consultants familiar with the sector, and representatives from the sector itself. These people were supported
by an experienced coordinator, a secretariat, and consultants,
most of whom were local. There was an agreed-upon objective,
time frame, and budget, and most of the work would be done in
small groups of about five people.

The participative planning method: a model for policy and strategy formulation

Establishing the project-management parameters

In a process-oriented or participative planning exercise it is not possible to predict the outcome because the contributions of the participants are needed to reach a conclusion by consensus. Therefore, in the first stage it was essential to clearly highlight to those involved the characteristics of this method:

- The method is process oriented, so more time than usual would be required to reach a conclusion.
- The method involves several participants, so the results would be more transparent than is normal in a policy-formulation exercise.
- The method would likely generate consensus.
- The method incorporates all the important issues and links them in their causal relationships, rather than simply prioritizing them, so the sequencing of interventions would be more pragmatic.

In addition, because participants would be from decision-making and implementing institutions, subsequent steps in implementing the strategy would be easier.

A preliminary workplan with the relevant milestones was prepared, and all other official issues were settled.

Choosing the team

In a participative process, the most important ingredient is people. Great care had to be taken at this stage to avoid the mistake of the first task force, which had overlooked individuals from the sector for its membership. The initial temptation this time was to include almost everyone who came to mind, on the assumption that no one should be offended by being left out. An objective "search" for local expertise began. The people who were contacted were those who had produced a significant paper on the subject, managed a past program in the sector, occupied a key position relevant to the sector, etc. The emphasis was more on finding articulate individuals with experience than on finding representatives of institutions.

To find out who was interested and available to participate in the process, the project managers phoned these individuals and asked them if they wished to take part in small, informal brainstorming sessions of about five or six people on topics related to small enterprises in which they had some experience. The topics included the sector's contribution to employment, entrepreneurship, rural industrialization, export, technology adaptation, subcontracting, and urban land-use planning.

In addition to giving project managers an opportunity to identify those individuals who had the firmest grasp of the issues and therefore would make good participants, these sessions helped the managers isolate key and recurring themes and identify publications that would be useful later. At the end of this stage, 25 people were selected to join the process.

Defining the sector and gathering information

At some stage when dealing with the subject of small enterprise, one is confronted with the issue of defining the sector. Most people perceive only a segment of the whole sector, and this limited perception becomes a source of confusion. Some governments already have definitions related to employment or capital or even technology. These definitions are helpful, but even they require further disaggregation so that participants can conceptualize different target groups when formulating interventions. After coming to terms with the question of definition and target groups, the next critical activity was the collection of relevant documents. These books, papers, and studies were mostly local, but international materials were also gathered to provide participants with information on the latest trends in the field. The major objectives of our collecting this information were to learn as many lessons as possible from the past and thus to avoid irrelevant themes in the future stages of the project.

Analyzing the problems: level 1

A strategy formulation workshop was held. It took place sufficiently far from the capital (Nairobi) that the selected participants were fully absorbed in the task. The workshop lasted for 5 days and was moderated by someone trained in the ZOPP method (the ZOPP — aim-oriented project planning — method was developed by the German Agency for Technical

Cooperation [GTZ] as a means of planning complex bilateral projects [GTZ 1992]). The 25 participants were not asked to write any papers but to come prepared for free, open, and frank discussions on the problems of small enterprises and how to address them in a practical manner. Selected background materials that had been collected in the previous step were copied and distributed to participants.

The ZOPP sessions began by generating consensus on a "core" or starting problem that was central to the subject. From that point the group derived the causes of that central problem and, going further down, the causes of the causes. In this way almost all problems related to small-enterprise development could be incorporated and their causal relations established. The main group reached a consensus on the first level of causes as well. The group then broke up into smaller working groups of five or six people to go into further detail. These problem clusters, which were essentially statements of negative conditions and their causes, were then reversed and stated positively as objectives. For example, if the core problem was "poor access to credit," then the objective could be formulated as "increased access to credit." Generally, the causes of problems when reversed and stated positively as objectives became the means to achieving the next higher objective. For example, if one of the causes of poor access to credit was "no long-term capital available," then "increased availability of long-term capital" became part of the solution to the problem of poor access to credit.

In the case of the CENTRE Project, the core problem was located at the very high level of "unemployment." Four causes were identified:

- high population growth,
- the inability of agriculture to absorb more jobs,
- a slowdown in the modern wage sector, and
- insufficient growth in small enterprises.

The insufficient growth in small enterprises was attributable to the high mortality rate and insufficient expansion of existing enterprises and to the lack of adequate startups. The working groups then discussed each of these last problems to elaborate on their causes and eventually the solutions. Discussions were animated and lively, and the working groups frequently met until the late hours of the night.

One of the successes of the workshop was the consensus the public- and private-sector participants reached on the critical problems and their causes. It became clear, however, that there was considerable overlap in some areas. For example, poor entrepreneurship could be the cause for high mortality rates as well as inadequate startups; similarly, a hostile business environment or limited access to credit could be the cause of both insufficient expansion and high mortality rates. A core group of about 12 participants, committed to seeing the process through to the end, was selected to examine the results from the workshop. This core group identified three main factors as common obstacles to growth in the sector:

- an unfavourable environment,
- limited access to credit, and
- a low quality of entrepreneurship.

These factors affected all levels of small business, but they were problems for which specific remedial measures could be designed.

Analyzing the problems: level 2

At this point it became clear to those involved that even with the synthesized ZOPP results, a further and deeper level of analysis was required. Of particular concern were the successes and failures of the more interesting programs in Asia. Furthermore, a thorough analysis of the existing institutional capacity in Kenya was needed before the team could recommend meaningful and pragmatic steps to be taken. The core group, therefore, broke up into working groups again. The three tasks at this stage were the following:

- to send one member of each group to one or two countries outside east Africa and to feed the knowledge acquired back into the process;
- to hire local consultants to examine the country's institutional players; and, when this was complete,
- to draft the chapter on this area for the strategy document.

Five main strategic themes emerged from this stage:

1. The Government of Kenya should abandon its position as an implementer and become a facilitator, and all

future projects should be planned against this background.

This theme reinforced the fundamental change in policy called for in the government's Sessional Paper No. 1 of 1986 (Kenya 1986). Approaches that exemplified this role change were identified. Hence, the emphasis was on additional projects to disseminate information rather than on additional extension services and credit.

2. The private sector must take a more active part in formulating and carrying out projects.

   Of necessity, this would mean shifting to the private sector much of the institutional support that had until then gone to the government. Hence, there was a scramble for new private-sector partner organizations.

3. Small enterprises are part and parcel of the private sector, and if there are serious constraints on the private sector, such as irrational interest rates or distortional foreign-exchange rates, the small business is just as likely to suffer as the larger business.

   In response to this theme, attention was directed to improving the enabling environment for investment and expansion. The proposed strategies included improving the sector's access to urban infrastructure; disseminating information on technology; simplifying licencing procedures; removing price controls; and switching from import quotas on raw materials to tariffs.

4. For significant vertical growth of existing businesses to occur (as opposed to simply adding new entrants of the same type, thereby achieving only horizontal growth), existing businesses should have access to formal credit.

   This would entail liberalizing the interest rates so that banks could make a profit on loans to small enterprises; developing alternative forms of security and collateral; initiating more credit schemes to increase the supply of finance; and improving the institutional base of the country to disburse thousands instead of hundreds of loans and to collect the repayments.

5. Even if all these improvements were made, the number of adequately qualified entrepreneurs had to increase, both in the long term and in the short term.

This was to be accomplished by celebrating the role of the entrepreneur as a creator of wealth (before this, the entrepreneur had been portrayed as an exploiter); introducing entrepreneurship into the education system; improving the quality of small-business management training through better needs assessment; and upgrading the indigenous apprenticeship system as a credible alternative to the formal technical training institutions, which in any case did not have the capacity to absorb the growing number of unemployed youths.

Producing the strategy document

Because none of those involved in the process was a professional writer, an editor was hired for the last 3 weeks of the project to work with the three groups and the project managers to produce a strategy paper with well-reasoned arguments and a strong internal logic. Each recommendation was tested for relevance and consistency with the overall direction of the strategy paper. In addition to the strategy itself, a separate set of recommendations was prepared for donors. The document also contained project profiles to illustrate the types of interventions considered appropriate for implementing the strategy.

Disseminating the results and developing the policy

Following the presentation of the findings to the Government of Kenya 9 months after the project began, the project team made several other presentations to various ministries and donor agencies. These presentations further polished the strategy and sensitized the ministries and agencies to the direction in which the government, in partnership with the private sector, wished to go.

More focused workshops were then held on specific aspects of the strategy with a view to initiating projects to address the major problem areas.

Donor agencies continued to support the core group of local experts through a second project called the Small Enterprise Development Policy Project. In May 1989 the core group presented their findings to government in a report entitled *A Strategy for Small Scale Enterprise Development in Kenya: Towards the Year 2000* (Kenya 1989b). Because of the involvement of all the key and relevant actors throughout the policy formulation process, the document was immediately adopted by the government. Furthermore, the document was widely acknowledged by many others outside government for providing valuable information and suggestions that they could use to improve their own enterprise-promotion programs in Kenya.

Two other important events taking place in Nairobi coincided with the publication of the strategy paper. The first of these was the formulation of the country's Sixth National Development Plan (1989–1993). Most of the key actors from government who were working in the core group were also involved in drafting the chapter on small enterprise for the development plan. As a result, the recommendations in the strategy paper were mirrored in the development plan (Kenya 1989a). The timing of the strategy paper had been optimal, and many of its recommendations were translated automatically into policy because of their inclusion in the development plan.

The second important event taking place at this time was a Mini-Donors Conference to discuss the future directions of government policies and strategies and major areas for further collaboration. The government took the opportunity to present to the donors the recommendations outlined in the strategy paper. Many donors (some of whom had actually participated in some of the activities surrounding the formulation of the strategy) expressed immediate interest in specific areas. Those donors who were most keen agreed to establish a forum to discuss how best to coordinate their activities. (The donors found the forum so useful that they have continued with it, meeting regularly on a quarterly basis.)

One of the major effects of the Mini-Donors Conference was growing support for the idea that the recommendations of the strategy paper should be introduced to Parliament as a sessional paper. This, in effect, provided the necessary policy framework within which implementation would take place.

The preparation of the sessional paper involved the four key ministries that had participated in the formulation of the strategy. The staff of these four ministries edited the materials previously produced by the core group and drafted it in the style of a sessional paper. The respective permanent secretaries of the ministries prepared the necessary briefs for their ministers, who jointly sponsored the sessional paper in its presentation first to Cabinet and then later in the same year to Parliament. The paper easily passed through both stages and was published as Sessional Paper No. 2 of 1992, *Small-Scale and Jua Kali* [small manufacturers] *Enterprise Development in Kenya* (Kenya 1992). Since its approval, 4 000 copies of the strategy paper and the sessional paper have been produced and distributed.

Project evaluation

The UNDP conducted an evaluation of the CENTRE Project and the follow-on project, the Small Enterprise Development Policy Project, and had this to say in the summary of its findings (Malkamaki et al. 1991):

> The CENTRE and Small Enterprise Development Policy projects represent one of the first attempts at formulating a comprehensive national policy and programme of action for implementing a small enterprise development strategy in Africa. The projects utilized a participative approach to achieve remarkable outputs at relatively low cost by using local experts in small enterprise development (SED) as the main technical resource for the projects' activities and outputs.
>
> The project achieved much in terms of creating awareness of SED issues and activities nationally through media coverage. Policymakers and implementors of SED programmes were sensitized through workshops and participation in committee meetings. The magnitude of the awareness created is evidenced by the creation of SED units in two ministries and SED departments in two commercial banks in the country.

The main distinguishing features of the approach were that it was highly participative, open, and transparent; fully used local expertise; generated wide consensus; and made implementation of the results easier.

On balance, although the approach has been considered successful, three criticisms of the results have been raised:

1. The recommendations failed to penetrate the highest levels of policy decision-making.

Despite the fact that almost all of the participants were senior government technocrats, heads of NGOs, private bankers and the like, the strategy was poorly understood at the political level, where recommendations such as those related to the use of market interest rates for small-enterprise lending schemes offer very little potential for winning votes. Although individual politicians have lent their support to the strategy and its proposals, this criticism still remains valid and accounts for some of the prevailing policies that continue to inhibit the sector.

2. In the initial stages of project identification that followed the development of the strategy, much of the donor assistance went to support government ministries instead of the private sector.

The justification for this was that the implementation of the recommendations required a more sophisticated government capable of understanding the long-term direction of the proposals being made. This naturally required the buildup of human resources within the government. At the same time, many of the private development institutions had not yet emerged with an adequate capacity for implementation. (In the last few years, however, the balance of assistance has shifted to the point where the private sector is implementing some of the projects recommended by the strategy paper.)

3. Some key recommendations have not been implemented. Most glaring is the continued involvement of the government in lending programs.

The cause of this is connected with criticism 1 — the recommendations are not well understood at senior political levels. The government has, however, recognized the inconsistency of continuing this activity in view of maintaining its posture of nonintervention in the sector. Such weaknesses in policy consistency underline the absolute necessity for the government to have a strong and effective monitoring capacity that is supported by the private sector.

What has been the impact of this process?

Almost any paper that has been written on the subject of small enterprise in Kenya quotes either the strategy paper or the sessional paper. The consequence of this has been a common recognition of the main problem areas. This alignment has led to improved coordination, better project planning, and little duplication. Coordination meetings are held quarterly to ensure that planned interventions are in line with the provisions of the strategy. As a result of this consensus, the implementation of the strategy has never been in question.

The following projects and programs, which were recommended by the strategy paper, are still working in Kenya today:

- Three significant micro credit schemes cover almost the entire country and have a portfolio of approximately 6 000 borrowers (KIE, K-REP, PRIDE).

- The Credit Reference Bureau helps small borrowers build up a track record as a substitute for tangible securities.

- The College of Banking and Finance has established regular courses to orient commercial bankers to the special needs of small entrepreneurs.

- An entrepreneurship education program offered by most of the country's technical training institutes trains young technicians to start and run their own businesses.

- Small business centres attached to these technical training institutes provide assistance to entrepreneurs who want to learn how to put together business plans for investment.

- A subcontracting exchange facilitates the expansion of small-enterprise markets and introduces small producers to new standards of production and quality through interaction with larger firms.

- An urban infrastructure program is increasing the access of small producers to long-term tenure of premises and to secure electricity, thereby improving their access to more modern technologies.

- A privately sponsored permanent national exhibition of small manufacturers' products tours the country each year, exhibiting the best that the sector can offer.

- A coordinating mechanism of government, donors, and the private sector allows for examination of outstanding policy deficits and discussion of major interventions that may be planned by any of the three partners.

- The National Federation of Jua Kali Associations is the embryo of a representative body for articulating the interests of the small entrepreneur.

Current initiatives for the coordination of SED policy in Kenya

In the course of implementing many of the above-mentioned projects it became obvious that some form of coordination was going to be necessary. Several organizations were, for example, working in the area of credit. Would resources be shared? How would complementarity be achieved? How would duplication be avoided? These were the main concerns of all parties. The donors continued to meet regularly after the Mini-Donors Conference, primarily to inform each other about their own potential project-intervention areas. The Ministry of Planning and National Development then established the National Coordination Committee, with representatives from government and some of the NGOs, to continue the information-sharing process between the implementing agencies.

Although there was ample communication between the comitttee and the donors, it was evident that neither group, on its own, possessed adequate influence with senior government decision-makers to avoid some of the inconsistencies that have been mentioned above. Both bodies were having their own impact, but there was still no accepted channel for different interest groups wishing to articulate new policy initiatives. To meet this need, the government and donors recently agreed on a configuration of committees and advisory groups that allows adequate access by all major parties to the policy-formulation process. The structure also provides a clearinghouse for information on existing and planned interventions.

The structure is as follows. At the highest level is the National Steering Committee, comprising only permanent secretaries from the Ministry of Planning and National

Development, the Ministry of Commerce and Industry, and the Ministry of Research, Training and Technology. The National Steering Committee is the main organ for policy development. Next comes the Advisory Group, made up of members predominantly from the private sector and the donor community, with some government representation. The purpose of the Advisory Group is to advise the National Steering Committee on relevant policy and operational issues of concern to any of the parties. Then comes the Small Enterprise Coordination Committee, which has working groups in the functional areas of credit and finance, entrepreneurship and training, and the enabling environment. The purpose of this Small Enterprise Coordination Committee is to identify problem areas and recommend technical solutions.

All bodies are supported by the national database, maintained by one of the NGOs. External support is still needed, however, so the Ministry of Planning and National Development is currently discussing with the Overseas Development Administration the possibility of its assistance in updating policy priorities and identifying new areas that need attention in a constantly changing policy environment. Although one of the criticisms of the process described above has been that far too much assistance went to government ministries, it should be emphasized that the policy implementation capacity in the concerned government offices is still weak.

Changing roles of the key actors

This new and as yet untested coordination mechanism has clearly delineated three fundamental interest groups involved in the development of policies for the small-enterprise sector: the government, the private sector, and donors. How have their roles in the process changed over the last 20 years? The following critique may sound harsh, but that's only because we are evaluating the actors of 20 years ago with the performance standards of today.

The government has a strong tradition of intervention in this sector. In the early 1970s all of the industrial estates, extension services, business training, and credit were implemented through either government ministries or parastatals. During this time, KIE was set up to provide industrial space and extension services, the Kenya Institute of Business Training was established, and credit was disbursed through the Joint Loan Board Scheme and two development finance institutions (DFIS), KIE and ICDC. The emphasis during this period was on building up indigenous entrepreneurship by providing subsidized services or credit to an embryonic class of African business owners.

The ideal private-sector business owners in this same post-independence period were perceived as small Kenyan industrialists running modern factories producing substitutions for imports. They were treated very much as "beneficiaries," and it was assumed that without the support of significant subsidies indigenous entrepreneurs would not survive. The Kenyan entrepreneurs were therefore the recipients of aid, and with more aid flowing than there were recipients, the challenge for most of them became how to maximize returns from assistance programs rather than how to succeed in business. These circumstances naturally attracted opportunists, who, because of their affiliations, were able to obtain large loans and subsidized facilities. This mistargeting led to poor recovery rates for the DFIS and low impact from the extension services.

The donors played the role of policymakers in this era of plenty. Projects were designed in Europe and North America for a sector of development assistance that often required more people-oriented skills than the technical qualifications of those assigned to the task. The emphasis of the donors was on disbursement. This required the development of institutional mechanisms that could handle large volumes of aid. Little attention was paid to impact or cost efficiency. The donors supported the interventionist role of the government and the paradigm of the entrepreneur as a recipient.

Fortunately, there has been a great deal of movement and change, albeit gradual, in the attitudes, skills, and capabilities of all three actors in policy formulation and implementation.

The government, both in policy and practice, has taken up the role of a facilitator. Tighter budgets, parastatal reform, and a more competent private sector have been the main stimulants in this change. Also important has been a growing recognition that past interventions were misguided and ineffectual because of an inherent weakness of government in implementing the type of business-promotion programs that we have seen in the last 20 years. The role of facilitator was clearly spelled out in Sessional Paper No. 2 (Kenya 1992), and evidence of the shift is seen in the kinds of projects in which the government is now involved. These include strategy and policy development, monitoring and evaluation, R&D, information supply, and the coordination mechanism discussed above. One of the major practical challenges that the government now faces is what to do with the institutional infrastructure that it has built up over the last 20 years. The mission statements of these institutions are for the most part outdated, and their existence creates a counterweight to the emerging role of the government as a facilitator.

The government is in the process of withdrawing from its interventionist role, and it is also handing over the function of implementer to the private sector. Moreover, the last 20 years have seen a phenomenal growth in the informal sector, under-lining a vast reserve of entrepreneurial talent that for many years had been overlooked. Large and medium-size enterprises have recognized the benefits of working with small businesses, as shown by the following:

- the creation of the Kenya Management Assistance Programme, an organization of large and medium-size enterprises providing counselling and training to small businesses;
- the expansion by two commercial banks of their small-enterprise lending programs; and
- the sponsoring by one large multinational of its fifth annual national exhibition of small-enterprise products and technology.

Also, private voluntary organizations (PVOs), providing credit as well as training, have mushroomed in the last 10 years. The implementation capacity of PVOs is far more effective and diverse than that of the government, and the targeting of their programs is much lower than what we have seen in the past. The implications of this are that the pool of entrepreneur clients is far greater than before, giving the promotional organizations far more flexibility in selecting those clients that are most likely to have a significant impact on the economy. The challenge of the private sector in its new role as an implementer is one of sustainability. The commercial viability of the private small-enterprise-oriented institutions will depend on their ability to both mobilize donor assistance and extract an adequate income from the target group they serve.

The donors continue to be deeply involved in the area of policy development. They are, however, now dealing with a technically far stronger and experienced government that is capable of engaging them in conceptual debates on the merits of some of the proposals that are put before it. This increased capability in the government has given the donors the space to sharpen their role as risk absorbers and to spin off their better projects into sustainable programs. Major improvements with the donors have been the willingness and effort that have gone into the coordination of their activities. Joint projects are frequently the outcome of this coordination. Examples are the database of all publications on small enterprise in Kenya, an inventory of projects being implemented, and the training-needs assessment study of informal-sector entrepreneurs. This joint funding is partly due to less money being available, but it is also a result of a greater emphasis on achieving a measurable impact with the projects that are operational or "in the pipeline." The challenge for the donors is to help the government identify appropriate projects that support its facilitative role and at the same time channel bilateral and multilateral assistance to alternative private-sector development partners that are strong enough to handle the magnitude of the tasks. All of this activity is in the context of building programs with long-term sustainability.

Conclusion

The Kenyan experience in the field of small-enterprise policy development has been deep and constructive. A widespread consensus on priorities exists among the fraternity of individuals and organizations that are active in the promotion of this sector. By extending its hand to the private sector, the government has created a fruitful partnership in which comparative advantages are recognized. The adoption of an open and participative approach to policy development has been an adequate preparation for continued implementation. This has been the unique aspect of the process of small-enterprise policy formation in Kenya. Because of the general acceptance of the policies, donors have found it easier to fund projects that are integrated into a long-term game plan. This has resulted in higher quality projects with a greater overall impact on the growth of the sector. ✻

THE ROLE OF THE NATIONAL SMALL BUSINESS ADVISORY GROUP IN PROMOTING SMALL-SCALE ENTERPRISES IN ZIMBABWE

Enoch Moyo
Friedrich Naumann Foundation, Belgravia,
Harare, Zimbabwe

Introduction

Like many developing countries that have in the past 10 years embarked on economic reforms with the assistance of the World Bank, Zimbabwe has come to realize that small businesses offer a real opportunity not only to create employment but also to get indigenous people to participate in the economy. For a country that for 90 years was torn apart by racial strife and for the first 10 years after independence in 1980 practiced socialism, the adoption of policies to promote small business presents unique challenges.

This paper describes the efforts of those working to implement these new policies. The first part of the paper describes the genesis of the policies that define the economic milieu in Zimbabwe today. The second part describes the impact of government policies in the first 10 years of independence. The third part describes the efforts of those interested in a change in policy on small business, principally the efforts of the National Small Business Advisory Group (NSBAG). The last part looks at future challenges in the work to change national policies to accommodate small business.

The genesis of economic policies in Zimbabwe

Historians from different ideological backgrounds generally
agree that the way the territory that is now Zimbabwe was col-
onized largely shaped the economic policies its rulers adopted
in its first 100 years (see Biermann and Reinhart 1980). Cecil
John Rhodes, after whom the new country was for a time
named, invaded the country in 1890, hoping to reward himself
with the mineral wealth he believed existed in the new territory. When it turned out that there was not as much gold as he
had imagined, the 1 000 mercenaries he had used to invade the
country were each rewarded with 3 000 "morgen" of land and
10 gold claims. To legitimize his actions, he gave the new territory to the British Crown as a new colony. The system of
rewarding with land those who had done military service for the
British Empire was pursued for most of the colonial period. Each
wave of settlers resulted in the inevitable displacement of
indigenous people. Effectively, this translated into the translo-
cation of indigenous people from their own lands to the less
hospitable regions of the country, where they still find themselves today. Precisely because of these displacements of indigenous people, that land became the single most important factor
in the war of liberation, and even today it remains the single
most important cause of conflict between the black majority
and the white farmers.

A deliberate zoning and licencing system, which effectively separated whites from blacks, geographically, economically, and socially, has left an indelible mark that even 14 years
of independence has been unable to erase. The system made
sure that blacks did not participate in the economy except as
workers or providers of very basic services like running buses or
little family stores. The system was also efficiently policed, and
penalties were instituted to deter any violators. When people
are systematically oppressed, it is quite probable that they will
end up believing that the way things are is as it should be. Many
researchers observe that a whole generation of black families do
not believe that blacks can operate businesses. These families,
in fact, believe that to run a business is evil. Because of such
beliefs, black entrepreneurs were labeled traitors or sellouts during the struggle for independence. Many of their businesses
were destroyed by nationalist insurgents during the war. The
absence of any meaningful economic activity in all areas

allocated to blacks is, thus, not a result of choice but a product of a deliberate policy to create a market for whites and a source of cheap labour for the settler economy. Through this institutionalized monopoly, the settler economy achieved its competitiveness. Through this system, the white community gained a considerable head start over black entrepreneurs.

What strikes most people visiting Zimbabwe for the first time is the stark differences between the living standards of blacks and those of other races. Even the war of independence took on the character of a conflict between blacks and whites. When the country became independent, the new government adopted a policy of reconciliation between races in a belief that the colonial policies had been driven by pure racism.

In this paper, I contend that the driving force behind the colonial policies was what L. Tager of the Law Review Project in South Africa terms "monopoly capitalism" in its purest form. Viewed in its simplest form, such a system appeared to thrive on legalized elimination of competition. Once firms were established, they made sure that no other firm would ever be started to compete with them. At the community level, it meant that once whites were in, they made sure no one else entered who was not of their colour. They then constructed a myriad of laws to prevent any challengers. Virtually every law passed in the 90 years of colonial rule made a reference to blacks and whites. All economic laws passed in this period deliberately restrict entry by blacks. Laws like the *Land Apportionment Act* of 1930 and the *Land Tenure Act* of 1969 were designed to totally separate races. Complementary legislation determined what blacks could do.

It is, therefore, not surprising that the socialism of the first independent government in 1980 was so popular with blacks in the first few years of independence. But the collective ownership espoused by socialism also explains why it is so difficult to make people in Zimbabwe today understand the advantages of competition in a modern economy, especially when in the past there were laws to stifle competition. This in turn explains why organizations like the Indigenous Business Development Centre clamour for legislation to protect enterprises formed by indigenous people.

The impact of government policies in the first 10 years of independence

The socialism of the Zimbabwe African People's Union (ZANU), the party that won the elections in 1980, was based on the general belief that the suffering of black people had been the result of the capitalism practiced by white people. Admittedly, the support that socialist countries gave to the nationalists during the fight for independence also influenced the decision to adopt socialism. However, this support would have been meaningless if people had not endured economic oppression at the hands of white settlers.

The new government saw private capital, whether that of blacks or that of whites, as essentially bad. Although not adopting a policy of wholesale nationalization of private firms, the government, through licencing, prices, labour, and foreign exchange controls, would exercise stringent controls over what it viewed as the inherent excesses of private capital. The government also saw itself as a protector of indigenous people against the threat of predominantly white capitalism. The parastatals were given a bigger role in achieving the social objectives of the new government. The government also adopted policies to empower black people through cooperatives and the so-called community-based income-generating projects. Very hefty incentives and nonmaterial support were given to those who adopted the economic modes promoted by the government. Many northern NGOs, which sympathized with the government's ideology, extended their support to these programs. In addition, most diplomatic missions in Zimbabwe established units to promote cooperatives and income-generating projects. Currently, only a few NGOs are willing to assist individuals who want to establish their own businesses.

Cooperatives and income-generating groups are generally exempt from the regulations that affect private businesses. Where authorities try to apply regulations, politicians and the officials engaged to assist them always intervene on behalf of the collectives and the income-generating groups. A recent study commissioned by Environment and Development Activities (ENDA, Zimbabwe) and undertaken by Imani Development (Pvt) Ltd (1993) clearly shows how officials turn a blind eye to the mismanagement of officially sponsored cooperatives and income-generating groups, even where basic laws on hygiene are not followed. In contrast, private black-owned retail businesses in rural areas are closely monitored by regulation-enforcement agencies, despite protests that these regulations are generally discriminatory against them. In the past, if hawkers wanted to escape harassment by police, they simply became members of a cooperative. If they happened to be arrested for violating a by-law, the registrar of cooperatives intervened on their behalf. Cooperatives were synonymous with socialism, and every politician of the ruling party promoted cooperatives as a way of appearing loyal to the party.

Many associations that were formed at independence to champion the needs of the small-business sector were, over the decade, completely marginalized by either the government or established private-sector institutions. For example, in 1980 there was a very strong association for hawkers and vendors. The Harare Vendors and Hawkers Association fought hard to have the laws that prohibit the operations of these types of business reviewed or rescinded. The ruling party expressed its sympathy with this group. Members of this group were encouraged to join the party. In Harare, for instance, a membership in the party became a passport to obtaining a vending licence. Most "legal" hawkers in suburban areas owe their positions to their membership in the party. Municipal councillors could easily assure themselves of a vote by promising a vending licence. The party could also protect its members from police harassment. Other members were enticed to form cooperatives in exchange for protection or a promise of resources. This is precisely why by 1984, registered cooperatives had swelled from a mere 300 at independence to more than 2 000.

Before independence, the only recognized business associations were for white businesses. Those representing blacks largely operated informally. Under the policy of one industry – one organization, black-owned associations were persuaded to join those already established. The Zimbabwe National Chambers of Commerce (ZNCC), which represents commerce, elected its first black president during that decade. The same applies to the Confederation of Zimbabwe Industries (CZI).

A close examination of these organizations clearly shows that the small-business sector was totally marginalized. At congresses, their concerns made a few headlines but were never taken up in the formal lobby sessions between the government and the private sector. The government white paper on the reform program makes it quite evident that the well-organized business associations had greater influence than the small businesses. The concerns of the small-business sector were expressed only in general terms.

The cooperative sector also experienced the same divisions and marginalization. The 300 odd cooperatives that existed at independence and operated exclusively as suppliers of agricultural input were roundly condemned as organizations of the elite among the peasantry. The Government Policy on Cooperatives of 1983 clearly states that the government favoured cooperatives of a productive type, as this encouraged collective ownership of the means of production, in line with the government's socialist policies. By 1983, there were two fiercely opposed groups representing cooperatives in the country: the organization of Collective Cooperatives in Zimbabwe represented the new and favoured cooperatives; the Central Association of Cooperatives was officially considered capitalist. To complicate matters even foreign donors took sides and helped to deepen the divisions.

The failure of the government's economic policies to stimulate investment and employment was most likely the impetus to reconsider the small-business sector. Reviews undertaken in 1987 and 1988 clearly showed that controls on the economy had stifled investment and employment. The cooperatives and parastatals, on which so much hope had been placed, had failed dismally. Through its planning control mechanism, the government had failed to steer the economy toward the desired ends.

As in all developing countries where this situation is reached, it was time to call in the World Bank and the International Monetary Fund (IMF). In 1989, in a white paper entitled *Zimbabwe: A Framework for Investment 1990–1995* (Zimbabwe 1989), the government endorsed the view that the way forward was through a market-led economy. In this paper, the government for the first time clearly acknowledged the need to promote small business as part of its economic development policies. Also for the first time, the government recognized the efforts of individuals to set up their own businesses.

Zimbabwe's economic reform program shares most if not all the features of reform programs assisted by the World Bank and the IMF in the past decade. The central features are monetary and fiscal reform, trade liberalization, deregulation, and the introduction of an instrument called the Social Dimensions of Adjustment, designed to cushion the blow for those most affected by the reforms.

It has been pointed out that most of the donor organizations have since 1980 confined their support to cooperatives and income-generating groups. Many reviews undertaken toward the end of the decade clearly showed that the donor's support had failed to achieve its objectives. Many groups that had formed as cooperatives had done so because that was the only way to gain access to resources. As soon as a cooperative gained access to resources it split up into individually owned enterprises. This clearly shows the outcome of a subsidized development process. Genuine development projects tend to be crowded out by many bogus ones in search of cheap resources.

A closer examination of the business environment in Zimbabwe of the 1990s clearly shows that very little has changed in the way small businesses are viewed, not only by the government but also by the population in general. The stereotypes that were used to describe small businesses well before independence are still prevalent. For example, hawkers are seen as dirty and, therefore, undesirable. Women who conduct cross-border trade are seen as smugglers. This is in contrast to the way people view similar trade practices of the elite (Gaidzanwa 1992). The policies that excluded blacks before independence now incorporate the new black elite, who through their positions in the government now help to perpetuate the exclusion of the poor, who are mainly black.

When the reforms were first announced, many institutions were extremely worried about the likely impact on the small-business sector. Although the government assured the general public that the Social Dimensions of Adjustment would shield all the vulnerable groups and businesses from the negative effects of the program, there were no instruments specifically designed to assist small businesses. There was also a fear that the private sector, through its well-developed lobby institutions such as the CZI and the ZNCC, could easily hoard all the benefits of the program. There was, therefore, no way the small-business sector could influence the outcome of the reforms for its own benefit.

There were basically two options open to institutions working with small business. The first approach involved trying to go along with what the government planned for the sector.

This was precisely the approach pursued by development agencies in the first decade of independence. It only led to frustration as both the promoters of small business and the small businesses, mainly cooperatives, tried to work with unpalatable and unworkable policies.

The second approach, which the small-business promoters eventually adopted, involved collectively working with the government to arrive at appropriate policies for promoting small business. Small businesses were also encouraged to participate in shaping the policies that would affect them. This approach obviously marked a great departure from the norms of law- and policymaking pursued by the government in the past. It also meant that small-business promoters would require a lot of tact and skill to persuade the government to change the way it implemented policies for the sector. An institutional framework for promoting small businesses became necessary.

In such work, there is always a risk of donors such as the World Bank and the IMF imposing their will on the government in the name of facilitating development. The Government of Zimbabwe generally tends to be very sensitive to outside influences.

Against this background, deriving a policy for small businesses was not going to be easy. As things stood there was no common ground for achieving consensus on policy for small business. Both government and the donor community lacked experience in promoting small business in a competitive environment. They were operating at cross purposes, they had yet to coordinate their efforts, and they were unsure how to go about doing so. Out of this morass NSBAG emerged.

Toward achieving consensus on a policy for small-business development: the work of NSBAG

The NSBAG is made up of all bilateral and multilateral aid agencies, NGOs, government ministries, private-sector business associations and financial institutions that support small business in Zimbabwe. Emerging associations for small business and the informal sector have also begun to take part.

Membership is open to all institutions, and there are no membership fees, no constitutions, and no elections. The position of chair is purely honorary. The current chair of NSBAG was nominated because he had time to spare to administer its affairs. Members volunteer to fund its meetings, and a small secretariat organizes meetings, supervises the production of a bimonthly newsletter (the *SSE News*), and also supervises and coordinates research sponsored by members. Membership does not carry with it any obligations or responsibilities. In the 2 years NSBAG has operated, there has seemed to be no need to formalize its operations.

The NSBAG had been formed by organizations that felt that unless something was done to help small business, economic reforms would leave it behind. Initially, many donors were concerned only about the sectors they worked in. For instance, the Canadian aid agencies, such as the Canadian International Development Agency (CIDA), were more concerned about the impact of the reforms on women. These agencies did a lot of research in 1989 and 1991 to find out how women would fare under the reform program.

In 1990, the Friedrich Naumann Foundation also funded several studies on how the general opening up of the economy would affect small businesses on the whole. At informal meetings of representatives of the foundation and NSBAG, it became apparent that although there would be slight variations depending on whether the proprietors of business were men or women, all small businesses on the whole would be affected to the same degree.

After several informal meetings, government ministries were also brought into the discussion. In Zimbabwe after independence, the government made policies and everybody was expected to abide by them. This top-down approach applied to all sectors of the economy. The willingness of the government to accept input from NSBAG marked a real departure from the past.

Obviously, the government had learned from past mistakes. For example, in 1983, it instituted a policy on cooperatives that both the cooperative and government workers were supposed to abide by. The policy was designed by government officials and passed by the government. The policy failed. The failure of this approach to policymaking is well documented. The objective of bringing government operatives into the deliberations of NSBAG was to create a partnership with all parties concerned with the development of small business.

The first step to building cooperation is building confidence. Past efforts to achieve cooperation in the development of small business failed because institutions tried to achieve uniformity. Under a development policy that emphasized "one correct approach," very little room was left for those who wanted to use different methods. The approach adopted by the founders of NSBAG is based on the conviction that there may be a need to agree on objectives, but there is certainly no need to specify how these objectives should be accomplished, let alone by whom. If all that is required of development agencies is agreement on broad principles, cooperation is possible. Institutions are, then, free to borrow from each other whatever they consider essential to their own work.

As a way of building the confidence of its members, NSBAG held seminars to identify the core problems that would constitute the focal points for support. At its inaugural meeting in May 1991, NSBAG identified the following broad areas of concern:

- *Financial problems* — Small businesses have a difficult time obtaining loans and credit. Banks have a negative attitude toward small businesses, and there is a lack of appropriate financial schemes for those who would normally not qualify for bank loans.

- *Regulation problems* — Problems relating to the environment under which small businesses operate, in the main, relate to the regulations that affect businesses in general and small businesses in particular. Local laws and regulations top the list of such problems.

- *Nonfinancial problems* — Nonfinancial problems relate to the attitudes of officials who may resist reforms that favour small business because they fear they will lose their power, influence, or even jobs.

From the start, NSBAG acknowledged that it is the government that has to implement the reform policies. The NSBAG members, therefore, accepted the fact that their role was only to assist the government in achieving its goals. To ensure success, the members adopted the following principles:

- They would not claim any credit for their achievements.

- They would endeavour at all times to make specific initiatives fully acceptable to the appropriate agency.

- They would adopt a piecemeal approach instead of tackling all the problems of the sector at one go.

Whatever NSBAG undertakes is done for either government or the small-business sector.

How NSBAG operates

After its inaugural meeting, when NSBAG identified the core problems that would constitute the focal points for support, the group developed an action plan, which member organizations are free to implement. At periodic meetings, members report on what they are doing within the framework of this plan. The periodic meetings also serve as an opportunity for the government to indicate the specific support it may require from NSBAG members. For example, in 1992 the government asked NSBAG to provide support in the area of deregulation. Several member organizations, including the Friedrich Naumann Foundation and the Overseas Development Agency of the British government, are now collaborating with the government of Zimbabwe in this endeavour.

Another approach is hosting major policy dialogues in the form of conferences that bring together researchers, government officials, and members of the small-business sector. Topics have included deregulation (Tager 1993), the role of small business in the economy, and the impact of monopolies on small business.

Achievements of NSBAG

The small-business sector has benefited from seven achievements of NSBAG so far.

1. NSBAG represents the first working network to assist the growth and development of small business. Perhaps, it works so well because the networking arrangement remains loose. Similar arrangements largely failed because they were rigid and required conformity. One indication of success is the fact that NSBAG continues to grow.

2. NSBAG has become a forum for sharing ideas and experiences, allowing members to "bounce off" ideas before implementing them. When the members meet (every

2 months), one important item on the agenda is "who is doing what and who is in town."

3. In the early years of independence, the "us versus them syndrome" was very prevalent among government officials. The government saw itself as the champion of the weak and oppressed. Reforms of the economy were often seen as forms of retaliation against some past injustice, usually of whites. NSBAG has succeeded in bridging the gap between the private sector and the government on matters relating to the small-business sector. There is increasing recognition that economic reform can only work in a win–win situation.

4. NSBAG has effectively pressed for change. Through a system of action plans, it has been possible to target specific inputs in support of SMEs. For example, in August 1992, NSBAG supported the removal of regulations that denied minibuses the right to serve urban commuters. The fact that these regulations have been removed shows the value of collective action. Because the government, NGOs, and the private sector interact freely within NSBAG, consensus is reached even before proposals are tabled in Parliament. Also, because of pressure from the member organizations, a project team has been set up to speed the removal of regulations that inhibit the development of SMEs.

5. It is perhaps due to the work of NSBAG that SMEs are now broadly accepted as a development option by a wide cross section of society.

6. NSBAG has supported a lot of research that has assisted policy formulation. Notable achievements of NSBAG in research include publishing compliance cost studies on metal works, textiles, and food processing. In addition, researchers and advocates of small businesses are invited from time to time to address specific policy issues. For example, L. Tager, of the Law Review Project in South Africa, has presented papers on the process of deregulation (such as Tager 1993) that have contributed much to the current deregulation work in Zimbabwe.

7. The effective communication of ideas, experiences, and policies among those who promote small business is a

major achievement of NSBAG. Communication is principally achieved through *SSE News*, the NSBAG newsletter that is published every 2 months. With a circulation of more than 500, the newsletter is read by many people, including policymakers. Conferences and seminars are another important means of communication. Each seminar or conference focuses on a specific aspect of the action plan. Members of NSBAG freely debate issues of concern, and resolutions constitute new action plans or re-enforce old ones. These resolutions are well received by both the government and other institutions that work with SSEs.

Through NSBAG, an open-ended network has been established. It is important to emphasize that NSBAG is merely a network. Real work takes place when NSBAG members embark on projects. The network can, therefore, not replace these efforts. Real credit belongs to individual members.

NSBAG as a catalyst

The NSBAG also acts as a catalyst. For example, in 1992 NSBAG targeted deregulation of the transport sector as a priority. A new Minister and Permanent Secretary for Transport was appointed that year. The British government funded a consultancy on transport reforms. NSBAG organized a number of seminars with transport as the major focus. In August 1993, NSBAG took a group of Zimbabwean civil servants and members of Parliament to South Africa to observe how deregulation was progressing in that country. They were very impressed with how South Africa had gone about deregulating the transport industry. On their return, they tabled an amendment to the *Transport Act*, and urban transport was deregulated.

The NSBAG is, in essence, merely a forum for consultation and coordination. No single member can claim credit for its achievements.

Future challenges

So far, NSBAG has concentrated on achieving results in its work with the government. To a certain extent, the major hurdles have been passed. But there is more to be done.

There is still a need for effective associations that owners of small businesses can join. As pointed out earlier, there
were many strong associations for small businesses before independence. They all saw themselves as fighting against an ille-
gitimate government that denied them their rights. When the
new government took over, it presented itself as the legitimate
authority that would not only meet all the needs of these
special-interest groups but also represent their interests in
future, and so there was no longer any need for them to exist.
History has proven otherwise. There are no associations that
really represent the interests of small business. If economic
reforms are to be of real use to small business, small businesses
themselves should be the ones to state their case.

The presence of small-business units at ZNCC and CZI
reflects the desire on the part of big business to contribute to the
development of the small-business sector. Such generosity is
nevertheless no substitute for the direct representation of the
small-business sector.

The real challenge for NSBAG is to facilitate the development of grass-roots institutions that really reflect the interests
of the sector. Otherwise, there is the possibility that the government will enter into a dialogue with institutions that do not
really represent small business. Carrying on a dialogue with
individual proprietors of small business is certainly not the
answer.

In an effort to involve small businesses in the national
development dialogue, individual members of NSBAG sponsor
seminars for small business. The objective is not only the artic-
ulation of special problems and the solutions desired by the sector but also the creation of a permanent platform for
articulating the views of those in the small-business sector.
This will not be an easy task. People operating in this sector
have endured oppression for a very long time and may also be
wary of those who with the best intentions may undermine or
defuse small-business owners' own efforts. They have also
learned not to vocally reject offers of support, as this never leads
anywhere.

The challenge is, therefore, to build confidence in these
entrepreneurs so that they can play a meaningful role in shaping the economic future of Zimbabwe. People in the small-
business sector have learned to survive on their own. It is now
very difficult to convince them that those in authority will ever

do anything to help them. The network format is the only way to assist them.

Conclusion

Changing policy is necessarily a very slow process. Each step forward is a pioneering effort that carries with it a lot of risk. Any mistake can easily erase all that has been achieved. To ensure sustainability, sufficient time should be allowed for each step to undergo the test of time, especially at the beginning. NSBAG has learned that government officials do not like to be hurried, but once government officials gain confidence the pace of adoption of new measures is hastened. In fact, sometimes officials set a pace that is too fast for the facilitators.

The success of any effort to help small business can only be measured by the extent to which the proprietors assert themselves in the process and form a true partnership with those helping them. But the poor are generally wary of those who promise to alleviate their condition. Out of sheer politeness, they may show an interest in all offers of support. NSBAG has still some way to go before it is genuinely accepted by the poor.

There are many signs that NSBAG has indeed achieved what it set out to do. But the work may be ongoing — as long as the small-business sector remains weak, NSBAG will be of use. *

CREATING A PRIVATE-SECTOR ENVIRONMENT IN TOGO

E.R. Assignon
Faculty of Economic and Management Sciences,
Centre for Business Administration,
Benin University, Lomé, Togo

M. Sow
United Nations Industrial Development Organization,
Lomé, Togo

Introduction

An outstanding fact around the world today, and especially in Africa, is the retreat of the state from involvement in economic activity. Because most state enterprises have ended in failure, we are now witnessing a new approach that aims to reinvigorate the private sector.

This new direction that African countries are taking means promoting a dynamic, effective, diversified, and competitive private sector, at the national level of course, but also at the regional and international levels. To make this possible, steps have to be taken to encourage private investment. This is essential because the business sector in Africa, and in particular the SMEs, is called on to take the place of the state as the main engine of the continent's economic and social development. But up until now, the African SME sector has been viewed as ineffective. Indeed, it has been suffering from tremendous problems, which have hampered and discouraged its development.

In Togo, the public authorities have set up support structures to help the private sector develop to the point where it can assume the tasks of public enterprises. Have these efforts achieved their goals? What impact have these structures had on the growth of local entrepreneurship? Is there a proper environ-ment for SMEs to grow and flourish? This paper attempts to answer these questions by analyzing some of the structures in place to promote SMEs in Togo.

The social and economic context in Togo

Togo is a small rectangle of 56 000 km², squeezed between the Republic of Bénin to the east, Ghana to the west, Burkina Faso to the north, and the Atlantic Ocean to the south. With a popu-lation of 3.5 million, Togo is essentially a land of farmers and merchants. It is especially famous for the *Nanas Benz* of the marketplace at Lomé.

Despite the changes that the Togolese economy has gone through since independence, the primary sector still con-tributes something more than 30% of the gross domestic prod-uct (GDP), as Table 1 shows. The secondary sector is not well developed and only accounts for about one quarter of the GDP. In contrast, the tertiary sector has been thriving and now con-tributes almost half of the GDP, despite having receded some-what during the late 1980s as a result of the world economic crisis. Table 1 shows that restaurants and hotels are the most

Table 1. Structure of gross domestic product (GDP) of Togo, 1987–1991.

Economic sector	Contribution to GDP (%)				
	1987	1988	1989	1990	1991
Primary					
Food production	18.22	19.05	19.56	NA	NA
Export crops	4.08	3.42	3.79	NA	NA
Total (entire sector)	32.37	32.89	33.24	33.91	33.70
Secondary					
Extractive industries	7.46	8.97	8.82	NA	NA
Manufacturing industries	6.38	6.24	6.64	NA	NA
Construction and public works	3.98	3.42	3.12	21.63	NA
Total (entire sector)	20.33	21.83	22.46	NA	22.66
Tertiary					
Commerce, restaurants, and hotels	24.70	23.59	23.13	NA	NA
Transportation	6.33	5.97	5.80	NA	NA
Public services	9.77	9.34	9.00	NA	NA
Total (entire sector)	47.30	45.28	44.30	44.46	43.63

Source: Compiled from data in the *Macroeconomic Framework*, published by the Togo Ministry of Economy and Finance.
Note: NA, not available.

developed among commercial activities. This is why we speak of Togo as a country of merchants.

The public authorities have taken many steps to overcome the weakness in the country's secondary sector and, especially, to help increase the contribution of industrial output to the GDP, or to help encourage the private sector. Let us look first at the formalities for starting up a business, to see whether this goal has been met.

Administration and taxation framework

Start-up formalities

Start-up formalities constitute four stages that an entrepreneur must go through to create a business. Each of these four stages requires visits to, respectively, six, seven, five, and one different locations. According to a report from the United States Agency for International Development (USAID 1990), start-up formalities in Togo are cumbersome and costly. In the best case, it takes 62 days and at least 60 000 XOF (in 1994, 570 CFA francs [XOF] = 1 United States dollar [USD]) to set up an individual enterprise with a capital stock of 700 000 XOF. (One French franc [FRF] = 50 XOF; these expenses are, therefore, 1 200 FRF for capital of 14 000 FRF.) This means that at least 9% of a company's capital goes to administrative formalities. The entrepreneur is penalized by having to pay taxes even before the business gets off the ground.

Clearly, some real barriers stand in the way of setting up a business in Togo. These formalities lead many entrepreneurs to set themselves up informally. Bureaucratic formalities and requirements can eat up an entrepreneur's time in Togo, compared with Florida, for example, where it takes only 3.5 hours to register a small enterprise (de Soto 1989).

Taxation

The Togolese entrepreneur has to start paying taxes in advance, even before he or she has the authorizations to launch a business. According to the tax officials, many small entrepreneurs "disappear into the woods" once the legal formalities are completed, to prevent this, advance payment for a licence (a professional tax) is required.

Generally, a business pays tax on the profits it has earned every year. In Togo, the normal rate of this tax is 40%. It is internationally acknowledged that paying taxes is always something of a problem for taxpayers. Because the tax payable by corporations is proportional to their profit at the end of the year, the tax officials say that many businesses escape paying tax because they end their year with a loss or with too small a profit. (During our research, we frequently came across two balance sheets for the same year and for the same enterprise. When we looked into this, we found that it was common practice for businesses to keep two or three sets of books for the same year: one for the owners [the only set that reflects the real situation of the firm], one for the banker, and one for the tax service.) To get around this currently widespread practice, the state charges all regularly established businesses a minimum tax of between 1.5 and 3% of their turnover, regardless of their profit or costs for the year (Togo Ministry of Economy and Finance 1983). In principle, this tax represents a down payment on corporate or income tax. At the end of the year, if the amount paid is less than the tax due, the business will pay the normal tax; if it is more than the tax due, the state keeps it anyway.

Having to pay this minimum tax can ruin a business that is having problems, especially if it has had a loss several years in a row. The direct result of the tax is the progressive reduction of its business capital. In the long run, the business may find its basic financial balance ruined. If the business has been borrowing from a bank, the business may find it is impossible to continue doing so, unless it agrees to put in fresh capital to reestablish its financial balance. So, it is easy to see why a Togolese SME subject to the minimum tax may well disappear over the long run if its profit cannot always cover its minimum tax obligations.

In the fiscal year 1990/91, there were 996 firms registered with the Statistics Office (Togo Ministry of Planning and Land Development 1991): 262 commercial firms (26.31%); 525 service firms (52.71%); 103 hotel companies (10.34%); and 106 industrial firms (10.64%).

These statistics confirm that commercial firms, hotels, and services make up the bulk (89%) of Togo's economic fabric beyond the primary sector. These are sectors that do not require a major investment. Togo's SMEs are preoccupied with the short-term bottom line, just like SMEs in general (Cloutier 1973;

Robidoux and Garnier 1973; Deeks 1976). In a study carried out for the European Economic Community (EEC 1991), company executives insisted that in light of the constraints weighing on them, they could never afford to go into a business where they would have to wait for results. Furthermore, if entrepreneurs have to wait for profits to appear, they may have problems with their financiers, who are not necessarily bankers. Under these circumstances, then, it is easy to appreciate that the levying of a minimum tax on all firms is just one more factor that can drive Togo's SMEs to early bankruptcy, particularly the weaker ones. By way of example, a study currently under way on joint ventures in Togo shows that between 1980 and 1991, 590 joint ventures, mainly involving French partners, were registered with the Ministry of Trade and Transportation. When an attempt was made to trace them, it was found that only 150 of them, or 25%, were still in business. This study is being conducted by our local team from the Entrepreneurship Network of the Association of Partially or Entirely French Language Universities – University of Francophone Networks (l'Association des universités partiellement ou entièrement de langue français – Université des réseaux d'expression française, AUPELF–UREF) and will shed light on all the factors behind the closing of these businesses. It is worth noting that the registry kept by the Ministry of Trade and Transportation reports only information on established firms and has no up-to-date data on which ones are still in business. Of the 590 joint ventures, only the 150 still active are listed among the 996 firms registered with the Statistics Office (Togo Ministry of Planning and Land Development 1991).

Levying the minimum tax certainly helps the state minimize its losses on corporate income tax, but it represents a real obstacle to the development of Togo's private sector. According to the National Employers' Council (le Conseil national du patronat, CNP), "under present economic conditions, this tax serves to impoverish firms and foreclose their futures" (CNP 1991, p. 14).

The Investment Code

The Investment Code became a part of Togo's economic system in 1965. The Code "represents a legal, fiscal and financial act by which the State undertakes to renounce certain of its prerogatives for a fixed period" (Togo 1989); its purpose was to attract investors to the country's industrial sectors by offering economic conditions favourable to their activities.

Under the first three versions of the Togo Investment Code, the sectors eligible for its investment benefits did not include many domestic SMEs, but the Code generally favoured foreign enterprises. Nevertheless, there were three areas of potential benefit to domestic investors:

- Industrial crops, fishing, and related activities were permitted under the Code to attract investment from domestic SMEs, but to this day these activities remain in the informal sector. There were some attempts to organize industrial crop producers into cooperatives, but these cooperatives soon disappeared because of their tremendous management problems.

- Although transportation businesses are largely controlled by Togolese citizens, these businesses are not organized to meet the terms of the Code or benefit from its investment advantages. There is an entire region of the country (the home of the Tem people) where the greatest part of investment goes into transport. This investment is often made by rich *El Hadj*, which are rarely organized as formal companies. This sector was in fact suppressed after the second revision of the Code, while the autonomous Port of Lomé was growing rapidly. The autonomous Port of Lomé serves Sahel countries like Burkina Faso, Niger, and Mali, and the development of this port was intended to encourage the creation of transportation firms to take advantage of the market for shipping goods to and from those land-locked countries.

- There is no doubt that social-housing societies could have attracted private-sector money, given the tremendous need for such housing in the country. But that business does not produce immediate profits. Domestic SMEs wanting to invest there will need special conditions to survive, and these the Code does not offer.

However, the new version of the Code promulgated in October 1989 (Togo 1989) does offer some real opportunities to Togolese SMEs. It incorporates new sectors specifically to encourage the national private sector. These include industrial equipment maintenance, local product packaging, and production-scale handicrafts.

The Investment Code is so cumbersome and ineffective that "it is of no interest to business" (EEC 1991, p. 41). As proof of this, only two businesses have been approved under it since 1989, and two others are under study (EEC 1991). (According to the EEC study, promoters are waiting for the Code to prove its effectiveness. Unfortunately, it can only do so if enterprises are interested in taking advantage of it.) Furthermore, in the period from 1969 to 1985, only 20 domestic SMEs were declared eligible for benefits, or fewer than two per year.

Yet this Code could be of real help and encouragement to SMEs if it were practical, effective, and simple in its application. If it were open to the traditional areas of Togolese entrepreneurial activity, it might promote the "formalization" of the country's countless struggling microenterprises and help turn them into true small businesses, better organized and more likely to be profitable.

The eligible business areas have not attracted investors from either Togo or elsewhere in Africa. Either the investors have no interest, or, as one businessman put it, the conditions they would have to meet are beyond the reach of local entrepreneurs, and the procedures for establishing firms are too cumbersome. Perhaps, what is required is a number of special hand-holding measures, simple procedures that would appeal to local investors, and also perhaps some education to help them see the value of participating.

Customs protection

One way of encouraging the survival and development of a national private sector is to provide it with border protection through customs measures. On this score, everyone agrees that Togo's customs service needs reorganizing. According to business people, customs tariffs increase the purchase price of imported products considerably. Customs formalities are costly and time consuming, and the tariffs themselves can vary, depending on the relationship between the entrepreneur and the customs official. This situation works to the favour of a few large firms whose owners are especially clever. It has been noted in fact that it is of great advantage to foreign enterprises established in Togo. It is common to see two merchants import the same goods at different tariff rates.

Institutional framework

Credit Guarantee Fund for Togolese Enterprises

The Credit Guarantee Fund for Togolese Enterprises (le Fonds de garantie des crédits aux entreprises togolaises, FGCET) is managed by the National Investment Corporation (la Société nationale d'investissement, SNI) "for the purpose of promoting national private initiative by guaranteeing access for Togolese enterprises to the credit necessary for their development" (SNI 1980, p. 1). To this end, "it assists by extending its guarantee for credits provided to corporations and individuals of Togolese nationality by banks, financial companies and suppliers, whether located in Togo or not" (SNI 1980, p. 2). FGCET also gives a counter guarantee to signed undertakings accepted by banks in favour of these same Togolese firms.

This should be an excellent initiative for encouraging the creation and development of SMEs in Togo. Unfortunately, the fund offers nothing as an incentive to banks or financial companies. It offers only a back-up guarantee, which means that bankers will turn to the fund only if their clients are unable to honour their obligations. In effect, the fund was stillborn. In any case, anyone wanting to make use of the fund's guarantee has to meet numerous conditions — the beneficiary firm has to agree to certain constraints and, in particular, to accept in writing the principle that SNI has control at all times of any business that is guaranteed and that credit obtained must be used according to conditions set by SNI's management committee. Togolese entrepreneurs often prefer individual enterprise over a corporate structure simply because they do not want other people meddling in their affairs. As a result, FGCET is unable to help many businesses, although they are nearly all in desperate need of funds.

We approached several Togolese entrepreneurs (20, to be exact) for their views of FGCET. Most of them (75%) would like to see the fund reactivated (as would the National Employers' Council), but they say the conditions of access should be changed. These entrepreneurs feel that if SNI is prepared to provide a guarantee, it should trust them to use the funds properly, without standing behind them like a policeman. The fund is now being reorganized and should be reactivated once the country returns to political stability.

The National Investment Fund

The National Investment Fund (le Fonds national d'investissement, FNI) was set up to encourage businesses to invest. The businesses contribute 0.5% of their annual turnover to this fund. This is deposited with SNI, and FNI issues a certificate. To get these forced savings back, firms have to make an investment within 2 years equal to three times that of the certificate. Otherwise, the deposits become FNI bonds with a 40-year term, at 3% interest.

The FNI was originally created to force foreign enterprises to reinvest part of their profits in the country. In practice, however, it represents a tax on all businesses.

This system amounts purely and simply to the blocking of funds for the term of the bonds. In light of the special financial risks that SMEs face anyway, participating in FNI is a serious problem for them. Because most SMEs are chronically short of cash, they have to resort to bank overdrafts to pay this contribution (CNP 1991, p. 16), and the rate they pay on overdrafts ranges from 14 to 16%.

Thus, the conditions of access to FNI, far from encouraging private-sector development, represent a distinct handicap, and, of course, FNI has failed to achieve its purpose. Its logic is contrary to any rational theory of finance. How can someone in an economy where capital is scarce be expected to borrow at 14% and invest at 3% for 40 years? How can any company pay the difference without draining its own resources? Even when a company does not resort to bank credit to pay FNI, how can its managers justify the investment of its owners' money at 3%, when there are risk-free returns available at 7–8.5%? In light of all this, entrepreneurs are justified in calling FNI a tax.

The irony is that Togolese SMEs (especially those prospering to some extent) will some day have a pile of FNI certificates worth more than their company; in the meantime, they are continuing on in acute need of working capital.

In developing countries, priority should be given to mobilizing savings in support of the private sector and making the best possible use of such resources. Schemes to be avoided are those that extract what few resources these companies have. In the case of FNI, its intentions may be good, but the way it is working is strangling the country's SMEs.

Conclusion

This paper examines only a few of the structures set up to promote the private sector in Togo, but from these it is possible to
conclude that public policies have a negative impact on the promotion of Togolese entrepreneurship. There are many brakes in
the system. The complex bureaucratic procedures, the failure to
recognize the realities faced by entrepreneurs, and the inaccura-
cies and inconsistencies in the ways officials apply the provisions make life difficult for business people. Far from helping to
promote private-sector development in Togo, this environment
is stifling such efforts.

The institutional framework that Togo has set up may
indeed be favourable for business development, but what kind
of business? It is certainly not much help to the local SMEs,
which make up the bulk of the national private sector.

This situation has in fact encouraged the emergence of
the informal sector. Thus, trade with countries of the Economic
Community of West African States (la Communauté
économique des États d'Afrique de l'Ouest, CEDEAO) and with
the rest of Africa is largely conducted in the informal sector.
Formally constituted SMEs play only a small role, as the official
statistics demonstrate. This trade is essentially carried on by
the women of the Lomé market. We talked with two of them —
two young women among the 30 or so who sell goods of all
kinds, ranging from cloth, to lingerie, to food products. The first
woman we talked with had customers mainly in Central Africa.
On each trip, she delivered about 5 million XOF worth of goods.
The second woman we talked with traveled between Togo,
Bénin, and Côte d'Ivoire, and on each trip she bought goods
worth 6–10 million XOF. If each of these women made one trip a
month, she would be doing between 60 and 120 million XOF
worth of business each year.

Each time the women pass through customs, the customs officers hold them to ransom for 5–10% of the money they
are carrying (the going rate is 10% in Abidjan). Of course there
is nothing in the agreements governing CEDEAO trade that autho-
rizes customs officers to impose levies on traders on their own
initiative — the customs officers simply issue no receipts.

So, these traders must set aside at least 6–12 million XOF
of their yearly turnover for bribes at customs. Of course, if the
start-up formalities were faster and simpler, the tax rate were

set more reasonably, and the rules were less constricting, then these traders might find it in their interest to set themselves up as formal SMEs, which would also give the state a new source of revenue.

From what we have now seen, it is easier to understand why the *Nanas Benz* are so active. They are happy to stay in the informal sector rather than formalizing their affairs. They are so well positioned that they are able to take on competition from the entire CEDEAO common market, something the formal SMEs are not ready to do. At present, these traders are the ones who are fulfilling the intention of CEDEAO.

Despite its good intentions, the state has not achieved its goals. In the laws and regulations we have reviewed, there was a definite intention to promote the private sector. However, the changes and measures that this implies are not yet taking place or being installed. The fact that the rules are out of step with the social context of the country poses a very serious problem for the expansion of Togo's private sector.

The rules and laws will have to be revised for the purposes of regional integration and allowing local SMEs to become more competitive. The government will have to cooperate with the private sector in developing a policy to promote SMEs that is more consistent and offers more incentives, so that everyone's interests can be reconciled.

Little use seems to be made of the business know-how of Togo's SMEs. Despite the plethora of assistance and promotion schemes — whether it is a World Bank project, a United Nations Industrial Development Organization (UNIDO) program, or any of the various other initiatives launched to improve the SME environment in Togo — Togo's SMEs are no better off.

This implies that the whole approach to promoting and helping Togolese enterprise should be changed for investment to be of any use. At the same time, there has to be better coordination of activities in this field — this is the goal of a project now under way to create a House of Enterprise. A lot of money has been invested, but so far its impact has been diluted because activities are not coordinated or consolidated. The political situation in the country for the last 3 years has not helped either.

In an attempt to improve this situation, a wide-ranging analysis was undertaken to design a master program for managing industrial development. It had the following main goals:

- dealing with institutional problems;

- creating greater dynamism in the financing of SMEs;
- studying the various routes to profitable investment;
- helping and encouraging SMEs;
- making use of local resources; and
- setting up free zones for export processing.

Despite the weak impact various initiatives have had, all the conditions are theoretically in place for promoting the private sector in Togo. The main objectives are to adapt bureaucratic rules and laws to present-day reality and to instill a greater sense of public morality in officials. ✳

Part III

Regulatory Reform

How the Legal, Regulatory, and Tax Framework Affects the Dynamics of Enterprise Growth

Donald C. Mead
*Department of Economics, Michigan State University,
East Lansing, MI, USA*[1]

Introduction

One of the most important challenges facing the countries of Africa is the creation of jobs. With only limited absorptive capacity in traditional agriculture and with stagnant or declining employment opportunities in the public sector and in large private firms, attention is turning to the capacity of small enterprises to provide productive employment for an increasing number of job-seekers.

Efforts to support the growth of small enterprises generally focus on one of three different target groups: newly established businesses or people starting up a new business; existing enterprises struggling to survive and perhaps to grow a bit; and existing small businesses seeking to graduate to the intermediate size. These diverse groups have the potential to contribute in different ways to employment. They also face different problems and constraints.

This paper explores some of the employment growth patterns of small enterprises and microenterprises and the ways these enterprise dynamics are affected by the policy environment, particularly the legal, regulatory, and tax framework

---

[1] The author is also Co-Director, Research on Growth and Dynamics of Microenterprises, with the GEMINI Project.

(LRTF), of countries in southern Africa. The paper starts with an examination of enterprise start-ups, then explores factors that have led some new enterprises to close. The third section looks at patterns of growth among existing enterprises, distinguishing between constraints faced by enterprises that expand only a little and those faced by enerprises that graduate to the intermediate size. The final section summarizes the findings.

Enterprise start-ups

Over the long term, most of the new jobs in small enterprises in southern Africa have come through start-ups of new enterprises. Studies indicate that 75–80% of all current jobs in small enterprises came into being when the enterprise itself was started (the remainder resulted from the expansion of existing enterprises some time after start-up). This growth in employment through new starts has several important characteristics:

- The rate of formation of new enterprises is quite high. The rate has been estimated at about 14% per year in Zimbabwe for the period 1981–1989, a figure that may be representative of the rates in other countries in the region. Contrary to what some have argued, there does not appear to have been an overall shortage of new starts of small enterprises in southern Africa.

- Most newly established small enterprises are very small, are located in rural areas, and rely heavily on the entrepreneur and unpaid family members.

- Many new enterprises do not last for long: the attrition rate of newly established units is substantial.

- There is considerable year-to-year variability in the number of new jobs created through start-ups of new enterprises.

Analysis currently under way will test the hypothesis that the rate of job creation through start-ups of small enterprises is inversely proportional to macroeconomic growth: when things are going well, there are fewer start-ups, but when the macroeconomy is under stress, start-ups increase. If this hypothesis is true, it would suggest that an important driving force behind many of these new starts is the unavailability of better alternatives.

How does the LRTF affect the rate of new starts of microenterprises? The answer appears to be this: at a micro level, very little.

Two sets of data support this answer. The first set is from an Organisation for Economic Co-operation and Development (OECD) study focusing on the impact of laws and regulations on small enterprises and microenterprises in Swaziland and Niger (Joumard et al. 1992). That study found that only about half of the small enterprises and microenterprises in Swaziland and two thirds of those in Niger had the requisite registration or trading licences. Those two countries were selected for study in part because it was expected that the burden of registration was much more onerous in francophone than in anglophone countries. When account was taken of other key variables (location, size, and sector), however, the likelihood of registering turned out not to differ significantly between the two countries.

As part of the OECD study, a survey asked those entrpreneurs who had the required permits how burdensome it had been to obtain them. It asked the entrepreneurs who did not have them why they remained unregistered and whether this had created problems for them. For those who were registered, the direct transaction costs of registration were surprisingly low. In Swaziland, for example, it took on average 2.2 months for an applicant to receive a licence; for more than half of the applicants, the waiting time was 1 month or less. The average amount of time required from the entrepreneur for this process averaged only 2.3 hours. In Niger, the comparable measures were even lower. These figures differ sharply from the "famous" 289 days required to register an informal enterprise in Peru (de Soto 1989). Of course, obtaining a licence generally implies subsequent obligations to comply with other regulations (including, especially, the payment of taxes), but the direct transaction cost of registration appears to be minimal.

Among those entrepreneurs that did not have a licence, only a few indicated that their not having one created problems for them. A few wished to advertise their products and were constrained from doing this by not having a licence. A few others indicated that not having a licence prevented them from obtaining loans from a bank (or, in a few cases, even from opening a bank account). For most, though, it seems to have mattered little whether they had a licence.

The same OECD survey asked owners of small enterprises two questions about the problems they had faced at the time of start-up. The first question asked them to identify the most pressing problems. The second asked specifically about regulatory and tax constraints. In response to the first question, only 5% of the respondents in Niger and 2% of those in Swaziland mentioned the LRTF as the most important constraint they faced at start-up. Even when prompted by the follow-up question to consider problems in the domain of government regulations and taxes, 88% of the respondents in Niger and 78% of those in Swaziland said that they had no such problems.

The second set of data is from surveys reported by Liedholm and Mead (1993). For those surveys, some 3 500 enterprises in six countries in southern Africa filled in questionnaires investigating the most important problems faced at the time of start-up. The resulting data are grouped in Table 1.

The most striking thing noted by Liedholm and Mead (1993) was the limited extent to which taxes and government regulations were reported as a serious problem for most newly starting small enterprises. These findings, like those of the OECD study, suggest that the problems and constraints faced by newly established small enterprises are much more likely to be in the realm of markets and demand or of working capital, credit, and finance than in the area of taxes, licences, and other government regulations.

South Africa is a partial exception that deserves special comment. Prior to the mid-1980s, government regulations governing economic activities in the townships of South Africa were extremely restrictive (Liedholm and McPherson 1991). Many types of economic activities were forbidden, including all manufacturing, wholesaling, and finance; ownership of nonresidential business premises by blacks was against the law, as were all sales outside the township. Although many of these restrictions have since been removed, they reflect the context in which many existing small enterprises were first established.

Restrictions on business start-ups in other countries of southern Africa reflect two principal motives on the part of the authorities: the confinement of small enterprise activities to particular localities and the maintainance of health requirements. Police sweeps of people doing business in the "wrong places" are common in several of these countries. Sometimes,

Table 1. Perceived problems of microenterprises and small entrepreneurs at the time of start-up.

Type of problem	Respondents (%)					
	Botswana	Lesotho	Malawi	South Africa	Swaziland	Zimbabwe
Working capital, credit, and finance	52.0	21.2	41.0	35.3	51.2	32.9
Markets and demand	16.7	37.9	23.5	28.1	21.6	23.3
Inputs, tools, and machinery	6.0	12.2	13.5	6.9	9.0	25.6
Taxes, licences, and other government regulations	2.0	1.5	5.5	10.9	4.0	3.7
Other[a]	23.3	27.3	16.5	18.3	14.0	15.0

Source: Liedholm and Mead (1993, Table A-1).

[a]The most important problems cited in this category were working space and location, transport, and labour.

this is due to a desire on the part of the policymakers to keep things neat and tidy. In other cases, police sweeps are aimed at protecting established traders from competition from informal sellers. Although a concern about health is appropriate, particularly with enterprises engaged in the sale of prepared foods, there is a risk of this becoming a cloak for protecting existing enterprises (such as when it is argued that the sale of used clothes constitutes a health hazard).

It should be recognized that these questionnaires were given only to existing enterprises. Some people surely have been prevented from starting new businesses by the LRTF. Although the start-up rates for enterprises in southern Africa have been high in recent years, they could have been even higher if regulatory constraints had been eased. This is particularly true for somewhat larger enterprises and for enterprises seeking to get started in product lines or in localities that are more strictly regulated. This suggests that the problem of the LRTF for new start-ups is not a general one but is specific to particular sizes of enterprise, sectors, and localities. For most newly established small enterprises, the LRTF appears not to have been a major issue.

Survivorship

In the developing countries of Africa, as in industrialized countries, many new small enterprises do not survive for long. Unfortunately, estimates of attrition rates among newly established small businesses are frustratingly imprecise. Survey work currently under way in Zimbabwe and in the Dominican Republic will provide more precise estimates of the small business attrition rates for developing countries. In the meantime, existing studies throw important light on the question of why small enterprises go out of business.

Available information is based on a survey approach involving interviews with people who had operated a small business that had closed (Liedholm and Mead 1993). Proprietors were asked to identify the principal reason for the closure of the business. The responses are shown in Table 2.

Table 2 shows that in most countries better opportunities and personal reasons (retirement, sickness, and the like) together contributed to a quarter to a third of the closures. This

Table 2. Reasons for closure of small businesses.

Reasons for business closure	Respondents (%)				
	Botswana	Kenya	Malawi	Swaziland	Zimbabwe
Business problems	41.4	39.4	53.8	55.9	47.5
Better opportunities in another business	4.6	12.2	8.0	5.5	6.5
Personal reasons	30.3	4.1	21.2	22.2	27.9
Legal problems or troubles with government	5.3	20.5	2.9	4.3	5.7
Other reasons	18.4	23.7	14.0	12.2	12.4

Source: Primary data from baseline surveys of small enterprises in each country. Detailed references are provided in Liedholm and Mead (1993).

reminds us that significant numbers of closures should not be considered business failures.

Except in Kenya, only a small proportion of the closures were attributable directly to the LRTF. The case of Kenya deserves special comment. Unlike the other surveys from which the data in Table 2 derive, the survey in Kenya was not nation-wide; rather, it was restricted to one urban slum (Kibera) on the outskirts of Nairobi. This is an area where the government was seeking to control and regulate economic activities of which it did not approve. Episodes of bulldozing and other forms of harassment were not uncommon. The government actions not surprisingly contributed in an important and direct way to firm closures in that setting. In the other countries, though, only a few respondents reported that laws and regulations were directly responsible for the closure of their small enterprises.

These results need careful interpretation; they do not mean that the LRTF was irrelevant to patterns of attrition among small enterprises. Some of the factors reported in Table 2 as business problems were in fact attributable to government regulations and policies. In several countries, a common reason given for closure was limited access to operating funds (20–25% of all respondents in Botswana, Malawi, Swaziland, and Zimbabwe). It is well known that "shortage of funds" is a catch-all phrase concealing a wide variety of problems, particularly poor management; yet nearly a quarter of the respondents identified the shortage of funds as what principally led to the closure of their firms. Although this constraint is categorized here as a business problem, it reflects a host of government policies that make it difficult for many small enterprises to obtain credit. In a similar vein, in Malawi and Zimbabwe, the principal reason cited for closure by nearly 10% of respondents was "shortage or expense of stocks or raw materials." But we know that this shortage is in large measure a result of government policies that channel existing supplies primarily to larger enterprises.

In sum, it appears that the direct effects of the LRTF on firm closures has been limited. Aside from the entrepreneurs in Kibera (Kenya), very few referred to the LRTF as the principal cause of their going out of business. Of more importance are the indirect effects of the LRTF, particularly lack of access to raw materials and intermediate inputs (in Zimbabwe and Malawi) and to operating funds or credit for working capital (in Zimbabwe, Swaziland, Malawi, and Botswana).

Expansion of existing small enterprises

Survey results from several countries suggest that 20–25% of all new jobs in small enterprises have resulted from expansion of existing firms. There are several points about this expansion that are relevant to the topic at hand.

1. Most small enterprises do not grow at all. In all the countries studied, only about one fifth of all enterprises had added to their workforce after they were first established.

2. Among the 20% that do grow, most grow only a little. The great majority of these start out very small, adding only a few workers to their labour force and ending up with well below 10 workers. This "small-growth" category accounts for about two-thirds of the new jobs that are due to expansion of existing enterprises.

3. Only about 1% of the enterprises that start out very small (with fewer than 5 workers) succeed in graduating to an intermediate-size group (with 10 or more workers). This type of movement from very small beginnings to medium size is of particular interest because it often represents the most dynamic segment of small-enterprise growth, creating jobs that may yield higher returns — such enterprises may be more heavily

engaged in export, which may be a particularly good springboard for further growth (Mead et al. 1993). Although less than 1% of all newly established very small enterprises succeed in making this transition, this select group accounts for a third of the employment growth in Botswana and a fifth of the increase in employment in Swaziland and Zimbabwe.

Some have argued that the policy context is a principal determinant of the ability of small enterprises to grow (Young 1993). What evidence can be advanced concerning the LRTF's potential to limit growth?

Surveys in several countries in southern Africa have investigated the principal problem small businesses face during periods of growth (Liedholm and Mead 1993). The main findings of these studies are shown in Table 3.

As in the case of problems at start-up, one must interpret these findings with care. These are the perceptions of entrepreneurs and may not accurately reflect the underlying forces at work. Again, the problem of access to inputs (raw materials and intermediate products, machinery, and tools) appears a serious one in a number of countries. This problem is frequently due to government regulations aimed at controlling the supply of imports and domestically produced materials. Once again, the direct effects of the LRTF appear not to have been of primary concern to respondents.

This set of surveys (Liedholm and Mead 1993) also investigated problems currently faced by the entrepreneur (at the time of the survey). These data are shown in Table 4 for low-growth enterprises and high-growth enterprises (those that had grown a lot — graduated to the intermediate size). The data are from Malawi (for which the most complete information on this topic is available).

The data shown in Table 4 suggest that small enterprises that have grown rapidly face a somewhat different set of problems than small enterprises that have expanded only moderately. Among enterprises that have grown substantially, access to working capital and inputs are more pressing problems than finding markets for their products. There is little evidence here that the direct effects of the LRTF are a serious problem for either of these groups of small enterprises.

Table 3. Perceived problems of microenterprises and small enterprises during periods of growth.

Type of problem	Respondents (%)					
	Botswana	Lesotho	Malawi	South Africa	Swaziland	Zimbabwe
Capital, credit, and finance	25.7	14.3	22.8	28.2	45.3	20.0
Markets and demand	21.8	21.4	14.3	23.4	4.5	24.0
Inputs, tools and machinery	23.0	14.3	28.3	7.8	9.1	24.0
Taxes, licences, and other government regulations	1.3	0	6.5	6.8	0	4.0
Other problems	28.3	50.0	27.8	34.1	40.7	26.1

Source: Primary data from baseline surveys of small enterprises in each country. Detailed references are provided in Liedholm and Mead (1993).

Table 4. Perceived problems at the time of the survey: Malawi.

Most important problem	Respondents (%)	
	Low-growth firms[a]	Graduating firms[b]
Finance	24.5	37.5
Working capital	22.0	37.2
Fixed capital	2.3	0.2
Other	0.1	0
Markets	26.1	1.9
Inputs	35.0	55.2
Tools and equipment	2.7	0.4
Raw materials or intermediate inputs	32.3	54.8
Government policies and regulations	3.2	2.3
Taxes	0.2	1.7
Licences	1.0	0
Zoning or location restrictions	0.1	0
Other	1.8	0.6
Transport	3.6	1.8
Labour	0.8	0.1
Other constraints	6.9	1.5

Source: Primary data from baseline surveys of small enterprises in each country. Detailed references are provided in Liedholm and Mead (1993).
[a]Proportion reporting problems: 88.2%.
[b]Proportion reporting problems: 97.6%.

Summary and Conclusions

Microenterprise dynamics involve a heterogeneous and diverse set of currents and trends. Looking at the four dimensions of change — start-ups, closures, small expansions, and transformations — one can clearly see that these categories of change reflect different forces at work, offer different opportunities, and are subject to different problems and constraints.

Examining the impact of the LRTF on these different categories of change, we find that some common themes emerge. The process of registration (licencing and authorization to operate legally) — steps that are sometimes grouped together under the heading of "formalization of informal-sector enterprises" — appears to have been of significance only to a few newly established enterprises. Exceptions were enterprises seeking to get under way in more closely regulated sectors (such as restaurants) or in localities where the government sought to protect existing producers or to control the geographic development of enterprises. For most new small producers, the process of formalization appears not to have been a major hurdle, at least, for

those who passed it, nor does it appear to have been a major constraint for those who have chosen to bypass or ignore it.

The impact of the LRTF on enterprise dynamics goes far
beyond that of registration. Two major themes emerge from this
discussion. Access to credit was a major issue for firms that
ceased production, as well as for those that have grown. Access
to inputs was also a major issue in several countries (although
not all). It is well known that complaints about the unavailability of credit can reflect a wide range of inadequacies in the management of the enterprise; conversely, an ability to establish
effective procedures for input procurement and inventory control is a characteristic of good management. Yet it is clear that
the ability of entrepreneurs to deal with these challenges is
strongly influenced by the policy environment in which they
operate.

In discussions of the process of change in the LRTF in
which small enterprises operate, it is helpful to have some idea
of which aspects of that environment are hindering growth in
enterprise. The discussion of this paper suggests that these two
areas — access to credit and access to raw materials and intermediate inputs — may be the most important factors affecting
the ability of small enterprises to get started, to survive, and to
grow. ✤

CREATING AN ENABLING ENVIRONMENT FOR THE DEVELOPMENT OF SMALL-SCALE ENTERPRISE THROUGH TAX REFORM: THE CASE OF UGANDA, 1986-1993

Justin Zake
Uganda Revenue Authority, Kampala, Uganda

Background

The economy in Uganda had been devastated in the early 1970s and 1980s, so the National Resistance Movement government, which came to power in January 1986, faced the monumental task of reviving both the productive and the financial sectors. In particular, the government had to control inflation, which was running at an annual rate of more than 360%, reduce the imbalances in the external accounts, improve producer incentives, improve the allocation and use of public resources, rehabilitate the infrastructure, and promote growth.

In 1987, with the help of the International Monetary Fund, the World Bank, and other donors, the Government of Uganda launched its Economic Recovery Programme. The program had a macroeconomic thrust: the intent was that an improved macroenvironment would create a suitable business climate in which the private entrepreneur could thrive. The results of the program, especially in relation to growth objectives and inflation control, are now being realized. Growth for the period 1986/87 to 1992/93 has been more than 5% per annum. Inflation has declined to a level of –2% per annum as of June 1993, although the underlying rate appears to be about 8% if the food element, which constitutes more than half of the inflation index, is removed.

During all the economic hardships, the resilience of Uganda's economy can probably be attributed to an underlying but vibrant sector of the economy, namely, small-scale enterprises (SSEs). The predominant sector, agriculture, is on the whole characterized by small-scale farmers in the monetary and the nonmonetary (subsistence) sectors. These farmers have sustained Uganda's export industry, particularly that of coffee. This pattern is slowly changing as diversification into other agro-based exports takes root, again led by the SSEs. At present, no large-scale mining and quarrying are taking place in Uganda; this sector is also dominated by SSEs. The manufacturing sector, too, is not devoid of SSEs, especially in agro-processing. The same phenomenon is evident in the construction, commerce, and transport sectors. SSEs have sustained the economy of Uganda. Thus, there is a need to focus on the characteristics of the business environment in which they operate and to evolve policies that would make it easier for the SSEs to grow and achieve economies of scale through better management and productivity techniques.

The nature of small-scale enterprises in Uganda

For the purposes of this paper, the definition of SSEs is quite broad, ranging from a one-person business or venture to a company registered under the legal provisions. The definition of a small enterprise often revolves around such parameters as size, turnover, or number of employees. However, it is the opinion of the author that SSEs have to be defined in the context of the economy and the cultural and social peculiarities of a particular country. Enterprises in which a small-scale operator is engaged in a gainful business activity, whether as an individual, in partnership, or (to take advantage of limited liability) in a corporation, are what this paper means by SSEs. More explicitly, in the context of the economic activities in Uganda, SSEs would include the following:

- sole proprietors in various retail trades;
- service organizations, such as beauty salons, small construction companies, secretarial service bureaus, artisans, and private taxi operators;
- small-scale farmers;
- small agro-processing industries;

- small mining establishments; and
- professionals under the categories of medical practitioners, lawyers, architects, engineers, and accountants.

There has been some concern over the lack of SSE promotion in the mainstream of government policy and, in this context, tax policy. This lack has sometimes been attributed to two causes:

1. SSE policy is confined to a small section in the ministry responsible for industry and

2. SSEs do not have distinct and identifiable associations or groups through which they can forcefully channel their policy requirements.

It is argued that as a result, policy formulation is left to the whims and desires of macroeconomic planners who do not have sufficient knowledge of the sector and thus put in place policies that may not be consonant with the needs of the SSEs. Although this position may generally be true, the SSEs in Uganda, out of the dire need to have government listen to their plight, have formed specific and general organizations to advance their concerns.

On the government side, the Tax Policy Division of the Ministry of Finance and Economic Planning has been receiving tax policy proposals from various groups, including those representing SSEs. After study, the division has taken some of the proposals into account in formulating tax policy. Because this Tax Policy Division is in the ministry responsible for fiscal policy, the channel through which representative groups, including SSEs, have to pass to present their interests is shortened considerably. Further, the Uganda Revenue Authority, the tax-collecting arm of government is charged by statute to advise government on tax policy matters. Because the authority is in continual contact with the tax-paying public, it can gauge the practicability of tax measures and their impact on compliance. In this vein, the authority has opened up dialogue with representative groups of taxpayers and has offered formal seminars for them. Its advice to government has included some proposals presented to it by these groups, including those representing SSEs. To a large extent, therefore, private-sector involvement in the formulation of tax policy in Uganda has been institutionalized with the objective of providing a balance between macro- and microeconomic needs.

On the SSE side, starting in 1988, powerful lobby groups, whose aim is to promote the needs of enterprises in general, began to emerge. These groups include the Uganda Manufacturers Association (UMA), which was formed to further the needs of local manufacturers irrespective of size. Not to be outdone, and in the belief that UMA represents the larger and more powerful middle- to high-class enterprises, other manufacturers formed the Uganda Small Scale Industries Association (USSIA) to solicit manufacturing incentives, especially credit, for its members. Another institution that would normally look after the interests of the trading community in general is the Uganda National Chamber of Commerce and Industry (UNCCI). This institution, which used to thrive in the mid-1960s and early 1970s, suffered from mismanagement and self-interest and is now only reviving, although its "industrial arm" broke away to form the UMA. Offshoot SSE groups with the specific aim of advancing their own needs have also emerged under UNCCI. These groups include the Uganda Importers and Exporters Association, formed as a pressure group against high taxes; the Kikuubo Traders Association, which looks after the interests of small-scale traders and importers in the hub of the capital city; the Uganda National Farmers Association, whose aim is to promote the needs of Uganda's farmers, both big and small; the Uganda National Coffee Association, which is an association of private coffee processors and exporters; and the Uganda Clearing and Forwarding Agents Association, which represents the licenced customs-clearing agents who interact with the Customs and Excise Department of Uganda Revenue Authority on a day-to-day basis.

Overview of the taxation system in Uganda

In Uganda, the major tax types can be divided into direct and indirect taxes as follows:

Direct taxes	Indirect taxes
Personal income tax	Customs duty on imports
Pay-as-you-earn (PAYE) personal income tax	Sales tax on imports
Income tax deposit	Excise duties
Corporation tax	Sales tax on local products
Withholding tax	Surtax
Stamp duty	Commercial transactions levy
Fees and licences	Re-export levy

All sses that are not incorporated as limited-liability entities, that is, those that fall in the sole proprietor and partnership categories, are subject to the personal income tax schedule, but as businesses, they qualify for certain deductions. Their net incomes may fall into any one of the personal income tax brackets within which they will be taxed; in addition, they are given a threshold level that attracts no tax. The limited-liability sses are subject to the normal corporate tax rate also enjoyed by larger enterprises, and it is a moot point whether this rate was necessarily designed with the large-scale enterprises (LSEs) in mind. However, the trend in Uganda's tax system is toward lower taxes over a broader tax base, so sses would stand to benefit from the lower tariff structure.

With the general lack of a tax-paying culture and the underdevelopment of the voluntary declaration and self-assessment modes of tax compliance, the majority of sses, whether in the formal or informal sector, are subject to a presumptive income tax deposit. This is normally payable as a lump sum at the beginning of a trading year. In Uganda, each trading enterprise is required to obtain an income tax clearance certificate indicating that income taxes were paid before the relevant licencing authority can issue an annual trading licence. Whereas the limited liability enterprises can obtain an income tax clearance certificate on the basis of their annual tax returns and tax payment record, the smaller business enterprises would normally have to pay a lump-sum deposit before they are issued with a tax clearance certificate that qualifies them for a trading licence. The demand for a lump-sum payment (which is income tax in advance) rather than installments may easily be perceived as inequitable.

All sses that are involved in the import trade must pay customs duty and sales tax on imports. They are also subject to local sales tax if they manufacture goods in the domestic economy and this tax was not charged on the raw material inputs. Many sses are not registered for domestic sales tax purposes — those involved in small-scale manufacture, for example, normally pay their sales tax on inputs. Excise duties are confined to a small group of products: alcoholic beverages and spirits, cigarettes, and mineral and carbonated waters. However, sses are not, in the main, involved in manufacturing these. sses that import these products have to pay an import excise rate. All service-oriented enterprises, including sses, are subject to a commercial transactions levy, which is a sales tax at the point of retail. It can be argued that this retail sales tax is a tax on tax; however, it can only be eliminated if a broad-based tax on value added is introduced.

The tax policy concerns of the SSE sector

The SSEs convey their tax policy concerns to government through their representative groups. Both UMA and USSIA have prepared various economic studies with the aid of international organizations and have invited government policy planners to seminars and workshops. The executive committees of these organizations act as advocates for their members to the highest levels of authority in Uganda. The Parliamentary Committee on the Economy has also received representations from these and other groups, and their submissions are considered in Parliamentary debates on fiscal measures. In present-day Uganda, there has not been a shortage of channels through which SSEs can make representations.

Representations of the Uganda Small Scale Industries Association

A study prepared by USSIA and the Friedrich Ebert Foundation (1992) and presented to the Ministry of Finance and Economic Planning raised a number of tax-related issues. The study contended that SSEs have little or no capacity to keep and prepare annual books of accounts. Because of this, the SSEs were not being assessed on profits but had since 1974 been paying an income tax deposit or presumptive tax that was considered unfair. This deposit system was also perceived as punitive to the SSE because it was paid in advance of earnings in one lump sum, and the levels were considered too high. The study concluded with a plea to government to undertake a careful analysis of the implications for SSEs of the tax policy, keeping in mind the following issues:

- The business tax should be equitable and based on actual performance rather than being a lump-sum prepayment or estimated assessment.
- Business beginners, regardless of size or type, should be exempted from tax deposits because investors are discouraged if they are required to pay income tax deposits before the business starts operating.

- Very small enterprises with capital assets worth 500–10 000 USD should be assessed a flat tax payable at the end of the year of operation. The SSEs with capital assets above this threshold could then be encouraged to pay taxes assessed on profitability, and only those that are unable to prepare books would be required to pay income tax deposits. All SSEs with capital assets worth less than 500 USD should be totally exempt from tax.

Apart from central government taxes, SSEs pay charges and levies to local authorities. These local fees include trading licence fees; a graduated tax or poll tax for individuals over 18 years of age; market dues, which are charged daily for market stalls; movement of goods licence (hawkers licence) fees; and ground rents. The USSIA study raised the complaint that the multiplicity of charges levied by different tax-collecting authorities had a negative effect on the profitability of the SSEs. Implicit was that these multiple charges inhibit growth of the SSEs and prevent them from graduating to formal status and thus from enjoying the benefits formal status provides.

The study also recommended the following reforms to government:

- To promote savings and investment, eliminate the distortions in personal income tax that affect business performance.

- Eliminate the indirect taxes that affect business performance; levy no tax on capital equipment and all imported raw materials.

- Strengthen tax administration and collection, increase taxpayer audits, and intensify efforts to identify taxpayers so that taxes are spread across a broader base to avoid overtaxation of individuals.

- Increase the tariffs on imported goods that have equivalents manufactured domestically.

- Severely restrict tax exemptions on imported goods.

- Discourage luxury commodities or regulate these through taxation.

- Streamline the procedures for setting up a business by removing high-cost impediments such as income tax deposits, registration charges, licencing fees, and complicated paper work.

- Simplify tax assessment procedures, tax forms, and tax payment processes because most small-scale entrepreneurs do not understand them.
- Increase the interaction between the tax assessors and the taxpayers by having the tax assessors visit SSEs, not only to carry out on-the-spot assessments, but also to educate and help the taxpayer meet the tax obligations.
- Tax authorities at the district levels should work hand in hand with the district USSIA offices while assessing taxes for their zonal members.

This last proposal was meant to enhance the tax education of USSIA members and encourage their compliance with income tax law.

The survey of small-scale enterprises

Although many SSEs have groups to represent them, some are not represented by the "industrially oriented" USSIA. For this reason, the author carried out a limited survey of 130 SSEs around the capital city, Kampala, to get views on the tax system from a cross section of SSEs. A questionnaire similar to the one used in the survey is presented in Appendix A, and Appendix B shows a breakdown of the types of SSEs surveyed. The survey sought taxpayers' opinions on tariffs, direct and indirect taxes, and tax administration. With respect to tariffs, respondents were asked whether they considered the taxes high, fair, or low. With respect to tax administration, respondents were asked whether they felt that assessments of tax, mainly direct tax, were made fairly or unfairly. It was also important to determine whether the taxpayers knew when taxes were due; whether at the time of payment the taxpayers knew the amount owing; whether at the time of payment the taxpayers had funds with which to pay their taxes; whether (because the author had the impression that in general account books were not kept by SSEs) the taxpayers preferred the deposit (lump-sum) system or an assessment based on account books (profit). It was also important to gauge whether the taxpayers in the SSE category understood the tax returns they were meant to fill out (if they had ever filled them out at all). The respondents were also asked whether they kept some form of accounts and whether these were prepared by an accountant, bookkeeper, or external auditor. Taxpayers were also asked what reforms they would auditor. Taxpayers were also asked what reforms they would like to see in the tax system.

The results of the survey

Responses on tariffs and tax rates — The majority of SSEs in the sample felt that the rates for the following were too high:

- customs duty,
- sales tax on imports,
- commercial transactions levy,
- corporation tax, and
- PAYE personal income tax.

In general, the respondents wished to see a reduction in the rates of the above-mentioned taxes.

Responses on tax administration — Of the 130 respondents, 66% felt that they were unfairly assessed. Cross tabulation of the results suggested that unfair assessment was attributable to high rates of tax and tax deposit, a taxpayer's not always knowing clearly the amount of tax payable, and a taxpayer's difficulty in understanding the tax return documents. The results did not indicate any preference for deposit or assessment of profits as the method of tax assessment. It is interesting to note that the majority of SSEs in the sample know when the tax is due and normally have the funds to pay the tax by the due date. Contrary to expectations, 78% of the respondents indicated that they keep some form of accounts; 49% keep comprehensive books, and 29% keep some form of income and expenditure account. This suggests that assessment of tax on income and profits should be relatively easy. Further, the results show that about 28% of the respondents employ both an accountant or bookkeeper and an external auditor; nearly 5% employ only an external auditor; and 19% employ only an accountant or book-keeper.

Other comments made by the respondents — The following is a summary of comments made by the SSEs on reforms they would like to see in the taxation system:

- Most of the respondents wanted to pay income tax in installments, as this would spread the payments out and alleviate liquidity problems.

- Some respondents suggested that the withholding tax be removed because it depleted their working capital.
- Without being specific, some respondents preferred to see the number or quantum of taxes scaled down and consolidated, especially those that may be related.
- Another suggestion was to increase taxpayer education; tax assessors should be friendlier and should offer more explanations to the taxpayer about the taxes due.
- Respondents suggested that it would be more convenient if they could pay their taxes through banks other than the only one used now (Uganda Commercial Bank).
- The sses suggested that taxation policy and tariff documents be circulated to the taxpayer.
- The sses wanted to be given incentives and tax relief of up to 5 years so that they could grow and prosper.
- The sses also suggested that the Uganda Revenue Authority design simple accounting documents in which income and expenditure could be recorded.
- Some respondents suggested that taxes be collected by local authorities (this implies that the Uganda Revenue Authority should use the local administrations as tax collection agencies).

The tax reform effort in Uganda

The tax concerns of sses as determined by both the ussia study and the author's survey can be classified under three headings: tax policy, tax-rate structure, and tax administration. Tax policy addresses the concerns of whether, in principle, particular tax types, such as withholding tax, should be in place at all and whether income tax should be paid through a deposit system. Other concerns are the issues of equity, the policy on luxury goods, and the protection of local industry from competing imports. Tax-rate structure addresses the issue of the severity of the tax rates already in place. Issues addressed by tax administration are using simpler documentation, increasing taxpayer awareness of the taxation process and tax obligations, paying taxes in installments, and increasing tax compliance from the existing tax base.

Tax policy

The Government of Uganda has made significant strides in tax reform since 1987, establishing the following framework of medium- to long-term objectives:

- to increase domestic revenue;
- to widen the tax base and gradually lower the tax rates to enhance equity, improve taxpayer compliance, and minimize tax evasion;
- to increase the share of domestic consumption taxes through the introduction of value-added taxes (VATs) or refined sales taxes, preferably at the retail level, taking into account the level of accountability skills at the taxation point;
- to minimize taxes and tariffs that inhibit export competitiveness and have a direct bearing on production or output decisions;
- to limit the application of excise duties to a few goods such as petroleum, alcoholic beverages, and tobacco (these excises would not discriminate between imported and locally produced goods);
- to simplify the system of tax administration by reducing the number of tax-rate bands while allowing for flexibility in implementation of fiscal policy;
- to use the customs duty on imports for protection and to use the sales tax or consumption tax for revenue generation;
- to improve tax administration by offering attractive remuneration incentives to tax collectors, by improving the training of personnel, by rationalizing tax laws to simplify implementation and enhance equity, and by providing adequate facilities for the effective collection of taxes; and
- to avoid meaningless and uncoordinated adjustments and instead to allow a period of stabilization and forward planning.

The results of the tax reform effort show that the government has addressed some of the concerns of the SSEs. More specifically, the government, through the Uganda Investment Authority, has offered local and foreign investors duty exemption on capital equipment and has offered other incentives, such as tax holidays. As a policy, raw materials are subject to an import duty — registered manufacturers of whatever scale remit the sales tax at the time of importation. This sales tax is now recoverable after manufacture or processing. Tax exemptions on imported goods have been severely restricted, and any exemptions have to be justified to the Ministry of Finance and Economic Planning before being granted. Excise rates have been applied on a narrow band of goods (both locally manufactured and imported) including petroleum, cigarettes, alcoholic beverages, soft drinks, and a few luxury goods. To mitigate the costs of setting up a new business, the Uganda Revenue Authority has made it a policy to charge tax on profits that are earned, so new businesses are not required to pay income tax deposits at the outset.

Although some SSEs had suggested the elimination of the withholding tax, the government is undertaking a review to exempt only taxpayers with a good tax-paying record. Because the tax culture has been eroded over the years and because the withholding tax is advance income tax that is credited to the final tax liability of the taxpayer, it is unlikely that this tax will be eliminated in the near future.

Tax-rate structure

Direct taxes

The corporation tax rate has gradually been lowered from 60% in 1986 to 30% in fiscal year 1993/94. This rate affects both the larger establishments and the SSEs. The personal income tax rates were cut through a gradual increase in the threshold, widening of the tax brackets, and lowering of the top marginal rate to the current level of 30%. All those SSEs with net incomes falling within the designated brackets will not pay any more tax than that paid by the larger entities with net incomes in the same brackets. This is because the top marginal personal income tax rate and the corporate tax rate are both 30%. The SSEs also have the opportunity to pay taxes of 10% on the excess of their net annual income falling between 840 001 and 2 100 000 UGS and 20% on the excess of their net annual income falling between 2 100 001 and 4 200 000 UGS (in 1994, 1 075 Ugandan shillings [UGS] = 1 United States dollar [USD]). There is a built-in cumulative relief in the personal income tax structure that is not available to the limited-liability companies. It could be argued, therefore, that the tax system may be offering an incentive for the limited-liability SSEs to deregister and move into the nonincorporated category. For loss carry-overs, the Uganda tax law allows a business to exhaust the loss incurred in previous periods before paying corporate tax. The same applies to businesses that are sole proprietors and partnerships, even though they are assessed on the personal income tax schedule.

Indirect taxes

Through the preventive arm of the Uganda Revenue Authority, the government has strengthened the machinery for monitoring and controlling smuggled goods that unfavourably compete with the activities of the SSEs. The maximum import duty rate has been reduced from more than 250% in 1986 to 30% in July 1993, and during the 1992/93 financial year, the government started paying taxes for all its imports. The government also reduced the maximum sales-tax rate to 30% to pave the way for the introduction of a VAT. In June 1993, in pursuit of the objective of lowering the tax rates over time, the government announced it was lowering the indirect taxes across the board (Uganda Minister of Finance and Economic Planning 1993a,b). The government is also streamlining the valuation of imported goods by requiring all importers with consignments valued over 2 500 USD to have their goods pre-inspected. The resulting "Clean Report of Findings" and the taxable value therein are acceptable for customs purposes. These measures affect the SSEs involved in the import trade or small-scale manufacturing.

Tax administration

Almost every year since 1986, the government has stressed the need to strengthen the tax-collection mechanism. It has improved incentives to the collectors, provided tax-collection facilities, opened up new offices for wider tax coverage, and revived the inspectorate function. In the 1990/91 fiscal year the government studied the possibility of setting up a tax authority. As a result of this study, the government set up the Uganda Revenue Authority in September 1991, which made tax collection autonomous, businesslike, and more accountable than before. The Authority is currently distributing tariff- and tax-related documentation to taxpayers, and work on a taxpayer's guide is in advanced stages.

The Uganda Revenue Authority has further strengthened the revenue-collection process by appointing experts in customs and excise, income tax, and investigations and audit to plan, train staff, and manage the new institution. The experts also have the authority to improve the mobilization of domestic resources and to simplify tax procedures. Part of the process, which has already started, includes the review of tax tribunals, the preparation of operational manuals, the consolidation of the tax laws, and the intensification of taxpayer education programs and of interaction with representative groups of all enterprises, including SSEs. In addition, the Uganda Revenue Authority has opened up a desk to cater to the small taxpayer. At this desk, the taxpayer will get the necessary explanation for filing a tax return and, more important, the need for self-assessment. Another task of this desk is to simplify the tax return to meet the needs of the small taxpayer.

In the field, tax officers have intensified their educating and explaining role. The basic theme is that the taxpayer should not be looked on as a criminal. This approach is already yielding massive dividends. The payment of taxes in installments has been revived in the target group, the SSEs. The government took this measure after recognizing that tax compliance is improving and that taxes can be spread over an accounting period for the "hard-to-tax" categories, once mutual trust, monitoring, and follow-up audits have been established. The introduction of taxpayer identification numbers (TINs) will help the monitoring process — each taxpayer will have a unique identification number linked to a taxpayer ledger in which all assessments and payments will be logged.

The government is studying the possibility of allowing more financial institutions to function as payment points in the tax-collection network. Opening up additional payment points would go a long way toward answering the cry of the SSEs for a more convenient way to pay their taxes. Furthermore, the government is studying the possibility of allowing agencies to collect taxes on commission. This would also reduce the Uganda Revenue Authority's collection costs, especially those associated with collections from the numerous small-scale operators.

Lessons from the Uganda experience

Tax reform in Uganda in the period 1986–1990 followed the macro-approach — the basic objective was to stabilize the macroeconomic environment for all business players. Further, the government's tax-reform objectives have been consonant with the concerns of the SSEs. Gradual but firm steps have been taken to create a tax environment conducive to business growth. The main features of the approach to tax reform in Uganda have been the following:

- The government encourages dialogue between the tax policymakers (Ministry of Finance and Economic Planning) and the tax collectors at the front line (Uganda Revenue Authority) and representative groups of taxpayers. These representative groups now have access to the Parliamentary Standing Committee on the Economy, which has considerable say in tax policy measures and takes the lead in fiscal debates in Parliament.

- The government also encourages small-scale operators to form associations or groups to interact with the Uganda Revenue Authority at the operational level and to provide taxpayer education for their members in partnership with the Authority.

- The government engages in research to predict the impact of tax measures on taxpayers so that it can propose policy changes that will simplify the tax system and set tax rates that will optimize collections.

- Linkages between the Uganda Revenue Authority and the local authorities are being forged to rationalize tax collection methods and to share information. Each taxpayer will have a TIN that will be used by both the central and local government authorities.

- The government has synthesized the taxation concerns of both the LSEs and the SSEs so that the interests of the LSEs do not overshadow the legitimate concerns of the SSEs. Indeed, in Uganda at present, some LSEs are accusing government officials of looking out more for the needs of the small-scale operator. However, the government favours a balanced approach to economic development because the mainstay of the economy has been, and is likely to continue to be, the small-scale operator.

Outlook for the future

One objective of the Government of Uganda is to mobilize more of its domestic resources through tax reform. At the same time, it is attempting to balance macro- and microeconomic needs. Tax collection in Uganda is now handled in a businesslike manner — the tax collector even has to market taxes like a storekeeper markets goods. This means that ultimately the tax collector has to woo the taxpayers by making it attractive to pay taxes and by listening more to their concerns. To achieve an effective and equitable taxation system, we should keep the following points in mind:

- There should be one tax-collection mechanism for both direct and indirect taxes and at all levels — the taxpayer wishes to see only one tax collector.

- The SSEs should form one strong and well-organized group that would have affiliates from different trades and sectors to, among other things, articulate tax concerns and present tax proposals logically and systematically. An apex organization for SSEs would make dialogue with the government more meaningful.

- The government has a duty to open up clear channels of representation and appeal, especially near the centre of fiscal policy formulation, so that the representations of the SSEs are not lost in a maze of bureaucracy.

- The government and the SSEs should undertake joint tax research to gauge the impact of tax measures and to identify areas of tax-base expansion so that the tax burden can be spread out and the government's objective of lowering the tax rates can be realized soon.

In conclusion, it can be said that in Uganda the government has progressively responded to the legitimate tax concerns of the SSEs and is continually reviewing its tax policy to find ways to eliminate taxation impediments to growth. The most feasible way of removing the sting of taxation for the SSEs, and indeed for other groups, is through partnerships between the tax collectors and the taxpayers. This approach removes ignorance of concepts and practices on both sides by bringing about transparency, and it can generate a responsive rather than a confrontational tax culture. ✳

Appendix A:
Questionnaire used in the limited survey of small-scale enterprises

1. Nature or type of business _____

2. Number of employees _____

3. Source of production inputs: [imported]   [local]

4. Ratio of imported to local inputs (estimate) _____

5. Indirect taxes paid

    Customs duty
    [high]   [fair]   [low]   [don't know]   [not appl.]

    Sales tax on imports
    [high]   [fair]   [low]   [don't know]   [not appl.]

    Sales tax on output
    [high]   [fair]   [low]   [don't know]   [not appl.]

    Excise duty on output
    [high]   [fair]   [low]   [don't know]   [not appl.]

    Surtax or surcharges
    [high]   [fair]   [low]   [don't know]   [not appl.]

    Commercial transactions levy
    [high]   [fair]   [low]   [don't know]   [not appl.]

    Import licence commission (2%)
    [high]   [fair]   [low]   [don't know]   [not appl.]

6. Direct taxes paid

    Income tax deposit
    [high]   [fair]   [low]   [don't know]   [not appl.]

    Corporation tax
    [high]   [fair]   [low]   [don't know]   [not appl.]

    Pay-as-you-earn (PAYE)
    [high]   [fair]   [low]   [don't know]   [not appl.]

    Withholding tax (2%)
    [high]   [fair]   [low]   [don't know]   [not appl.]

    Stamp duty (3%)
    [high]   [fair]   [low]   [don't know]   [not appl.]

7. Tax administration

    a. Are your taxes assessed fairly?
       [yes]   [no]   [don't know]

    b. Are you always sure of the time when you should pay
       your taxes?
       [yes]   [no]   [don't know]

    c. Are you always sure of the amount of tax that you
       should pay?
       [yes]   [no]   [don't know]

    d. Do you make tax deposits against your tax liability
       when you have the funds?
       [yes]   [no]   [don't know]

    e. Do you prefer tax assessed on profits or the current
       system of tax?
       [assessment] [tax deposit] [combination] [don't know]

    f. Do you understand the tax return forms you use?
       [difficult] [satisfactory] [easy] [never filled] [don't know]

8. General

    a. Do you keep comprehensive account books?
       [yes]   [no]

    b If the answer to 8a is "no," do you keep an
       elementary account of income and expenditures?
       [yes]   [no]

    c. Do you employ an accountant or bookkeeper?
       [yes]   [no]

    d. Do you have external auditors?
       [yes]   [no]

9. What modifications in the tax system would you prefer to see?

Note: You do not have to indicate the name of your business.

Appendix B:
Type of businesses polled in the
limited survey of small-scale enterprises

Table A1. Types of small-scale enterprises in the Kampala area.

Description of SSE activity	Number
Food processing and preparation	12
Entertainment	3
Legal practice	3
Medical services — human and animal	11
Metal fabrication and carpentry	25
Retail and wholesale trade	21
Hospitality — bars, restaurants, accommodation	14
Other professional — consultancy, secretarial, educational	7
Beauty parlours or salons	5
Building and construction	1
Motor vehicle repair garages	7
Coffee processing	4
Photographic studios	3
Filling stations	2
Cobbling or shoemaking	3
Other trades	9
Total	130

REGULATORY RESTRICTIONS AND COMPETITION IN FORMAL AND INFORMAL URBAN MANUFACTURING IN BURKINA FASO[1]

Meine Pieter van Dijk
Netherlands Economic Institute and Economics Faculty,
Erasmus University, Rotterdam, Netherlands

Introduction

An unfavourable policy environment and strong competition can constrain small-scale enterprise (SSE) development. Despite regulatory restrictions, Burkina Faso has a highly competitive environment for SSEs. SSEs compete with medium- and large-scale units, male entrepreneurs compete with female entrepreneurs, and the formal sector competes with the informal sector. All face competition from imported products, which are relatively cheap because of smuggling and an overvalued CFA franc.

This paper analyzes the effects of the regulatory framework on the informal and formal manufacturing sectors and of competition between the two sectors in Burkina Faso. It also describes the impact of government policies and regulations and recommends policies to integrate the development of small- and medium-scale manufacturing enterprises.

---

[1] This paper, focusing on the comparison between surveys undertaken in 1976 and 1991, is one of a series. Other papers in the series discuss methodological problems of informal-sector research (van Dijk 1992b), the relevance of flexible specialization in the informal (and formal manufacturing) sector in Burkina Faso (van Dijk 1992a,d), the relations between the informal and the formal manufacturing sectors, the institutional problems of SSE promotion (van Dijk 1991, 1992c), and the importance of women entrepreneurs in the informal sector in Burkina Faso (Dijkman and van Dijk 1993).

Informal and formal manufacturing
in Burkina Faso

Informal-sector SSEs functioning outside the regulatory framework play an important role in the economy of sub-Saharan African countries (World Bank 1989a). They account for 59% of sub-Saharan Africa's urban labour force and contribute, on average, 20% of the gross domestic product (GDP). The sector supplies one-quarter of Burkina Faso's GDP, second only to agriculture's contribution. The informal urban sector provides more than half of the value added of the secondary and tertiary sectors and employs about three-quarters of the urban working population. According to a 1985 census, the informal sector in Burkina Faso provides 70% of nonagricultural employment. Only 10% of the nonagricultural jobs are provided by the formal sector; about 15% by the government.

The industrialization process in Bobo Dioulasso started in the 1920s with vegetable oil production; in the 1950s, a cotton gin and a furniture factory continued the process of industrialization. In Ouagadougou, industrialization only started in 1954 when the railroad from Abidjan reached the city, an electricity plant was built, and part of the city was reserved for industrial activities. After independence in 1960, the number of enterprises in Ouagadougou jumped, particularly in the 1970s. By the time of the 1989 industrial and commercial census, 906 enterprises were located in Ouagadougou and 270 in Bobo Dioulasso.

The industrial sector contributed 26% to GDP in 1989. The sector grew at 3.9% per year in the period 1980–1989, or 1% per year in per capita terms. Manufacturing made up 15% of GDP in 1989 and grew only 2.4% in the same period. The difference can be explained by a construction boom in the early 1980s.

Exported manufactured goods contributed only 11% to total exports in 1989, with machines making up the biggest share, followed by textile products, tires, tanned leather, and metal household products (Chambre de commerce 1990, pp. 135–136). Informal-sector activities contributed 40% to the value added of the manufacturing sector and two thirds of the value added in the services sector. The formal manufacturing sector employed 9 000 people.

Investment in industries reached its peak in 1982 but was heavily concentrated in the food and textile industries. The economic crisis that started that year was related to a drought and an international economic recession. Droughts (including ones in 1983 and 1984), political instability, and a worldwide economic recession certainly contributed to the decline of the manufacturing sector in the first half of the 1980s. At the same time, international competition became stronger, the economic climate for the manufacturing sector weakened, and the prices of locally produced manufactured products increased.

The result of all these developments was a large number of bankrupt enterprises and enterprises losing money. According to the United Nations Industrial Development Organization's (UNIDO 1989) industrial development review for Burkina Faso, one third of the companies stopped their activity and more than half the enterprises ran at losses in 1982.

Comparison between 1976 and 1991

The analysis in this paper is based on the results of two surveys of SSEs in the informal and formal manufacturing sectors in Burkina Faso, one in 1976 (van Dijk 1986) and a follow-up in 1991 (van Dijk 1993). The definition of an informal-sector enterprise in the 1976 survey was "a unit without a legal status such as the *société anonyme* or *société à responsabilité limitée*, where the employees do not receive the legal minimum wage and do not benefit from the social security system." The 1991 study used this last criterion because it was easier to verify the accuracy of reported information by checking whether any employees were registered for social security.

In the 1976 survey, 300 SSE entrepreneurs from the informal sector were interviewed; in the 1991 survey, 350. (Seven of the entrepreneurs interviewed in 1991 were later reclassified as belonging to the formal sector because they had registered some of their personnel at the Caisse de sécurité sociale. For the current analysis, all 1991 percentages are based on the sample of 350.)

Nine different activities were studied in 1976. For the 1991 survey, a complete census of economic activities was carried out in three neighbourhoods of Ouagadougou to determine the type of activities to study. Eighteen activities were selected on the basis of three criteria:

- comparability with the previous survey;

- involvement of women in the activity (female-dominated activities turned out to make up 50% of the informal sector in one of the neighbourhoods where a complete census of economic activities was undertaken); and

- the promise shown by some activities to exemplify recent developments in the sector.

Results of the two surveys

The average entrepreneur in 1991 was 33 years old (32 in 1976), but 50% of the entrepreneurs were under 30 years old and 80% under 40. Almost half were literate (39% in 1976), and 17% had received some vocational training (8% in 1976). This shows that education and training had improved somewhat in this period.

Job histories showed that about 60% of the entrepreneurs were farmers or still farming. The majority were also farmers in 1976. Less than 50% had learned their trade through apprenticeship (60% in 1976). In 1976, 12% of the entrepreneurs had some accounting system. This increased to 17% in 1991. Entrepreneurs in the informal sector who had work experience in the formal sector increased from 10% in 1976 to 13% in 1991. These indicators suggest that entrepreneurs in Ouagadougou's informal sector are better educated and have more experience.

These enterprises employed an average of 2.78 people (the entrepreneur included), slightly fewer than in 1976 (3.04). Number of employees by sector varied from 1.3 in the transport sector (1.81 in 1976) to 5.0 in the construction sector (5.62 in 1976), showing a similar decrease. In particular, the number of apprentices, workers, and daily workers had decreased, probably because in most cases they required a salary. For those who received a salary, the average salary had increased slightly.

The informal sector in Ouagadougou in 1991 was more dynamic than in 1976. There were more SSEs, there were all kinds of new activities, and new technologies were used. The range of available products had increased, and the quality of the products had often improved. In the neighbourhoods where a complete census of all economic activities was organized before, the number of activities had increased almost 70% since 1980. In one of these neighbourhoods, Wagadogo, half the number of entrepreneurs counted in 1991 were women; in a second neighbourhood, Tiendpalogo, just over one-third were women.

There were also changes in the composition of the informal sector (van Dijk 1993). Wagadogo and Tiendpalogo had a number of new activities. The most visible ones were photocopying, yogurt production (typically by women at home), and door-to-door services provided by manicurists, tailors, barbers, and bucket repairers. Other services that had not been available in 1980 were secretarial services and electrical engine and generator repair. Traders were also selling products that were not sold in 1980.

From 1976 to 1991, the informal sector also underwent a process of differentiation — this left only a few successful enterprises and marginalized a large number of artisans and traders. Examples of entrepreneurs who had poor prospects because of this differentiation were tailors who traveled by foot carrying their sewing machines on their heads and the door-to-door barbers, bucket repairers, radio repairers, and manicurists.

In 1991, the entrepreneur was no longer typically the head of a large family. One third of the interviewed entrepreneurs were unmarried men or divorced women.

In the informal sector, entrepreneurs tended to buy most of their raw materials and sell their products in their own neighbourhood. Entrepreneurs cited various reasons for choosing a location to set up business. In decreasing order of importance, these were

1. Because they lived there;

2. Because they owned or rented the place;

3. Because they expected more clients at that location; and

4. Because it was on a public road.

Entrepreneurs who gave the fourth reason said it was because that is where the clients were and nobody was chasing them. By contrast, formal-sector industries have the entire country as their market, although they rarely export a large part of their production.

Between 1979 and 1991, the number of formal-sector (modern industrial) establishments increased substantially from about 120 to about 150. The numbers are estimates because there is a somewhat fluid distinction between industries and some trading companies (for example, in the leather sector and the fruit and vegetables sector), and the demarcation between the informal and formal sectors is unclear.

The formal manufacturing sector is also dynamic: there were a number of new entrants, and many enterprises disappeared. In the sample of 50 enterprises studied in more detail in 1991, one-quarter had started or restarted during the previous 2 years. Nine enterprises (18%) were not operating either because of "technical unemployment" or because of bankruptcy. At least five enterprises in the sample needed to be reorganized to become profitable. Another five enterprises were waiting to be privatized. Others were looking for foreign partners, but most did not know how to go about this.

Is low demand a problem in Burkina Faso? Demand depends on the development of consumption, of backward and forward linkages, and of government and foreign customers. Macroeconomic developments and the preference of the population for informal-sector goods also affect demand. Several studies argue against the general validity of the assumption that informal-sector products are inferior goods, but there are insufficient data on expenditure patterns for different income groups to allow one to determine the income elasticity of the informal sector. Still, demand seems to have increased both relatively and absolutely over the period under review, although the informal sector had to compete with the formal sector and with imported products. Some formal-sector entrepreneurs complained about the lack of demand, but a number had managed to increase their sales.

In 1991, 60% of the entrepreneurs claimed that their sales had gone down, but a comparison of their reported turnover in 1993 and 1990 shows a substantial increase (not corrected for inflation). The perceived decline may be related to a jump in the number of enterprises. The entrepreneurs claimed that the lack of demand was related to decreased government spending and increased competition with other SSEs, formal-sector producers, and imported products. The situation in 1976 was certainly less gloomy — at that time 81% of the interviewed entrepreneurs reported that their sales had increased. These increases were probably related to increased foreign aid after the years of drought at the beginning of the 1970s.

The makeup of the client base changed as well. In 1991, the informal sector had the general population more often as its major client and had fewer business clients from either the informal or the formal sector.

Interactions: backward and forward linkages at the subsector level

Several questions in the 1991 survey were designed to elicit information on the backward and forward linkages between the formal and informal sectors. The following summarizes the findings:

- To what extent did SSEs buy raw materials from the formal sector?

  Barbers, tailors, people processing food or running a breakfast table, electricians, woodworkers, and metalworkers bought one-half to one-third of their raw materials from the formal sector.

- Did SSEs sell to the formal sector?

  Less than 10% of the entrepreneurs (23), particularly metalworkers and electric motor repairers, had the formal sector as their major client.

- Did formal-sector enterprises subcontract to informal ones?

  Two construction firms and three upholstery firms worked mainly for the formal sector. The arrangements could hardly be called a subcontracting relation, although it boiled down to it in the case of some metalworkers, construction firms, and upholstery firms.

- Had SSE entrepreneurs learned the skills they would need to run their businesses by working in the formal sector?

  In practically all informal-sector activities, entrepreneurs could be found with work experience in the formal sector. The largest number were among the metalworkers and construction workers. In general, these entrepreneurs fared somewhat better in terms of income and turnover than the entrepreneurs without this experience.

- Were the two sectors competing for the same market?

Artisans, barbers, tailors, fruit and vegetable sellers, woodworkers, metalworkers, and furniture makers, in particular, complained about competition from the formal sector.

• What was the role of the government in relation to taxes and registration?

The statistical evidence concerning taxes and regulations shows that SSEs paid many different taxes and were registered with a number of government services. The SSEs needed all kinds of permits, such as a market permit if they wanted a stall at a market, or proof that they were registered with the tax office if they wanted to obtain government orders.

Backward and forward linkages are limited in the informal urban sector, as well as in the formal sector. They exist for agro-based and agro-related activities, but many other activities require imported raw materials, tools, equipment, and spare parts. On average the small-scale entrepreneurs buy more raw materials in the formal sector than in the informal sector. Government orders and foreign customers are rare for small-scale entrepreneurs, who largely depend on the development of purchasing power in the local population.

Competition

The informal sector in Burkina Faso creates more jobs than the formal sector (World Bank 1989b). The formal sector is hampered by its lack of competitiveness because of high production costs and stifling regulations. The informal sector does not have these constraints to the same extent and could play an important role in developing an entrepreneurial class. It can be argued that because of the informal sector's innovative capacity, the artisanal part of the sector should be further developed (van Dijk 1992a).

The number of artisanal activities diminished substantially in Ouagadougou between 1976 and 1991 in both neighbourhoods where a census was undertaken. The productivity of the remaining enterprises had not increased enough to account for the difference. An additional census of economic activities in a peripheral neighbourhood found that artisanal activities had not moved to these neighbourhoods. This subsector of the informal urban sector has often been considered its most dynamic part. It was concluded that the number of artisanal activities declined because of competition from the formal sector and from imported products.

Agroprocessing

In the agroprocessing subsector the informal-sector enterprise operates at a very small scale with simple equipment, whereas the formal-sector enterprises are typically large scale and technologically advanced. Consequently, the two are not competing very much. For example, the most dynamic formal-sector activity, fruit and vegetable processing, is not open to SSE entrepreneurs because of the high cost and the complicated administrative procedures involved in exporting and arranging air transport. However, the appearance of so many new formal-sector enterprises in Burkina Faso proves that people there do have entrepreneurial skill and can mobilize the necessary capital. More integration between the informal and formal enterprises in this subsector is possible. SSEs could be encouraged to do more processing, and the formal enterprises could use SSEs more for selling their products, for supplying goods and services, and — to save on transportation costs — for processing.

Beer brewing is an example of an agroprocessing industry for which the Sankara government (1983–1987) increased competition. It did this by discouraging the consumption of modern beer by stimulating the consumption of the traditional beer, *dolo*. Sankara actively discouraged the modern breweries during the time he was in power. In 1991, sales of beer produced by modern beer breweries were still not at the level of the early 1980s. Two factors constraining sales for the formal sector are related to current regulations. SOBBRA is not allowed to sell beer to traders who are not *agréé*. The traders' card runs out every 3 months and will be renewed only if they have paid all their taxes. The breweries also have to sell their beer through a limited number of local traders. The breweries have the impression that those traders do not deliver outside the Bobo Dioulasso–Ouagadougou axis. When the breweries themselves used to do the transporting, they also delivered to clients in villages. Formal-sector brewers consider this a lost market for the time being.

Textiles

Informal tailoring has suffered from all kinds of competition from, for example, the formal sector, illegal imports, and secondhand clothes. Besides the few bigger formal textile enterprises, there are quite a few small-scale tailors who have tried to formalize their businesses. They were eager to get bigger orders from local formal enterprises or from the government. One such entrepreneur interviewed in Bobo Dioulasso had set up a unit in the industrial zone of that city. However, the firm is now back to its old tailor workshop in the centre of town. The advantage of producing in series with electrical machines in a modern building didn't pay for itself.

Leather

The formal sector in leather competes with illegal imports. An entrepreneur from a formal-sector leather firm complained about the competition in the market, which has tarnished Burkina Faso's reputation as a quality exporter. The owner of a shoe factory complained about competition from illegally imported shoes and the problem of producing the models desired by customers. The owner of a plastic products factory, rather than keeping the factory running, was studying what was necessary to become competitive again.

There is only limited scope for traditional tanning and production of small-scale leather products in Burkina Faso. Traditional shoemakers cannot compete with industrially produced shoes, especially not with plastic ones. Their work was described as "traditional models for a traditional group of clients, who now prefer plastic products."

Plastic shoes provide work for plastic shoe repairers, who did not necessarily repair leather shoes before. At some of the city's markets one can see these "modern" shoe repairers, using plastic and iron threads instead of textile ones.

Metal

Metalworking firms operate in a very competitive market. In this subsector a great many formal enterprises started as informal units and gradually expanded their business. Two such entrepreneurs were interviewed in 1991. Their problems were different from those of the average formal-sector entrepreneur. One complained that many of his clients do not pay for their

One complained that many of his clients do not pay for their orders because they feel "he is one of them."

The formal-sector entrepreneurs complained about the price of electricity and the difficulty of getting credit from a bank. They also felt that it was becoming more difficult to get orders. Some complained that it was hard to find foreign partners and skilled labour.

The informal metalworkers felt that they were losing one of their major clients: construction firms. These small-scale entrepreneurs said that they rarely worked for construction firms any more because most construction firms now had their own metalwork departments.

Wood

Formal-sector entrepreneurs in the woodworking sector face a lot of competition from the informal-sector SSEs. Informal-sector producers have the advantage of lower production costs, particularly if they have managed to ignore payment of the different taxes. Two entrepreneurs from the informal sector complained that they were working at only 40% of their capacity at the moment, whereas a competitor was working at 70% of his capacity. They clarified this by saying that their competitor offered a wider range of products and that he was seriously involved in metalwork and construction activities.

The number of furniture makers went down substantially because of the emergence of more modern and bigger firms. At the same time, international competition became stronger, the economic climate for the formal sector became less favourable, and the prices of locally produced industrial products increased. Several entrepreneurs complained that it was difficult to be competitive given the high costs of production in Burkina Faso.

The impact of policies on informal and formal manufacturing

Government policies related to the informal sector went through three distinct phases during the 1976–1992 period. In the 1976–1982 period, the government was advised to help the informal sector by providing credit, technical assistance, appropriate technologies, and government orders. Very few of these ideas were implemented, and those that were carried out were not very successful or had little effect.

During the Sankara period (1983–1987), government interest in the informal sector mainly consisted of attempts to control the sector by registration, taxation, and *regroupement* (*groupements d'intérêt économique*). The industrial policies of the Sankara government stressed the development of SSEs and microenterprises. The medium- and large-scale industries were concentrated in the two big cities, often required protection and subsidies, but had little impact in terms of employment or relations with other firms. The Sankara government was not willing to continue providing support for formal-sector industrial enterprises. The number of years for which investment regimes were granted was not extended. The 1984 investment code encouraged private and foreign investment but was intended to ease the transition from special regimes to common rule and to increase the taxes to be collected from the formal sector. For most enterprises the new regime reduced import duties by 65%. This situation will continue until the new investment code, announced by Sankara's successors, comes into effect.

After Sankara's death in 1987 the government adopted a more positive attitude, as shown by the *Plan directeur pour la promotion de l'artisanat au Burkina Faso* (1990) and action program. In this third phase, SSEs were no longer closed immediately if they could not pay their taxes. The directors were no longer obliged to wear traditional clothes or pressured to drink traditional beer. Economic liberalization created a positive environment for SSEs. It seems that 50% of the SSEs surveyed started up during the last 2 years (1990–1991) because the people expected difficult times but felt confident about starting their own business.

Institutionally, the Direction de développement industriel is still officially responsible for industrial policies, although there is no corresponding department or service for the informal sector. Institutions like the Ministry of Economic Affairs, the Chamber of Commerce, the Office national de la promotion de l'emploi, banks, and NGOs all play a role, but their efforts are not coordinated.

Over time, registration has become more important for informal-sector enterprises. Almost 10% of the 1991 sample was registered by the government in some way. Only 10 entrepreneurs were registered or had registered some of their personnel at the Caisse de sécurité sociale, sometimes for very different reasons. Often the personnel had been registered in their previous job or were registered because they still worked in the formal sector (three cases). Other entrepreneurs were registered by the Chamber of Commerce (33, or 10%), the municipal authorities (29, or 9%), l'Office national de promotion d'emploi (16, or 5%), or the statistical office (4, or 1%).

Officially, all the entrepreneurs interviewed in 1991 paid taxes; 113 (35%) were registered for that purpose. In fact, a limited number of enterprises paid several taxes — professional, turnover, value added, and municipal. Other enterprises managed to avoid taxes, often because the business had started only recently or was mobile. Entrepreneurs often did not know how frequently they had to pay, what kind of taxes they had to pay, how much they should pay, and for what purpose the government uses the money.

In the informal sector, capital usually came from private sources and not from credit institutions. Friends and family were typical sources. Often, clients provided the working capital. Only nine entrepreneurs in the 1991 sample ever got a loan through a bank (18 in 1976), usually from a government-owned institution. One got a loan from an NGO to raise pigs. The other loans were for an investment (four cases), for buying a stock of raw material (three times), or for consumption (two cases). Most entrepreneurs would like a line of credit; on average they ask for 800 000 XOF, more than five times their average actual total investments (in 1994, 570 CFA francs [XOF] = 1 United States dollar [USD]).

Conclusions

The informal and formal sectors can contribute more to production, employment, income generation, and tax revenues if the government encourages their development and explains to small-scale entrepreneurs, for example, how much tax they have to pay and how often and for what purpose.

Successful SSE development policies require support from all parties concerned: small-, medium-, and large-scale entrepreneurs, existing business organizations (for example, the Chamber of Commerce), and different levels of government (particularly national and municipal). Donor organizations need to understand the government approach before we can expect to get their support for these policies. But Burkina Faso needs better donor coordination. The nine initiatives to start a centre for innovation and technical assistance show the need for such a centre, but they also show the need to avoid duplication.

Burkina Faso's structural adjustment program will try to improve the economy; the informal sector should also benefit. Burkina Faso also needs an integrated development policy for the informal and formal sectors. Such a sectoral policy program should be part of a broader industrialization or development policy, such as a sectoral adjustment program.

Structural adjustment policies and programs will affect the informal sector, but the magnitude of these affects is unknown. One potentially harmful effect could be a decline in purchasing power because real wages may decrease. On the other hand, this may also increase demand for informal-sector products if certain formal-sector products then become too expensive. Increased unemployment may lead to the establishment of more SSEs and microenterprises, which may mean more hardship for existing firms. Also, the informal sector is usually not a source of exports. It uses imported raw materials, tools, equipment, and spare parts and, therefore, may be limited in its ability to manufacture substitutes for imported products.

Potential benefits of structural adjustment include the possibility of manufacturing substitutes for imports if imported and formal-sector products and services become more expensive. The disappearance of inefficient (protected) formal-sector enterprises could mean that SSEs would take up some of the slack. SSEs and microenterprises should also benefit from the improved economic environment created through structural adjustment policies, particularly the correction of distorted prices. The number of structural adjustment projects to benefit the informal sector is limited, but some initiatives are forthcoming.

The Burkinabe government has indicated its willingness to encourage development of the informal sector. Burkina Faso will move to a more market-oriented economy by reducing state intervention and allowing the development of the private sector, of which the informal sector is an important part. The government will have to provide more incentives to the informal sector.

Deregulation should also involve administrative measures affecting the informal sector. It will be necessary to harmonize macroeconomic, fiscal, financial, and other policies with incentives for sses and microenterprises.

A strategy to develop the urban informal sector

The purpose of this research was to discover the optimal combination of economic, social, and institutional arrangements to allow informal-sector enterprises to compete in national and, eventually, international markets. This aim has become even more important in Africa since private foreign capital fled Africa in the 1980s. The research findings suggest the following strategy.

1. Take an integrated approach

The private sector is weak in Burkina Faso. But strengthening it depends on the integrated development of micro-, small-, medium-, and large-scale enterprises. The formal sector in Burkina Faso shows insufficient growth and a lack of competitiveness; it is made up of industries lacking forward and backward linkages. Integrated development would be hampered by the institutional setup because two different ministries formulate policies for informal and formal enterprises. The new Ministry of Handicrafts and Small Enterprises was created only in 1991, setting off a dispute over where the cutoff point between small- and medium-scale enterprises should be. Some claimed an sse could have annual revenues of up to 30 million xof. In the Burkina Faso economy, however, this figure seems too high.

The new investment code should not make a distinction between small-, medium-, and large-scale enterprises, but it should consider the existence of economies of scale (or the lack of such economies) as one of the criteria to support enterprises of a certain size. Second, the code should aim to integrate modern industries and sses. There are still too many enterprises importing almost everything and achieving a very low value added.

2. Develop innovative entrepreneurship

Some dynamic enterprises that changed their business strategy to survive focused on producing a product appropriate for the local situation, as far as taste and price were concerned. They selected technologies that were not too sophisticated. This allowed them to easily change the production process or the kind or quality of the product.

A few entrepreneurs realized that they had to be competitive to survive and looked to export. In the textiles sector, enterprises have been using cooperatives to produce products whenever there is a demand. An increasing number of formal-sector firms are using local SSEs to supply products or provide specific services.

Given the important role of women in the informal sector, some special initiatives for women are justified. Some training centres train only girls and women. A number of projects for women in the informal sector are under way or ready to begin. Vocational training for women also needs to be stimulated because it can enhance innovation. Such training should also explain the practical aspects of starting small- and medium-scale enterprises in Burkina Faso. For a separate analysis of this issue, see Dijkman and van Dijk (1993).

3. Restructure taxes and reduce other production costs

Many informal-sector entrepreneurs complained about taxes. The tax base needs to be broadened in this sector. Currently, one-third of informal-sector enterprises pay 80% of all taxes collected. In the formal sector, entrepreneurs are waiting for the new investment code. They expect tax benefits for their additional investments. It is important for the government to tell them soon what can be expected.

The government should be tracking the prices of imported raw materials and spare parts. Cheaper raw materials can give small-scale industries a chance to become competitive. Lower prices can be achieved by revising the system of import duties. Electricity costs also need to be reduced by the introduction of differentiated prices (lower prices for off-peak use). Finally, transport costs could be reduced through a transport and infrastructure project.

4. Stimulate the development of private-sector institutions

The government should stimulate the development of genuine private-sector organizations — the Chamber of Commerce is currently controlled by the government. Both the United States Agency for International Development (USAID) and the World Bank are interested in working with the Chamber of

Commerce, but the two agencies require that it be free of government control and have an elected chair.

More consultation with the private sector implies that the government would accept a different role. Its role would shift from directly providing credit training and technical assistance to encouraging private initiatives in these fields. Government policies should not focus on artisans or formal-sector industries but should apply to all private-sector activities, informal and formal, trade, transformation, rural, and urban. The aim should be to develop and implement an integrated approach to private-sector development, taking into account how various activities are related, weighing the interests of enterprises of different sizes, and acknowledging that the informal sector is an important part of the private sector.

5. Provide space and infrastructure

Officials and formal-sector entrepreneurs often claim that not enough areas have a proper infrastructure, such as roads and power lines, for new industries. However, the industrial estate Kossodo is not fully occupied yet. Some tracts of land need to be reclaimed from their current owners and then redistributed among entrepreneurs willing to invest. Some of that space should be reserved for SSEs.

The government provides hardly any infrastructure specifically for SSEs and microenterprises. There are no special zones for the informal sector in Ouagadougou, and only one third of the entrepreneurs in the 1991 sample had access to electricity or had water connections. Usually, electricity is used only for lighting.

An industrialization strategy based on flexible specialization would promote clusters of enterprises of different sizes (van Dijk 1992a). Industrial zones should be open for establishments working in different subsectors. Cooperative competition could develop at such locations. Clusters of enterprises would also stimulate the formation of networks and encourage subcontracting relationships. The government should support such arrangements as a way of strengthening the industrial base.

6. Provide more access to credit

The entrepreneurs surveyed felt that the financial sector was not really supporting the development of the manufacturing sector. Entrepreneurs found it difficult to borrow money, even when they could offer some collateral. Entrepreneurs mentioned that factories, equipment, and villas offered as guarantees were valued far below their market price. The banks argue that these assets may be difficult to liquidate in times of hardship. The banks also do not accept land in the industrial estate Kossodo as a guarantee because this land is not currently the property of the entrepreneur. Letters of guarantee are difficult to get and expensive. The banks debate such issues as the problem of arrears, the merits of individual versus group loans, the interest rates to be charged, the securities to be provided, and the collateral to be requested.

Does the informal sector need credit? If so, how should it be provided? Donor agencies currently favour minimalist credit approaches, but no schemes with real impact exist at the moment in Burkina Faso.

The World Bank has provided credit to the informal sector in Burkina Faso through the Artisanat and SSE promotion project, which started in 1979. This project proved how difficult it is to reach a target group through government institutions. A better approach is to interest the private sector, particularly commercial banks, NGOs, and savings and credit institutions, in a cooperative approach (like the Caisse populaire Desjardins) to making loans available to informal-sector enterprises.

To improve SSES' access to existing credit (and other development) programs, the following are needed:

- policy support for NGO initiatives;
- innovations in requirements for collateral;
- availability of and access to financial resources for venture capital; and
- windows in existing savings and credit institutions for SSE and microenterprise financing at the national and regional levels.

Several donors in Burkina Faso have considered setting up a credit scheme for SSES and microenterprises. The Caisse centrale de co-opération économique (CCCE) will provide a line of credit to the Caisse nationale du crédit agricole to improve the marketing system and to promote small- and medium-scale agroindustries that process, for example, grains, shea nuts, anacarde, groundnuts, milk, meat, or fish. At the same time, CCCE will provide some technical assistance.

The Fonds de promotion de l'emploi is an interministerial initiative coordinated by the president. It envisions, among other things, a guaranteed fund for private-sector initiatives, particularly concerning "the self-employed, the informal sector and micro enterprises." The UNDP commissioned a study identifying SSE projects that could be financed as part of the Fonds de promotion de l'emploi.

7. Create technology and training centres

The creation of a centre for innovation and quality improvement — helping entrepreneurs with product design, production methods, and the use of multipurpose equipment — requires support. A centre like this was created through a structural adjustment loan for Chad. The centre could recommend the use of multipurpose equipment, particularly for small production enterprises, and promote its introduction. This is in line with the flexible specialization strategy, which was tested in Burkina Faso and turned out to be relevant (van Dijk 1992a).

Several donors are considering financing SSE service centres. The main problem will be the coordination of these efforts. As part of the CCCE project already mentioned, the service centre would be for small- and medium-scale enterprises processing agricultural products. The centre would help small-scale entrepreneurs select projects, would provide technological advice, and would assist them for a period after the enterprise started operating.

8. Promote exports

It is impossible for Burkina Faso to control all its borders. Instead it should develop exports for sectors in which it has a comparative advantage: agroprocessing, fruits and vegetables, and skins and hides. The government could increase exports by instituting export subsidies, as is done in Senegal, or by devaluing its currency. Regional markets, particularly in west Africa, need to be explored.

Summary

The policy and institutional framework within which informal-sector activities could develop has never been adequately defined in Burkina Faso. But there are now many initiatives to develop the informal sector, so these efforts must be coordinated. Too many different Burkinabe ministries and agencies want to get involved. This could lead to an unclear division of responsibilities, an illogical division of the work, or duplication of activities. Donors should also coordinate their efforts and avoid doing the same thing twice or doing what others have found absolutely not feasible or useful. Recently, the Conseil du plan has invited all donors interested in SSEs and microenterprises to discuss coordinating their efforts.

Government policies can contribute to the development of the broadly defined industrial sector by encouraging more industrial development. Policies for the industrial sector should consider the following recommendations:

- Revise the tax system to bring down production costs and eliminate pricing distortions.
- Revise the new investment code so that support is not based on a distinction between small-, medium-, and large-scale enterprises but rather on economies of scale; it should also give more weight to the interrelatedness of industries.
- Reduce electricity costs by introducing differentiated prices (that is, lower prices during off-peak periods).
- Reduce transport costs through a transport and infrastructure project.
- Revise the system of import duties to lower the cost of raw materials.
- Increase export through export subsidies or a devaluation of the currency.
- Explore the possibility of developing regional (West African) markets.
- Concentrate on industries in which Burkina Faso should have a comparative advantage: agroprocessing, fruits and vegetables, and skins and hides. ✽

Part IV

Financial Services

Obstacles to Financial Innovation for Small Business Development in the Formal and Informal Private Sectors: Case Studies from the West African Monetary Union

Douato Adjémida Soedjede
Faculty of Economic and Management Sciences, Benin University, Lomé, Togo

Introduction

The economic health of any country is intricately linked to the vitality and dynamism of its business sector. Business is in fact an economic agent that produces the goods and services needed to meet public demand, and its development and survival, therefore, represent sure guarantees of economic prosperity. This is why since the dawn of their independence and until the end of the 1970s, the countries of sub-Saharan Africa have been making efforts to set up a wide range of new national and regional production units, based on the availability of raw materials.

It is hard enough to create a business, but it is no easier to keep it on the path to smooth and ever-increasing growth and profitability. The growth and profitability of a business depend not only on the quantity and quality of available natural resources, but also on the way all production factors are combined to make a given product. This presupposes proper management of all these factors, and the most important of these is the human factor.

It is a fact that governments in sub-Saharan Africa have underestimated the importance of the private sector — the businesses these governments have launched have generally failed or are now being privatized. The last few years have, thus, seen a new dynamism in both the formal and the informal private sectors.

Yet in many countries of sub-Saharan Africa, which is characterized by a rapidly growing informal economy, the efforts both of governments and of international agencies to promote the private sector have run into obstacles. These originate partially in African culture itself, with its traditions of family solidarity, the insistence of entrepreneurs on building up their own businesses, confusion between social success and business creation, mistaken notions of time and credit, and so on. To these obstacles must be added technical and production problems, unrealistic feasibility studies, ever more pressing burdens of taxes and border customs, the business and financial culture of entrepreneurs, and so on. Overwhelming competition and problems of access to some subregional markets are merely a reflection of the failure to carry out reliable market and feasibility studies.

In addition, small enterprises most frequently cite lack of access to bank credit as the most serious handicap to their growth, and they blame this mainly on the inadequate and short-term nature of bank lending. Governments and international agencies have attempted to deal with this financing problem (which affects mainly the formal private sector but also affects the informal sector to some extent) by making long-term lines of credit available to business and development banks. Yet, in most cases, these lines of credit have been so poorly managed by sluggish bureaucratic structures that they have produced feeble results, if any.

More than 25 years of financing by both traditional and international financial institutions in Africa has not improved the financial balance, economic impact, and social appropriation. If we are to find mechanisms that would be appropriate in this socioeconomic context, we must bear in mind the informal financing mechanisms that the African people know and understand. We will have to adopt indigenous mechanisms to complement those imported from abroad.

One such indigenous mechanism that mobilizes savings in developing countries, especially in Africa, is the *tontinier ambulant*, or itinerant banker. These individuals visit the markets and urban and rural neighbourhoods to collect daily, weekly or monthly savings from the many minor operators and the small to medium-sized enterprises and industries (SMES–SMIS) in the informal sector. Were it not for the presence of these itinerant bankers, even the most enterprising business operators in the informal sector would be condemned to stagnation.

To gain a full appreciation of this problem, we shall look at the obstacles facing the development of SMES–SMIS; banking deregulation in the West African Monetary Union (WAMU); lines of credit from international agencies; informal financial innovations that have sprung up in Togo and Benin; and regulation of the informal sector. In this work, I used information obtained from surveys and interviews conducted in Benin, Côte d'Ivoire, Senegal, and Togo and supplemented it with my own bibliographic research.

The failure of selective credit policies and the impact of banking deregulation on SMES–SMIS

The banking reform undertaken in 1975 by the Central Bank of the West African States (la Banque centrale des États de l'Afrique de l'Ouest, BCEAO) eliminated the regulatory distinction between commercial and development banks. In addition, BCEAO introduced a selective credit policy, differentiating priority and nonpriority sectors. The goals for implementing this selective credit policy were to be defined each year by national credit committees. The impact of the policy on the priority and nonpriority sectors of Togo during the period 1985–1989 is shown in Table 1.

The 5 years of data in Table 1 show the effect of this selective credit policy on credit-access rates for the priority and nonpriority sectors. In agriculture, the goal for the period was never once achieved, and the SMES–SMIS exceeded their target only once, in 1985. For these SMES–SMIS, the average rate of attaining credit in 1986–1988 was generally around 7%, whereas the goal was 15%. The goal for 1989 was reduced to 12%, and the actual rate for that year was 9.2%. This brief analysis of the SMES–SMIS in the sectors classed as having priority shows that results fell far short of the hopes of the monetary authorities and demonstrates that the selective credit policy was a failure. Access to credit is very difficult for these SMES–SMIS, mainly because of their weak finances and the heavy

Table 1. Selective credit policy for the priority and nonpriority sectors of Togo and its results.

Sectors	1985 (%)		1986 (%)		1987 (%)		1988 (%)		1989 (%)	
	T	A	T	A	T	A	T	A	T	A
Priority										
Agriculture	15	10.4	15	6.5	14	12.9	12	10.7	9	8.6
SMES–SMIS	20	23.4	15	7.1	15	7.4	15	7.7	12	9.2
Social housing	7	5.8	8	4.3	8	3.9	3	4.3	5	4.4
Livestock, fishing	—	—	2	0.5	3	0.3	3	0.2	3	0.2
Nonpriority										
Industry	28	18.8	28	22.5	28	26.5	28	26.8	28	26.7
Commercial	20	27.9	20	43.1	20	38.7	27	40.1	31	40.9
Construction, public works	5	8.3	5	8.7	5	3.7	5	2.7	5	3.4
Transportation, communications	5	3.1	4	4.4	4	3.6	4	4.5	4	3.6
Misc. services (such as tourism)	0	2.7	3	3.0	3	2.9	3	3.1	3	2.9

Source: CEAO-Lomé.

Note: T, target; A, actual.

guarantees that are demanded of them. It can be seen from Table 1 that the commercial sector — not a priority area — succeeded in obtaining the most credit, not only surpassing goals but actually doubling the target for 1986. The gap between goals and achievement is also very high for the other years.

After the failure of the 1975 banking reform, the monetary authorities decided in 1989 on a new approach to economic adjustment and restructuring in the WAMU countries to create the right conditions for sound and sustainable financing of growth and development (BCEAO 1989).

According to BCEAO (1992), "At the regulatory level, stricter prudential standards were set for the banks, without discriminating among them, and in accordance with the nature of the activities being financed." Under these conditions, the banks will finance only the activities they judge creditworthy, which means that they will increasingly ignore the SMES–SMIS. According to our calculations, which are based on data from the credit risk bureau of the BCEAO in Lomé, short-term credit represents on average 64.5% of all credit approved from 1987 to 1991.

Because of the problems of financing SMES–SMIS in both the formal and informal sectors, lines of credit were made available to commercial and development banks in the form of long-term resources. The use made of these long-term resources is examined in the next section.

Lines of credit from international agencies

SMES–SMIS cannot get financing from conventional banks, which are much more interested in providing short-term credit to major firms. Generally speaking, conventional banks do not have long- or medium-term resources because their term deposits are renewed for a maximum of 1 year. Many think that lines of credit might solve this problem, and at the present time direct financing to small business is being tried by some international agencies (OECD 1990).

Senegal

In Senegal, as in most of the WAMU countries, nearly all lines of credit provided to governments through the central banks have failed. The reasons for this lie basically in the conditions that have to be met for these lines of credit. This is especially true in Senegal, where the line of credit from the International Development Association (IDA) went unused for 5 years until a redefinition of its guidelines made it operational. (This is based on several interviews with private and state business managers and international organizations based in Dakar, which we conducted in March 1993 as part of our university research work.)

In Senegal, the Economic Promotion Fund (EPF) is a line of credit of almost 39 billion XOF (in 1994, 570 CFA francs [XOF] = 1 United States dollar [USD]) from the African Development Bank (ADB). EPF's main innovations consist of making it possible to benefit from an equity loan for 10% of the project cost, which reduces the required personal contribution from 30% to 20%. The annual interest rate is 13%, including a spread of 4%. Applications for credit are processed according to joint criteria of the bank and the EPF, and the risk of default (loss) assumed by each of the parties is 50% (CCAI-Dakar 1992). According to interviews with various business people in Senegal, EPF would have had better results if there had been a specialized financial structure for SMES–SMIS. In 1993, almost 140 financing applications were approved, 70 of which were of the new kind and made use of self-investment loans. Funding for EPF was only released in May 1992, and we shall have to wait until the end of the fiscal year 1993/94 to learn the first results. According to an officer of the ADB who we met in Abidjan in March 1993, the "EPF recipe" is succeeding in Senegal and Nigeria. Yet, for the Chambre de commerce d'agriculture et d'industrie de Dakar (CCAI-Dakar), the development finance problem remains, because financing goes to the big companies at the expense of the SMES–SMIS.

Togo

In Togo, IDA has provided the government with a line of credit under the Private Enterprise Promotion Project (le Projet de promotion de l'entreprise privée, PPEP) for 2.8 billion XOF, or 80% of the amount approved in the credit agreement. This agreement was signed 30 March 1988, but it had a slow start because of various problems arising in 1990. This line of credit is intended to finance SMES–SMIS for periods of 2–15 years, as well as to assist micro- and small enterprises, mainly in the informal sector.

The government of Togo set up the Equity Fund for Services (le Fonds de participation aux prestations de services, FPPS) to conduct feasibility studies and is making an initial contribution of 150 million XOF. The ministerial decree creating the fund was only signed on 12 October 1990. If a feasibility study results in going ahead with a project, the promoter must pay 50% of the cost of the feasibility study. Otherwise, the promoter does not have to bear any of the cost.

In 5 years, fewer than 10 projects have been financed. The basic reasons for this modest record are largely institutional:

- There was a delay in signing the ministerial decree.
- Two mutual-guarantee societies — one for the SMES–SMIS and one for artisans — were not created as planned.
- There were disagreements on the interest rate spread, 4.5%, which the banks wanted to raise to 6%. (This problem was finally resolved in February 1991, when the final interest rate was fixed at 11%.)
- Promoters have a difficult time finding their 30% of the project cost when their feasibility study is accepted. (It is often hard to put this money together even if the promoters ask other investors to participate.)
- A pilot project on micro- and small enterprises was never launched.
- The bureaucrats carrying out and coordinating the project weigh it down.

The credit agreement will have to be revised to make it fit reality in Togo. There are other lines of credit that are going unused, as well, such as those of the West African Development Bank (WADB) and the ADB — the funds are simply being placed in the money market, mainly by the commercial and development banks.

Analysis

Analysis of projects financed with lines of credit shows that the approach of the EPF and the ADB seems more realistic than the approach of the PPEP and the IDA.

Informal financial innovations in Togo and Benin and their regulation

Although the problems of financing the informal sector's activities have been ignored by the conventional financial institutions, I have been observing these problems for several years (Soedjede 1987, 1990a). My work has consisted of identifying the problems faced by so many business people in the informal sector and providing help to the people who finance them (Soedjede 1990b). Two of my publications were about the role of women, whose dynamism makes them the main players in national economic development (Soedjede 1993a,b). In addition to these publications, I have expanded my work and writings on the activities of itinerant bankers (Soedjede 1995a,b) and have helped in creation of the Lomé Itinerant Bankers' Mutual Solidarity Fund (la Mutuelle de solidarité des tontiniers ambulants de Lomé, MUSOTAL). (At my initiative, a meeting of all Togolese tontiniers was held in Lomé on 17 October 1992, under the patronage of the Principal Secretary of the Ministry of Economy and Finance.)

This paper focuses much more on innovative, informal financing methods and will deal with the products that itinerant bankers offer their customers. It is not my intention to cover all the work we have done on informal financing but rather to discuss the various innovative products offered by some of Togo's itinerant bankers and those operating in Cotonou, Benin.

In the case of *tontines* (itinerant bankers' financial schemes), according to Lelart (1993), what debtors and creditors are looking for is not the best rate of interest but the availability of funds that they can exchange among themselves every day. This is the justification for the freedom these itinerant bankers enjoy in setting the interest rate on a loan to increase the working capital of a client in the informal sector.

Togo's experience with itinerant bankers

The itinerant bankers of Togo offer a variety of financial products to their customers, as we shall see.

Risk capital

An itinerant banker and an entrepreneur may enter as two partners into an agreement to put together a risk capital operation. Some itinerant bankers in Togo and Benin already engage in this practice, although it is not formally recognized, as far as we know, in any WAMU country .

In the case of Togo, my survey of 29 itinerant bankers showed that 14 of them, or about 48%, engage in risk capital activities. The most commonly used technique is to monitor the growth of the customer's working capital. The daily or weekly visits that the itinerant bankers make to collect payments from their customers give them a chance to find out whether and how much the business is growing. Risk assessment is based on studying the profitability of the customer's business. Some of these bankers limit their share of the risk to 60% of the project's cost (Soedjede 1992).

A survey I conducted of itinerant bankers' customers in Cotonou, Benin, showed that 54% of customers would be willing to use risk capital. This result was little different from the survey of itinerant bankers in Togo (48%) and confirms that this is a source of financing for some activities in the informal sector.

Daily savings deposits

In another scheme, customers make daily deposits with the itinerant banker. If the customers do not take an advance, they will later recover 30 out of 31 units from their deposit; the first unit is the itinerant banker's remuneration. This represents an attempt at savings and the building of economic security.

Carte blanche

Carte blanche is a guarantee fund to meet the ever-growing demand for credit. Deposits are made monthly and range between 30 000 and 50 000 XOF. To make management easier, the itinerant banker will, after 6 months of savings, give a credit for the equivalent of 9 month's savings to a first group of customers. Three months later, another group will get a credit, and so on. The monthly savings and the credit carry no interest. The itinerant banker does not take any remuneration from these deposits, but this is implicit.

Weekly deposits

Another of the itinerant bankers' arrangements involves collecting between 3 000 and 10 000 xof from customers every week for 12 weeks. The customers get their deposits back 3 months later to finance their business. This kind of service allows the itinerant banker to give the customers short-term credit on favourable terms.

Back-to-school special

What is called a back-to-school special is a type of credit extended to regular customers for 3 months at a rate of 6% for the entire term of the credit. This service lets the itinerant banker gain customers' confidence by helping them meet specific needs, especially at the beginning of the school year.

Joint-liability groups

In a joint-liability group, members are jointly responsible for repaying the credits granted to each member in turn, as is the case with customers of the itinerant bankers in Cotonou (this topic will come up again in a later section).

No-bidding financial *tontine*

A no-bidding *tontine* is one where deposits are made weekly over a period of 52 weeks. The amount saved plus interest cannot be recovered until the 52 weeks are up (Soedjede 1990c). The itinerant banker makes a profit on this arrangement because it builds up a stable pool of money while meeting the customers' needs for credit. This product differs from the financial *tontine* with bidding, as practiced in Cameroon (Bekolo-Ebe and Bilongo 1988; Henri et al. 1991), where the funds are taken up by the highest bidder (that is, the one who offers the highest interest rate). In the no-bidding variety, the interest rate is fixed in advance.

Turnkey financing for profitable activities

After studying the borrower's motives, honesty, and profit record, an itinerant banker may decide to put up working capital.

Summary

The relationship between these different products becomes clear when we realize that the pool of funds from a financial *tontine* can be used to provide credit to customers using other forms (commercial) of *tontines*. This is useful because the flexible nature (generally, monthly repayments to clients) of the commercial *tontine* means that the itinerant banker does not always have money available, whereas funds from the no-bidding financial *tontine* are usually left with the itinerant banker for a year, so the pool of funds available for lending out is more stable. Furthermore, the customers of the itinerant bankers' commercial *tontine* may participate in the financial *tontine*. The latter fund can also be used to buy goods to make loans in kind, for example, to help set up new merchants and encourage them to join the itinerant bankers' *tontine* or to win back former clients who see their business falling off.

Benin's experience with itinerant bankers

For analytical purposes, I conducted a survey among the customers of itinerant bankers in Cotonou, Benin. Of the 386 people interviewed, 267 (about 70%) were clients of individual or associated itinerant bankers. The customers surveyed were chosen at random, after I verified that they had permanent market stands. I did the same thing with artisans, and I am working with some of the results of the surveys conducted in early August 1993 to understand the role of informal finance in the resurgence of informal business activity (Soedjede 1994). A study of customers at the St Michel market in Cotonou was completed earlier by Lelart and Gnassounou (1990).

Risk capital

The survey of the customers of individual or associated itinerant bankers in Cotonou confirms that there is risk capital activity. Out of 267 customers, 145 (about 54%) would be willing to have an individual or associated itinerant banker take an equity interest in the financing of a selected piece of business in the form of risk capital and let the itinerant banker share in any profit or loss, as Table 2 shows. Of the 145 customers who would participate in a risk capital scheme, the main reasons given were (a) for additional financial support (37%); (b) for sharing profits and risks (31%); and (c) for the good of both parties

Table 2. Opinions of 145 customers in Benin who would participate in a risk capital scheme.

	Respondents	
Response	No.	%
Would do it for supplementary financial support	53	37
Would do it to share the profits and the risk	45	31
Would do it for the good of both parties	26	18
Would not accept profit sharing	9	6
Frequently use such schemes	4	3
Prefer doing business alone	2	1
Would do it for other reasons (small share and no alternative)	2	1
No response	4	3
Total	145	100

(18%). I found that 6% would not accept profit sharing, whereas 3% do so "fairly often."

Of the 120 who responded negatively to the idea of equity in the form of risk capital, 101 (about 84%) were afraid of the risk involved, 2 (about 2%) simply preferred to take care of their business themselves, and the remaining 17 (about 14%) gave no reason.

Daily savings deposits

Daily deposits were made by merchants (128 of 267 respondents, or about 48%); by artisans (82 of 267, or about 31%); by taxicab and motorcycle taxi drivers (45 of 267, or about 17%); and by salaried employees (12 of 267, or about 4%).

Joint-liability groups

We asked the 267 customers for their opinion on setting up joint-liability groups of three to five people to get credit, knowing that each member would be responsible for the default of any other. On this point, 112 (about 42%) would agree to set up such a group. These 112 customers cited the following advantages of doing so: (a) mutual guarantee or group solidarity (71%); (b) greater creditworthiness (15%); (c) business development (10%); and (d) responsibility and independence (4%). This is a good result because, even in the formal financial sector, innovation is not always readily accepted. The main drawback to setting up groups of three to five people was lack of confidence or the possibility of default by individual members, according to 198 (about 74%) of the 267 respondents.

Other financial products

Out of the 267 survey respondents, 162 (about 61%) obtained credit or advances at least once from other itinerant banking schemes. This credit was used for, among other things, (a) business expansion (about 62%); (b) financing a specific deal (about 10%); or (c) school or funeral expenses (6 and 4%, respectively). For 80% of the customers, the largest amount they borrowed was between 50 000 and 200 000 XOF. Four of those surveyed had borrowed 700 000 to 2 million XOF. The repayment terms ran from less than 1 month to 10 months for the majority of the 162 who obtained credit or advances. One of them was able to get 2 years.

The other (non-credit-taking) 105 of the 267 (39%) surveyed gave the following reasons for not having obtained credit or an advance: (a) they never asked for credit (about 68%); (b) their itinerant banker did not give credit (about 18%); (c) they didn't request it in time (about 3%); or (d) they had doubts about their own creditworthiness (about 2%). Only 10 out of the 105 surveyed (about 10%) did not give a reason.

Summary

Those interviewed clearly saw these financial innovations (risk capital, joint-liability groups, various other financial products) as potentially of help to them in their business. Although there is now regular contact between these business people and the itinerant bankers, more will have to be done to make people in the informal sector aware of how effective these innovations can be.

Regulation of the informal financial sector

In one of my articles (Soedjede 1995a), I suggested that

> A genuine relationship should be established between the Togo Federation of Itinerant Bankers, once it is established, and the Professional Bankers' Association for planning the future of the Togolese economy. This is the only way to get these two sources of finances mutually integrated. We have had almost twenty-five years of experience and involvement in the work of various types of *tontine* organizations, and we believe it would be a serious mistake to try to stamp out this informal financing business by

imposing strict regulations. If this were attempted, it would only lead to spectacular growth in the informal financial sector, for, as everyone knows, the informal sector has plenty of innovative ideas, and they will flourish very well underground.

Within the Central Bank of the West African States...at Dakar, thought is being given to developing an "adequate" legal framework within which the various *tontines* and savings and credit cooperatives could grow. Because there are so many different types and methods of intervention, it will be necessary to undertake the following:

- Make everyone aware that there is no question of trying to forbid these forms of mobilizing savings and credit; instead, encourage those who are pursuing these financing activities after the failure of the development banks.

- Involve these people at every step of decision-making during the development of the institutional framework, and in particular get their input and comments on the statutes, internal regulations, and so on.

- Avoid the error of focusing on the semi-formal financial institutions; always keep in mind the previous point.

- Try as far as possible to design a number of institutional frameworks suited to each of the many types of business.

A working group on banking reform should look first at ways to stimulate and increase the volume of savings from firms and households and then determine how to keep these savings in place and how to invest them in the most worthwhile and profitable business activities. We should not regulate or suppress the informal financial sector but rather help it to "piggyback" on the formal banking sector by building two-way links between the informal and the formal financial sectors (Zeral 1990).

There is much to be learned from all the experience gained in promoting mutual societies and cooperatives in both rural and urban settings. Business and financial managers are now discovering the virtues of cooperative and mutual structures in the field of banking. According to Zeral (1990), what is needed is to encourage this positive approach by defining the operating rules that such structures should follow. This is all the more important because of the losses that the shaky practices of commercial banks have caused in the absence of banking regulation.

Conclusion

Throughout this article, I have been examining the failure of the selective credit policy created by the 1975 banking reform. The failure of this banking reform led the monetary authorities to adopt a new money and credit policy in October 1989, which resulted in banking deregulation. The main tools adopted to reach this goal were the prudential ratios and the classification of some companies as a credit risk. These two tools, however, have not done much for the SMES–SMIs.

The rise of various types of *tontines*, including itinerant bankers' services, is an innovation in the area of financial products. Customers turn to these sources even though the cost of credit is very high by conventional banking standards. The efficiency of the informal financial system no doubt led to the lowering of the maximum interest rates in October 1993 in the WAMU countries. Zeral (1990), of the French Treasury, noted this phenomenon.

After his 1989 communication on the setting of interest rates, Zeral (1990) was critical of the maximum margin of 5% allowed in the WAMU zone and was worried about how the banks could afford to lend at a 5% margin, given the risk factors and the management costs, when the informal sector can lend at 30 or 40% per month. Zeral added that the informal sector was a characteristic reflection of the liveliness of African society. But competition needs to be fair, and restructuring will not be of much help if at the same time the banks are not allowed to make a profit (Zeral 1990).

Some customers of itinerant bankers attempt to cover themselves against loss by getting quotes from several different itinerant bankers, keeping part of their savings in their own hands and taking part in mutual or no-bidding financial *tontines*. But now, with the itinerant bankers forming associations, such as MUSOTAL in Togo and the Cotonou Tontiniers Association in Benin, and companies or groupings of itinerant tontiniers, especially in Benin, customers are beginning to have more confidence. ❊

CHANGE AGENTS IN THE DEVELOPMENT OF FINANCIAL SERVICES FOR SMALL-SCALE ENTERPRISES IN GHANA

Gloria Nikoi[1]
AKUPEM *Rural Bank, Accra, Ghana*

Introduction

This paper examines the financial services available to the informal and small-scale enterprise (SSE) sectors in Ghana. These sectors have hardly any access to institutional credit in Ghana. Formal financial institutions find offering services to these sectors risky, costly, and unprofitable, and the various informal financial arrangements available to these sectors offer too little financial resources at too high a cost to enable them to sustain growth. This paper, therefore, shows that other providers of financial services should bridge the gap between the formal banks and the informal financial economy.

The development of financial services for the informal and SSE sectors will be looked at in the context of the continuing pervasive development crisis in the African continent and the fact, noted by the World Bank, that our continent is the only one where poverty is increasing. The informal and SSE sectors contain the majority of the economically active, indigenous population and provide the means of livelihood for the majority of the poor. The Ghana Statistical Service, which is conducting a study to determine the exact scope and output of the informal

[1] I am grateful to William Steel of the World Bank for his most helpful comments, which were of immense use in the revision of this paper.

sector, at the lower end of the SSE sector, estimates that the informal sector's contribution to GDP could be about 50%. If the output of the upper end of the SSE sector were included, this contribution would appear even higher. If the African continent is to achieve self-reliance and self-sustaining growth and the seemingly inexorable slide to poverty is to be reversed, the production, productivity, and incomes of the private entrepreneurs in the informal and SSE sectors must grow, and this growth will have to be accomplished through innovative and bold policies.

These policies must be targeted at the rural and inner-city areas because most of such enterprises are in those areas, and these policies must have a gender focus because women's activities are prominent in these sectors. For instance, the 1984 Ghana Census (Ghana 1984) indicates a total population of 12.3 million people, of which 8.4 million (67%) live in rural areas. Out of a total of 5.4 million employed persons aged 15 years or older, 3.3 million work in agriculture (for example, food crops, livestock, fisheries, and cocoa).

Providers of Financial Services in Ghana

The main agents for providing financial services in our economy are listed in Table 1. I shall briefly discuss why some of these financial agents are not providing effective and sustainable financial services to the SSE sector.

Commercial and development banks

There are 14 banks in the formal banking sector of Ghana, 8 of which are government owned. All operate as commercial banks, although three of them started out as development banks.

The deposit structure of commercial banks is essentially short term, and their decision-making is highly centralized. Therefore, they concentrate preeminently on meeting the short-term financial needs of public and private enterprises at the top end of the commercial and business market in urban centres. The risks of such lending are minimal, transaction costs are relatively low, turnover is quick, and profits are high.

Commercial banks do not lend in any significant way to SSEs. The banks consider such lending too risky and too costly. SSEs in the agriculture and related sectors in the rural areas are scattered throughout large, remote areas subject to natural

Table 1. Agents providing financial services in Ghana.

Formal		Informal
Banks	Nonbanks	
The Bank of Ghana (BOG)	Savings and loans companies (S&Ls)	Private money lenders
	Credit unions	Susu collectors
Rural banks	Discount houses, building societies, leasing and hire purchase companies, and venture capital funding companies	Rotating savings and credit associations, such as the susu system, and other self-help associations, such as business associations, Amassachina groups, and work groups
Commercial and development banks		
	Bodies that cater to the financial needs of SSEs, such as the National Board for Small-Scale Industries and the Fund for Small and Medium Enterprises Development, which administer various donor-sponsored credit funds	
		Traders and distributors of farm inputs
	NGOs	
	Guarantee funds	Friends, relatives, and personal savings

hazards, such as droughts, floods, and pests. These SSEs cannot give the type of collateral, such as immovable property, that commercial banks usually require. They do not meet the credit criteria of commercial banks. Their activities are not amenable to the normal feasibility studies, and they do not have the assets required by commercial banks. These SSEs require relatively small loans, largely unsecured, which commercial banks find costly to make, monitor, and retrieve. The location of the commercial banks, their operational guidelines, and their limited human resources make them unable to meet the financial needs of the informal and SSE sectors.

The ongoing Financial Restructuring Programme in Ghana has led commercial banks, in their quest for efficiency, to close down a number of their branches outside urban areas and to concentrate on a few centralized outlets in urban areas, thus making these banks less accessible to SSEs. The same can be said of the development banks, which engage in commercial banking and provide banking services for specific sectors of the economy, such as agriculture, construction, housing, and industry. They provide financial services to large and medium-scale clients in their areas of operations and are unable to cater to the needs of the SSE sector owing to their structure, mode of operation, and limitations in human resources.

Some formal nonbank providers of financial services

Some formal nonbank providers of financial services in Ghana's financial system are unable to seriously provide financing for SSES, owing to fairly stringent and rigid regulations. There is one consolidated discount house and one securities discount house. There is also one building society and four leasing and hire purchase companies. These are fairly strictly regulated by the financial authorities. For instance, the minimum capital requirement for consideration for registration is 100 million GHC (in 1993, 601 Ghanaian cedi [GHC] = 1 United States dollar [USD]). There are also fairly rigid capital, liquidity, and other requirements that they have to meet, and penalties are imposed for noncompliance.

These stringent regulations ensure that there are very few formal nonbank providers of financial services and that these, to remain viable, competitive, and profitable, cater only to medium- and large-scale enterprises. There are about 20 insurance companies and a social security and national insurance trust that cater to medium- and large-scale enterprises. A stock exchange has operated since November 1990, and its listing and membership regulations, despite the recent introduction of a "Third List," effectively bar the exchange's facilities to SSES.

The National Board for Small-Scale Industries

The National Board for Small-Scale Industries (NBSSI) was established in 1985 to implement policies and programs for the accelerated development of small-scale industries in Ghana. NBSSI's main activities facilitate access of SSES to credit and promote nonfinancial programs, including training and business advisory services, such as extension, support to business associations, and dissemination of business information to SSES.

NBSSI's endeavours are impeded because of the absence of any nationally established development policy clearly defining the different types of sses and the roles of various institutions in implementing such a policy. NBSSI has, therefore, to deal with enterprises ranging from the micro, to the medium sized, to the large. It has also found itself doing the same things for sses as other agencies, such as training of entrepreneurs, without being able to coordinate these activities. The result is that NBSSI's impact has been very diffuse, to say the least.

But much more important, NBSSI's efforts have not been effective. First, it tries to facilitate access to credit by linking up enterprises and individuals (whom it trains) with financial institutions. This has not been very successful. The sses cannot meet financial institutions' collateral and equity requirements. Commercial bank officials perceive the sector as risky and costly to lend to and are not attuned to offering credit to this sector. The borrowers' skills and managerial experiences are also considered inadequate to support traditional loans.

Second, since 1991, when NBSSI merged with the Ghana Enterprises Development Corporation, which was giving loans, it has itself been operating a number of small credit schemes. This credit program has a number of problems. The source of funds is neither stable nor sustainable. For instance, NBSSI was promised funds totalling 340 million GHC from the Programme of Action for Mitigating the Social Costs of Adjustment (PAM-SCAD), but so far only 150 million GHC has been released to it. The PAMSCAD program is itself being wound up. NBSSI also fails to meet some demands from applicants for these funds. The loans committees — with representatives from relevant departments and ministries, such bodies as the National Council on Women and Development, and the commercial banks — established to help select loan recipients, also work poorly.

The best way for institutions to promote the development of sses would be to divest themselves of their credit and financial service functions. They have neither the institutional capabilities nor the staff to perform these functions. Furthermore, they do not have access to regular sources of funds to make their financial programs sustainable. Their financial functions could be taken up by the banks or the credit unions and savings and loans (S&Ls), which can forge operational links with commercial banks. Strong links can be established between these financial agents and such bodies as NBSSI through their nonfinancial programs. Institutions such as NBSSI, with sufficient funds and adequate and appropriate human resources, could build up good databases on sses to strengthen entrepreneurial development and to provide advisory service programs to identify and develop entrepreneurs eligible for loans from the banks. Such institutions could help the banks and intermediary financial institutions, such as credit unions, monitor and follow up on loans. They could thus help the sses develop into viable enterprises beyond the limits of self-finance.

The Fund for Small and Medium Enterprises Development

The Fund for Small and Medium Enterprises Development (FUSMED) is the administrative unit established by the International Development Association (IDA) of the World Bank to pass a credit line on to participating banks to finance the development of private, small- and medium-scale enterprises in the productive sectors. FUSMED has provided 25 million USD since March 1990. The Development Finance Department of the Bank of Ghana (BOG) passes on proceeds from FUSMED to about 11 participating commercial banks to lend to their clients.

The procedures used to administer FUSMED are cumbersome and actually raise the transaction costs. For instance, participating banks are expected to prepare feasibility studies or to have them prepared by consultants. They or the banks are to apply to the BOG for the facilities. Furthermore, participating banks are to contribute 10–15% of the cost of the investment project from their own resources. If the application is approved by the World Bank and BOG, the credit is made available to the participating bank at an interest rate equivalent to the average cost of the 180-day deposits mobilized by the bank. The bank then, in turn, passes on the credit and other costs. The procedures actually raise rather than lower transaction costs, and not many banks are prepared to incur such outlays or go to such trouble for SSEs who are not their clients.

Other conditions make FUSMED unsuitable for SSEs. For instance, eligible enterprises should have total fixed assets not exceeding 2 million USD. Theoretically, therefore, any enterprise with fixed assets of any amount less than 2 million USD is eligible, other things being equal. Most SSEs usually have very modest, if any, fixed assets. Again, the applications of those seeking to benefit from FUSMED are to be channeled through their banks. Most SSEs at the lower end of the sector do not have bank accounts. Another limiting factor is that private enterprises are eligible only if they are engaged in productive sectors other than primary agriculture, trading, and real estate. This effectively bars large numbers of SSEs. Finally, participating SSEs are required to contribute at least 25% of the cost of their projects in equity or from their own resources. Most SSEs are unable to meet this condition.

For all these reasons, FUSMED has supported the relatively large enterprises. But even for such large enterprises, the cumbersome and lengthy procedures of FUSMED, which do not facilitate quick disbursement, make it unattractive as a source of funding. Indeed, as of September 1991, according to BOG sources, actual and potential commitments under the FUSMED scheme amounted to 11.3 million USD. The lowest was for 9 091 USD for working capital for a printer of stationery, and the highest was for 500 000 USD to a lumber products industry for importing equipment. A BOG source further states that FUSMED has not generated new lending to SSEs since September 1991. Banks were using FUSMED largely to provide loan funds to preferred SSE clients when the banks lacked their own funds.

Nongovernmental organizations

A number of NGOs — mostly the foreign ones — usually offer credit as part of their programs to rural and other low-income communities. In Ghana, some of the NGOs in the developmental field have programs with credit components.

The problems with credit from NGOs derive from a number of factors:

- Whereas banks mobilize savings and lend these resources to borrowers, NGOs rely on financial allocations from their governments and grants from foreign benefactors. The amounts are usually too small for the tasks. The regularity and availability of such financial resources are also not usually assured. This puts the financial programs initiated by NGOs at risk.

- NGOs that offer credit often lack guidelines clearly specifying whether such funding is a loan or a grant. If they are loans, there are uncertainties, for instance, about what interest and repayment rates to charge. If they are outright grants, the precise conditions for them are unclear. Recipients may sometimes take the funds, thinking they do not have to account for them in any way, and generally divert them to other uses.

- NGOs also lack the machinery, mechanisms, and staff to offer, monitor, and control the end-use or to collect interest or recover assets. Questions about the effectiveness of NGOs inevitably arise. For instance, project officers of NGOs are seen hurtling around rural areas on their mopeds, hanging on to large sacks of coins they are supposed to be giving to their clients. The danger posed to the security of such funds is obvious.

- The fact that NGOs usually do not coordinate their activities with the development priorities of either other NGOs or the government makes their impact as financial intermediaries diffuse at best and not too relevant to the country's development priorities.

NGOs should, therefore, leave the role of financial intermediary to those institutions specifically established and equipped to undertake this function.

NGOs can cooperate with intermediaries in areas where they are peculiarly suited to work, that is, by providing information about clients and by supporting training programs of all kinds for small-scale entrepreneurs who are unacquainted with the credit system.

Guarantee funds

Guarantee funds have not been effective in improving the access of SSEs to credit from institutions in Ghana. They are usually established to bridge the gap between formal banking institutions and small and microenterprises and operate by a mechanism that should make it easier for banks to help small borrowers, at minimum financial risk. The fact that they are operated through the commercial banking system with operational procedures that are not geared to lending to SSEs poses problems. The procedures involved have been cumbersome and in some cases unrealistic, and the banks have usually not been interested in making even minimal changes in their procedures to successfully operate these schemes, with the result that these funds are ineffective. The schemes either do not take off or just peter out.

Women's World Banking (Ghana) — Women's World Banking (Ghana) (WWBG) started its operations as a credit guarantee institution. It established an arrangement with one of the leading commercial banks in Ghana, whereby it used some seed money from the Women's World Banking (New York) as a guarantee fund for women who as small-scale entrepreneurs sought loans from that commercial bank. But the bank's normal eligibility and operational criteria were used. As a result, only a few, relatively large loans went to women with SSEs, mostly in the urban areas. The program ignored the women with very small SSEs in the rural and urban informal sectors. WWBG hoped that the commercial banks would leverage their guarantee fund by lending as much as four times the amount of the fund. But the banks never actually lent more than was deposited as a guarantee.

Mutualist Credit Guarantee Scheme — There is a Mutualist Credit Guarantee Scheme (MCGS) for micro- and small enterprises under the FUSMED facility. Under MCGS, mutualist guarantee associations (MGAs), expected to be formed by groups of 20–25 entrepreneurs, are registered to act on behalf of the members. Members then contribute to the MCGS through the payment of registration fees, monthly dues, and a guarantee fee calculated at 3% of the loan. The FUSMED contribution to the MCGS consists of 33.33% of the total contributions of the members of the MGAs. Both the participating financial institutions and the SSEs have found the eligibility rules and the loan appraisal, approval, and other procedures too cumbersome and unrealistic. The banks have not been anxious to encourage the formation of MGAs. The result is that since July 1993 only one MGA has been formed with one participating financial institution, and the bulk of the MCGS funds remains unused.

Informal providers of financial services

There are a variety of providers of informal financial services all over the rural areas and in the urban informal sector. Organized by individuals or groups of entrepreneurs for their own benefit, these agents provide different kinds of credit and support to entrepreneurs with SSEs. These informal providers of financial services include private money lenders; *susu* collectors; rotating savings and credit associations, such as the *susu* system; other self-help associations, like business associations, *Amassachina* groups, and other work groups; traders and distributors of farm inputs; and friends, relatives and the SSE owners themselves, with their personal savings.

The informal financial services satisfy both economic and social needs. They are fully participatory, are based *inter alia* on personal references, mutual trust, convenience, simple procedures, and easy access to resources, and are truly self-reliant. Their main disadvantage is that they do not serve many SSEs. Furthermore, the limited amount of credit they give does not significantly increase the production, productivity, or income of the SSEs. Innovative links with formal and intermediate financial institutions may improve their impact.

Agents of change

Commercial banks cater to the financial needs of large-scale public and private enterprises. Commercial banks find lending to SSEs risky, costly, and unprofitable. The informal financial system also does not adequately meet the growth needs of SSEs. Many banks and nonbank financial institutions are or will be, if adequately nurtured, effective agents of change, bridging the gap between formal financial institutions and the informal financial market and offering adequate credit access to SSEs.

Rural banks

Ghana's rural banks were established to provide institutional credit and banking services to small-scale farmers and rural entrepreneurs, to arrest a growing rural debt and a consequent pervasive stagnation in agricultural production, to make sure that resources mobilized in rural areas are used in rural areas, and to promote growth in the rural sector. Rural banks are unit banks operating as limited liability companies in accordance with the *Companies Code* of 1963 and the *Banking Act, 1989* P.N.D.C. L 225. Since 1976, 123 such banks have been established, spread all over the rural areas of Ghana.

Rural banks mobilize savings from their catchment areas and lend these resources to deserving rural SSEs. In 1992, the rural banks mobilized some 9.68 billion GHC and lent 4.81 billion GHC to a variety of SSEs. During the same period, rural banks bought 3.06 billion GHC worth of treasury bills. Rural banks have also participated effectively in the *Akuafo* cheques scheme whereby cocoa farmers are paid for their cocoa with cheques issued through the banking system. Indeed, in the 1991/92 cocoa-purchasing season, rural banks collectively purchased 20 billion GHC out of a national total purchase of 61 billion GHC — the highest purchase of cocoa by any of the banks in the formal sector.

The rural banks are able to be such effective financial intermediaries for rural SSEs because of a number of factors:

- They are decentralized and accessible. They are located in the rural areas among the people they serve and are expected to operate in a catchment area with a 32-km radius. In this catchment area, they can establish agencies to take banking services virtually to the doorsteps of their rural clients.

- They can make decisions locally and thus quickly.
- They are owned, managed, and controlled by the local communities and are thus fully participatory, operating under community sanctions and mores.
- Their operational guidelines are flexible. These banks use simplified procedures and clearly established eligibility criteria with a built-in equity system to ensure that credit goes to rural SSEs, especially those in priority areas of the economy.
- They emphasize savings as essential to credit, thus helping to inculcate a certain banking culture among rural populations.
- Their procedures are realistic. For instance, borrowers are required to find two people of standing in the community or account holders in the bank to be guarantors.
- They rely on locally mobilized resources for their operations. The survival of these banks thus depends on local initiative, local commitment, and local innovation.

The rural banks are basically self-reliant institutions, owned, managed, and controlled by the people of the community, mobilizing resources from the community and providing the institutional framework within which deserving members of the community can use these resources to improve their productivity and income.

Rural banks face some major difficulties. These derive, in part, from the sheer lack of basic amenities in our rural areas. Other problems include the following:

- There are many hazards to agriculture. Agriculture depends on rain, and we have not found any adequate responses to natural hazards such as drought, floods, and pests. This adversely affects agricultural production and, therefore, loan repayments.
- Because of the seasonal nature of agriculture, all the farmers' financial needs tend to occur at the same time. All the farmers want to take loans or to make deposits

at the same time. This makes it difficult to balance net savings and net loans at any one time.

- Although dependence on local initiative, leadership, commitment, and integrity is an advantage, banks find it difficult to survive where these qualities are absent in a community.

- Most of the rural banks are short of the capital required by the *Banking Act*, and this restricts their banking services.

- Most important of all, it is difficult for banks to recruit and retain qualified and honest management and support staff for the rural areas. The greatest problem facing rural banks, therefore, is the problem of human resources.

The Association of Rural Banks and BOG are pursuing a vigorous program of training for all cadres of rural-bank staff in all areas of banking, including operational procedures and financial-assets management. Customer service training programs are also being started. These training programs have greatly improved the efficiency of rural banks.

Under the Rural Finance Project, the World Bank is assisting the Association by helping it develop training materials and strengthening its capacity to deliver training programs.

The latest figures indicate that 19 of the 123 rural banks are in trouble financially and are to be phased out. Forty-three have met the capital adequacy and other prudential requirements of the *Banking Act* and are operating satisfactorily, and 61 are working hard to fulfil the requirements of the *Banking Act*.

The fact that 19 out of 123 rural banks are "distressed" should not lead to pessimism or despair about rural banks. The majority are providing effective financial services to the informal and SSE sectors and making critical improvements to the rural economy. The experiences gained during the 17-year history of rural banking should be used to help those 19 distressed banks survive and to help the good banks become even better.

Savings and loans companies

S&Ls have been on the Ghana scene since 1985. These operate by collecting savings from entrepreneurs and accumulating them for at least 6 months to build a deposit base for the saver. At the end of this period, the saver may withdraw his or her savings and also receive a loan proportional to the amount saved.

S&Ls can be good financial intermediaries for SSEs. The S&Ls usually locate where SSEs are, in markets and near workplaces. The S&L structures and procedures are very simple. The S&Ls operate with low overheads; they handle small amounts; and their transaction costs are low. Their personnel are usually knowledgeable about the entrepreneur and his or her experience and ability to save and handle credit.

Unfortunately, the kind of people who initially established the S&Ls in Ghana did not have the liquid resources to sustainably meet loan demands. Most also did not have the technical expertise and integrity to follow prudent financial management practices. Some defaulted. Others collapsed. Public confidence in them ebbed, and BOG was obliged to impose stringent laws regulating their establishment. These laws, among others, enjoin all those wishing to establish S&Ls to register with BOG, deposit 100 million GHC, and have permanent premises. S&Ls are also to follow certain regulations regarding capital adequacy and liquidity ratios.

Few people can readily meet these conditions. According to BOG, as of mid-1993 only eight companies had applied to be licenced. Of these, none had been licenced before, although two, CITI Savings and Loans Company and WWBG's Mutual Assistance Susu Ltd (MASU), are operating. We are awaiting approval for revisions to the *Financial Institutions (Non-Bank) Act, 1993* P.N.D.C. L 328 to reduce the minimum capital requirement for S&Ls from 100 million GHC to 20 million GHC and to establish more realistic capital adequacy and liquidity ratios.

To improve SSEs' access to financial services, it will be necessary to look at the whole regulatory framework for S&Ls. The amount paid for registration will have to be flexible. There should be greater monitoring and supervision of the S&Ls' operations to ensure that sound financial management practices are being followed. We should encourage innovative links with commercial banks, with mutual benefit to both the banks and the S&Ls. Two important examples of S&Ls are CITI Savings and Loans Company and WWBG's MASU.

CITI Savings and Loans Company operates as a limited service bank in one of the thriving markets of the capital city. It mobilizes savings from all its customers and has current accounts for customers who wish to put in their day's earnings. Initially, it concentrated on short-term revolving loans for wholesale and retail dealers operating in the food trade and those who process foodstuffs in the market. In addition to providing overdrafts to the food processors, the company has a hire–purchase system, under which the food processors can purchase equipment like cornmills, grinders, and cauldrons.

CITI Savings and Loans Company helps customers develop their own forms of collateral through savings, bank balances, fixed deposits, certificates of deposits, and Ghana Government securities. The company accepts savings bank balances as security and is making efforts to establish a loan insurance fund, which will be equivalent to a certain percentage of the value of all the loans granted. This fund is expected to be used to cover cases of involuntary loan defaults, such as those resulting from the sudden illness or death of a customer. CITI Savings and Loans Company has a direct relationship with commercial banks operating deposit accounts and shares overdrafts with them.

MASU, licenced in 1991, operates more as an S&L than a bank and has less direct relationships with commercial banks. MASU has evolved from the *susu* system, which female entrepreneurs established to help themselves. Becoming operational in 1992, MASU seeks to improve the traditional *susu* system. It offers services such as security, deposits, loans, hire–purchase financing, and payment to female entrepreneurs of interest on deposits that accumulate for 6 months without withdrawal. The sustainability of its operations can be assured if it can establish effective links with the commercial banks.

It is clear from the examples of CITI Savings and Loans Company and MASU that S&Ls can mobilize savings from a wider spectrum of customers than commercial banks. S&Ls could keep these savings as deposits in commercial banks and be eligible for loans and advances, which they could in turn lend to their customers. This would increase the commercial banks' resources and improve the S&Ls' liquidity and their ability to give reliable credit to their clients.

Because S&Ls are already effectively supporting microenterprises and SSEs, such links with commercial banks will improve SSE access to credit and make S&Ls good intermediate agents.

Credit unions

The 300 or so credit unions in Ghana are concentrated in two regions of the country (the Upper West and Brong Ahafo). There are "closed" unions, catering exclusively to certain categories of people, such as teachers and members of certain churches. There are also "open" credit unions, which anybody can join and where small-scale farmers, traders, and tradespeople make deposits and borrow to finance their activities. The credit unions pay dividends on the members' shares and charge an interest rate of between 1 and 2% monthly on credit.

The advantages of credit unions for SSEs are the easy accessibility of funds, simple procedures, a system of mutual trust, and the links between savings and credit that are characteristic of credit unions. On the other hand, credit unions have limited funds and weak management and operate with untrained staff. Credit unions also lack the machinery and mechanisms for adequately offering, monitoring, and retrieving loans. Their funds are usually at risk. To make credit unions more efficient financial intermediaries for SSEs, their operational systems, policies, and procedures should be strengthened, especially in areas such as accounting, auditing, and loans policies. The credit unions could be one of the best intermediatary agents for SSE financing if they had links with commercial or rural banks. In this way, the strengths of the credit union system — namely, customer orientation and trust — would be combined with the better refinancing and better trained management of the commercial and rural banks. The monitoring and inspection activities of BOG should encompass the activities of credit unions to help them strengthen their management and their working operations, to enable them to become institutions that cater effectively and reliably to the needs of the SSEs.

Recommendations

If banks and nonbank financial institutions are to effectively and reliably fill intermediary roles in the provision of financial services, BOG will have to provide the enabling environment.

BOG is the overall regulator of the financial system. BOG approves new financial institutions and supervises the operations of all financial institutions. It sets monetary and credit policies and supervises the implementation of these policies. As the regulator of the financial system, BOG's role is crucial to ensuring that SSEs have access to credit and other financial services.

Currently, the commercial banks control the bulk of the assets in the banking system in Ghana and offer minimal services to the majority of the economically active, indigenous population, who support the poor. Sustainable growth and the alleviation of poverty cannot be achieved unless commercial banks improve their services to this segment of the population.

Accordingly, BOG should consider taking a number of measures. First, BOG should initiate reforms to encourage commercial banks to develop innovative links with the intermediary banks and other financial institutions, such as rural banks, S&Ls, associations, and credit unions, which provide the bulk of the services to the SSE sector. This should deepen financial intermediation all around and make more resources available for growth in the sector.

Second, BOG will have to exercise its regulatory functions with some imagination and flexibility to enable these institutions to grow, rather than stifling them. As BOG itself recognizes, a minimum capital requirement of 20 million GHC, which BOG has recommended (awaiting approval), is more realistic, although even this may be changed, depending on experiences in the field. The same applies to the more realistic prudential regulations relating to capital adequacy and liquidity ratios that BOG has recommended.

Third, BOG's monitoring and supervisory functions will have to be stepped up, especially those for rural banks, S&Ls, and credit unions, to ensure that their operations are efficient and conducted in accordance with the regulations and also to ensure that the interests of depositors and borrowers are effectively protected. Such constant and regular monitoring and supervision should reveal areas in need of improvement. BOG needs to cut down and simplify the myriad returns that it requires the rural banks to complete. It should ensure the prompt analysis of these returns to aid in policy formulation and to improve operations. Indeed, it will be necessary for BOG to establish a databank, especially for rural banks, S&Ls, and credit unions, where current information about them (based on prompt analysis of returns they submit) will be available to those financial agents themselves and to others.

Fourth, BOG should promote training for the staff of rural banks, S&Ls, and credit unions. This should improve the financial services they offer the SSE sector. With the help of the Rural Finance Project (established under World Bank auspices) the Association of Rural Banks has in place an expanded program of training. Happily, the Association has funding from BOG to broaden and improve its training programs. BOG should help S&Ls and credit unions establish similar training schemes for themselves.

Conclusion

The development of the SSE sector is crucial to the overall development of Ghana and of Africa and to the alleviation of poverty and the creation of employment.

Properly developed, rural banks, S&Ls, and credit unions can bridge the gap between the formal banks and the informal financial system, bringing much needed financial services and development to the SSE sector.

By helping to promote these SSEs, BOG and the intermediary institutions can together be agents of change. ✻

THE EXPERIENCE OF FIDI IN DEVELOPING FINANCIAL SERVICES FOR MICRO- AND SMALL ENTERPRISES IN CÔTE D'IVOIRE

A. Boissau
Côte d'Ivoire Fund for Development and Investment
Abidjan, Côte d'Ivoire

Introduction

The Côte d'Ivoire Fund for Development and Investment (Fonds ivoirien de développement et d'investissement, FIDI) is part of an international network of local financing companies, inspired and launched by the International Investment and Development Corporation (Société d'investissement et de développement international, SIDI).

SIDI is a French limited-liability corporation with capital of 1 billion XOF (in 1994, 570 CFA francs [XOF] = 1 United States dollar [USD]). Its main shareholder and founder is the largest French NGO for development, the Catholic Committee Against Hunger and for Development (Comité catholique contre la faim et pour le développement, CCFD). Other individual and institutional shareholders are banks, credit unions, the Caisse française de développement, and foundations.

SIDI has made direct investments ("participations") in micro- and small enterprises and has developed a network of local finance companies and structures around the world, including Latin America (Bolivia, Chile, Colombia, and Uruguay), Africa (Côte d'Ivoire, Madagascar, Mauritania, Morocco, Senegal, and Uganda), Asia (Laos, Sri Lanka, Thailand, and Vietnam), Europe (Poland), and the Middle East (in the occupied territories).

Local companies participate in the financing of projects for creating or expanding small enterprises through the use of various techniques (direct investments, loans, lease–purchase arrangements, guarantees), according to local needs and conditions. SIDI is trying to use the means at its disposal to create an international network of local finance companies. It also provides technical assistance to various companies in response to their internal requirements or other needs associated with their activities.

FIDI and how its role has changed

FIDI arose when the World Bank asked SIDI to help set up a local finance company in Côte d'Ivoire. FIDI-SA is a public company (société anonyme, SA), created on 11 July 1991 with its own capital of 217 million XOF. Besides SIDI, its shareholders include some large Côte d'Ivoire companies — the Côte d'Ivoire Oil Refining Company, the Côte d'Ivoire Water Company, BLOHORN, SHELL-CI, and TOTAL-CI — a bank, COFINCI; and various individuals and associations. The members are united by their desire to contribute to the development of a class of profitable micro- and small enterprises in Côte d'Ivoire.

FIDI's uniqueness lies in the fact that its shareholders are interested in entrepreneurs who, without its intervention, would have no access to bank credit. FIDI has set itself two main goals. First, it participates in financing the creation or development of small enterprises, in particular ones that are considered feasible but that cannot meet the restrictive socioeconomic criteria needed to gain access to conventional financing. Second, FIDI follows the progress of promoters and business leaders and provides technical assistance where it is needed: both upstream (by counselling and by assessing a project and helping to launch it) and downstream (by offering advice and management assistance).

The initial goal of FIDI is basically financial — to help small enterprises get started when their promoters cannot gain access to bank credit. The process of FIDI's providing financial support begins as follows:

- FIDI works directly with the project promoter and places great weight on the promoter's abilities and motivation.

- FIDI prefers productive activities that use local resources and are labour-intensive.
- FIDI insists that the promoter provide a 50% share of the financing.
- FIDI invests directly in the capital of formal companies, supplementing this with working capital support. FIDI's contribution is always less than that of the promoter.
- FIDI's contribution ranges from 3 to 20 million XOF. All financing depends on the appropriate guarantees.

FIDI's role has evolved as follows:

- FIDI asks the promoter to initially put up a share of 15–30%. This can be done either in cash or in kind.
- FIDI tries to promote the development of existing small enterprises, rather than continually creating new ones.
- FIDI is broadening its field of financing activities to embrace all economic sectors, including the commercial and services sectors.
- FIDI is trying to design ways to help the so-called structured, informal sector.
- FIDI is hoping to use new formulas for lending and lease–purchase arrangements that are better suited to the needs of promoters.

As a general rule, were it not for external technical support, at least 5 or 6 (or maybe more in some countries) out of every 10 new enterprises would disappear, with the attendant economic, financial, and social costs that such loss entails.

On the other hand, people engaged in providing technical and cooperative support to entrepreneurs claim that the chance of survival for small firms exceeds 80% after 5 years if they take advantage of such support. Here is clear proof that properly adapted or personalized support can have an important impact. FIDI, therefore, offers a range of services to project promoters — initial consultation, counseling, studies, documentation, and so on. At the same time, FIDI provides the firms it finances with continuously updated tools to monitor the firms' progress. FIDI has a permanent research team and a network of experts to mobilize at any time.

FIDI's willingness to provide technical assistance is rooted in the need to secure its investment, of course, and its desire to ensure the survival of the companies it is helping to launch or promote. This activity has its costs, however, which we might call the extra costs of development. These extra costs include, in particular, those of providing expert supervisory support:

- attending to the management and technical aspects of a great number of small investments;
- screening and monitoring to ensure that project and promoter are properly matched; and
- taking an active part in setting up and monitoring the business, ensuring the best possible conditions.

The extra costs of providing such support can, of course, neither be completely recovered from the small entrepreneurs themselves nor be borne indefinitely by financing agencies like FIDI. This explains why the conventional banking system has given up financing small enterprises. Groups involved in small enterprise development, however "voluntary" they may be, must find a way to cover these extra costs — basically, they will have to be assumed by other partners.

Public authorities, financiers, and business people will have to choose — either they pay for the kind of technical cooperation that will prevent the premature failure of an enterprise, or they pay the price for the noncreation or nondevelopment of enterprises. In the short term, the choice may be difficult, because the question is, Who is going to pay? In the long term, however, the choice is clear if we consider the following consequences of refusal to pay:

- loss of capital when an enterprise fails;
- unpaid invoices from other firms;
- loss of workers' jobs and of their dependants' subsistence; and
- lost tax revenue.

The results of 18 months of fieldwork

Working method and support system

FIDI's method of supporting small enterprises consists of four stages, for each of which support systems have been created.

Stage 1: Selecting the entrepreneurs

The first stage, the initial consultation, is a key part of the overall process. The initial consultation provides a first screening filter to identify those would-be entrepreneurs who have the ability and the wherewithal to go further. This first stage of the process consists of one or two individual interviews that must take place on the promoter's own geographic and cultural turf. In the first 18 months, we met with 300 promoters, listened to them, gave them advice, and provided some of them with further technical assistance.

FIDI has created a series of computerized files for each of the promoters we have had contact with. These might involve a preselection file, for assessing the promoter and his project; a project creation file, for developing a feasibility study of the project; a business plan created with a business-plan software program adapted for small enterprises; and an assessment file on the promoter and project.

Stage 2: Providing upstream technical assistance

In the second stage, FIDI provides the project promoter with technical assistance on several aspects of business planning, including an analysis of the project to be launched, developed, or restructured; periodic management advice; a study of potential market niches; and guidance and help in performing feasibility studies.

The promoter receives ongoing and personalized support from the FIDI training team. In this way, we help promoters develop their own ability to act independently, instead of doing everything for them. The training team has helped an estimated 150 promoters. Depending on the case, this second stage can last anywhere from a few months to 2 years.

Stage 3: Helping to launch the project

Everyone knows how closely production, sales, human relations, and financing are linked in a small firm. If one of these functions is poorly managed, the whole operation is at risk. This is why FIDI always tries to look at each project in its entirety. This, in turn, means the advisers must give the promoters psychological support and advice and help them overcome difficult obstacles. About 50 promoters have already had the benefit of this approach. In this stage, FIDI helps with the actual setting up of the project (the launch plan), finds financing partners, and leads the promoter through various procedures and formalities. In addition, when the need arises, FIDI can use its team of specialists to advise on the best legal structure for a given project.

In its role as a financing agency, FIDI's Board of Directors has voted to approve investments in seven sectors: (1) rice hulling, (2) salt grinding, (3) aluminum-plate production, (4) candy making, (5) hotels, (6) butcher shops, and (7) charcoal making. This may seem like a modest number, but it must be viewed in the Côte d'Ivoire context and in light of the financing tool that FIDI has used to date, that is, having a direct stake in the company.

Stage 4: Providing downstream technical assistance

In the fourth stage, FIDI provides technical assistance in business management and control. This is an essential part of FIDI's approach because it gives the best assurance that the enterprise will survive. Bookkeeping assistance is always provided in close cooperation with the young operator of the business and can take two forms, depending on the size of the business:

- For microenterprises, FIDI can set up simple support mechanisms for recording and keeping accounts, with a view to gradually training a member of the business.
- For formal small enterprises, we will enlist the help of a professional accountant who specializes in small business. This accountant will deal with social and tax issues and handle accounting matters.

Management assistance covers every aspect of good business: interpretation of accounting data, personnel management, relations with suppliers, sales management, and so on. This type of assistance is provided by a person specifically assigned to the case, who knows the business and its promoter well and can offer full and personalized support.

FIDI's place in the socioeconomic system

FIDI's operating methods mean that it is involved in the very fabric of national and regional socioeconomic life. We strive to develop a synergy of efforts and abilities among the various players interested in promoting private initiative in Côte d'Ivoire. We create a real working network that can include both volunteers and professionals (experts, NGOs, accounting firms, financiers, and so on).

For FIDI, it is essential in any small-enterprise development project to articulate a dual strategy for helping promoters:

- offering technical support to the promoter or entrepreneur in setting up or expanding his or her enterprise; and

- offering the financing tool best suited to the entrepreneur's capacities and the specific needs of the project.

If it is to be effective, this dual strategy must lead to a partnership where roles and responsibilities are clearly delineated among the promoter, FIDI, and any third parties. In this regard, FIDI has been trying (so far without success) to engage the cooperation of local banks in the joint handling of small- to medium-scale enterprises (SMEs). It has also proposed two avenues of approach for large firms:

- expanding their subcontracting service by inviting tenders from small firms; and

- supporting laid-off personnel who are trying to start their own businesses.

Sectoral economic studies

There has never been a detailed sectoral study specifically focused on small enterprise in Côte d'Ivoire. It would, indeed, be useful to have surveys of all the economic sectors where small enterprise could potentially operate profitably and successfully, but the lack of reliable economic data makes it difficult to perform market and feasibility studies. As a consequence of our approach and the cooperation of various promoters, we have had occasion to study the following industries: charcoal production, rice growing, mining, fishing and aquaculture, water pumps, poultry raising, commercial beef operations, and the manufacture of aluminum housewares.

Other industries are under study, and we hope to make documents available soon to promoters looking for information on techniques and methodology.

Services offered to promoters and young entrepreneurs

FIDI has so far developed two main services:

- technical assistance (initial consultation, feasibility studies, setup, advice, monitoring, and so on); and
- financial participation in the project, through either a direct investment in new or expanding formal companies or setting up a joint venture, where a formal structure is unnecessary.

FIDI is now studying how it might act as an "outside incubator." In other words, we are trying to expand our range of services to microentrepreneurs to include the following:

- providing work space;
- organizing orientation and training sessions for setting up a small enterprise;
- organizing sessions on various themes about business and its environment; and
- establishing a database and library of business-related information (technical books, financing sources, and so on).

We will have to introduce these services gradually, depending on demand and resources; the objective is to provide answers to the practical needs of promoters and young entrepreneurs. Those who benefit from these services will be expected to make a financial contribution.

Lessons from the breaking-in period

To assess the past record of and future prospects for a structure like FIDI, we need to look at it from two perspectives, the short and the long term.

In the short term, FIDI's technical assistance record shows that it has handled applications from more than 300 promoters. FIDI has listened to these applicants and tried to sensitize them and guide them. Thus, it has played a role rather like that of a small-business promotion bureau — a necessary function, even if the results have been less than spectacular. By contrast, the results have been more modest for the enterprises that we have tried to help finance — in about 50 cases examined, FIDI's efforts have led to only seven investment decisions. Still,

FIDI is more interested in quality than in quantity, both for its own sake and for the sake of the promoters.

It is hard to make a long-term, objective assessment of these first few months of activity. FIDI has taken time to make itself known, both to the public and to the professional circles and organizations working with SMEs. We are, on balance, satisfied with the network we have established, although we have been somewhat disappointed by the lack of closer involvement of others working in the SME sector.

What lessons, then, can we draw from this breaking-in period?

Strategic choices in the launching of FIDI

From the experience that we share with all those people who took part in the creation of FIDI, we have learned that it is useful to involve both individuals and companies — to try to have both private citizens and businesses engaged in a common project. FIDI has managed to put together a diverse group of shareholders, a point of some significance, I think, in the context of Côte d'Ivoire. Let me emphasize one point: our shareholders made their contributions to FIDI's capital more as an investment in society, with a business angle, than as a strictly financial investment.

FIDI chose to organize itself legally as a limited-liability corporation. This is an advantage because a corporation is governed by clear and incontrovertible rules of management, a fact that no doubt attracted many of our shareholders. But this is a costly route, both in terms of launching the company and managing it day to day (particularly owing to the taxes). It is unclear whether our shareholders would still have invested their money if the company had been organized as a partnership of some kind.

Consider FIDI's method of involving itself in the financing of projects. FIDI has worked essentially by taking a direct interest and providing working capital as a partner. FIDI has favoured financing the expansion of formal businesses in sectors where there is high value added.

It quickly became apparent that in Côte d'Ivoire this approach was too restrictive and that for the micro- and small-enterprise niche we needed to offer simpler instruments (loans and lease–purchase arrangements) and to open up our services to all business sectors (commerce, service industry, and so on), indeed to get into the financing of the "structured" informal sector. In trying to recast its activities in this way, FIDI faces the problem that the central bank requires lending organizations to comply with the banking laws in the West African Monetary Union (WAMU) zone. FIDI is, in effect, being asked to transform itself into a financial institution.

Promoters interviewed and projects presented

We have seen a great number of candidates wanting to launch small enterprises, a fact that has two explanations:

- The current economic situation implies a fair number of bankruptcies and people who are victims of downsizing.
- There are few employment opportunities available to young people, even those with education.

We thus face a dilemma: are we a social or a business organization? (We know, of course, that the two are closely linked.) To the extent that we are trying deliberately to act as a business, FIDI has had to set up a selection process for projects and promoters, based on their profitability and economic feasibility. This of course does not exclude taking account of the personal and human aspects of a project.

Although our small entrepreneurs are loathe to admit it, our business culture is very underdeveloped. Too often, promoters will reduce the complicated question of launching a business to one of financing it, neglecting the market potential or the sources of supply that regular production will have to rely on. Promoters often lack basic business awareness or training.

To sum up, we find, at present, that about two out of every three projects presented have to be turned down at the outset, for any one of several reasons. Here are two:

- The project may be proposed for a business sector that offers few prospects. To this must be added a certain lack of foresight on the part of the promoters, who often think they can create a business in a sector that is already saturated — this is the case with dry cleaners, bars, and soap makers in Côte d'Ivoire.
- The promoters may have no personal savings, in which case FIDI has to turn them down.

Continuing support and follow-up for business managers

Managing a small enterprise these days is difficult enough in Western countries; to manage a small formal enterprise successfully under conditions prevailing in Africa is a real feat. This is where FIDI's technical assistance is most important: even if an apprentice manager is a true orchestral conductor, he or she cannot do everything alone but has to be able to delegate and maybe even use outside help (for example, to keep the books). We have repeatedly found new managers in difficulty when it comes to dividing up the work or putting in place simple but essential rules of management.

For one thing, it is very hard to persuade young business operators to set up internal procedures for collecting accounting data. Yet foresight of this kind is what management is all about.

It is also hard to instill a climate of trust or to convince entrepreneurs that they need help in managing their business. We have found that a promoter may always be ready to accept cooperation in the form of financial support, but he or she may be reluctant after the business is launched to submit the documents and data FIDI needs despite having signed the agreement and despite FIDI's having met its obligations to the operator.

FIDI's limitations in the Côte d'Ivoire setting

It takes patience and perseverance to pull together private funds to finance private initiatives in a country where, until recently, the state was omnipresent. Roadblocks and constraints are everywhere. Then too, we have to remember the lack of dialogue and coordination among the various players involved in the SME sector in Côte d'Ivoire.

The sociopolitical environment

We have experienced limitations linked to the sociopolitical environment. In the days when Côte d'Ivoire had the means, it would rather launch grand industrial projects than promote the birth of a class of local SMEs in productive sectors. This attitude tended to stifle any individual spirit of enterprise, or "daring to take risks," in those sectors where value added was high. Thus, from our vantage point, we have received many demands for assistance to set up commercial or service companies but very few for engaging in resource-processing businesses.

Then too, we must realize that for a promoter, launching a business is an adventure that requires something of the attributes of both a priest and a soldier. It takes a real sense of civic duty to take the risks involved in setting up a formal enterprise in this economy. We estimate that the cost of doing so is 20–40% higher than it would be in the informal sector — even then, the entrepreneur has to count on wasting at least a quarter of the time fiddling with administrative details, time that could be better spent looking after customers or improving the quality of the product. After all, as everyone knows, the small-business entrepreneur must do everything for everybody.

Key questions then are, What role should the public authorities play in the creation and expansion of SMEs? Should the authorities try to expand the scope of formal enterprises through tax incentives or would it better to see economic activity "informalized"? This is a vicious circle. The state, of course, is in desperate need of resources to finance its budget outlays, and business taxes represent a considerable part of its resources. But a fruit does not give as much juice if you pick it green as it does if you leave it to ripen. This is a strategic issue that the authorities must address, and, unfortunately, we must admit that even the current tax incentives are not working very well.

The economic environment

Conditions are very difficult for those in small-business development. The world recession has had especially dramatic effects on African countries: reduced demand for raw materials (owing to structural adjustment programs) has put thousands of people out of work and has led to a drop in household purchasing power.

Côte d'Ivoire has furthermore suffered a serious banking crisis, which has precipitated the failure of some institutions and has forced most commercial banks to reduce or even suspend their support for SMEs. Individuals and companies alike are losing confidence in banks and financial institutions.

This state of affairs has had several effects on the emergence and growth of the small-business sector in Côte d'Ivoire:

- potential markets have shrunk;
- promoters have no savings; and
- lines of credit are hard to get.

The legal and legislative environment

We have also encountered a number of limitations linked to the legal and legislative environment. We must clearly warn prospective creators of small businesses that the promoter has every incentive to remain in the informal sector. We have drawn their attention to bothersome bureaucratic meddling and how difficult it is to take advantage of existing tax incentives. But could there not be a framework that is really adapted to the emergence and operation of small businesses? Shouldn't it be possible to set up a simple legal framework, one that would not require establishing limited-liability corporations but that would give legal recognition to entrepreneurs and offer them the assurance that they can defend their rights and interests before the courts? And one that would let entrepreneurs do business without putting at risk all their personal belongings on some chance mishap that is not the fault of their own management?

The new banking law for the WAMU zone poses some real problems for companies that have a legal status like FIDI's. Here is a perfect example of the pendulum effect: we have gone from one extreme to the other. Thus, until recently, any individual or company could set up a business to collect and use savings, with every imaginable leeway. Then, along came promulgation of this new law, a necessary law no doubt, but one that forces any person who engages in direct investments, loans, or lease–purchase agreements to become a financial institution, with all the constraints that implies, regardless of the source or end use of the funds. To turn FIDI into a financial institution would alter completely the spirit in which it was created, and, indeed, it is not at all clear that businesses like FIDI would be able to meet the regulatory requirements to become financial institutions.

Thus, setting aside for the moment SME development projects that are financed through bilateral or international cooperation and that, therefore, have a transnational status, it is impossible today for an organization like FIDI (which does not draw on the savings of the general public) to engage in lending or lease–purchase agreements. This is a severe limitation on our ability to promote SMEs in Côte d'Ivoire. Lending and lease–purchase arrangements are in fact two instruments that are more flexible and suitable for SMEs than taking a direct investment interest, which can only be done within a formal legal framework.

The sociological and cultural environment

Let us look finally at the limitations stemming from the socio-logical and cultural environment. These influence, first of all, the social and personal pressures that surround the new entre-preneur, and, second, the ability of promoters to become pru-dent and wise business managers. You can set up all kinds of financial instruments for microenterprises and provide all kinds of technical assistance and lines of credit, but if the family and friends of the entrepreneur are not interested in the project's success or if they do not realize that a new business cannot be treated like the goose that lays golden eggs, then there is no point in the promoter's undertaking an adventure like setting up a business.

The sociological and cultural setting is hard to manage — after all, how can FIDI know how all these people feel about a project? As everyone knows, African families are large. One solution, already tried in some countries, might be to make financial assistance conditional on setting up a joint-and-several liability grouping within the family. But that takes time, and time is money, even for organizations like ours.

Entrepreneurial skills are, of course, a function of edu-cation, and it is clear that the people who approach FIDI do not have a high level of education. How can this situation be improved? We think there should be short and simple training modules available to help teach the ABCs of business — the skills needed both for launching a project and for managing a small enterprise. This of course would be outside FIDI's scope — it is up the public authorities to act on the issue of education.

Conclusion

FIDI's experience has been too brief for a proper assessment of its performance and impact. We must admit, in all humility, that we are still learning while we are doing. It would be unfair to judge the soundness of FIDI's activities solely from the economic viewpoint (on the basis of whether it makes a profit). Neverthe-less, FIDI's long-term goal is to be self-financing.

From my own experience in the field, I offer the following observations on developing a class of micro- and small enterprises. I believe, first of all, that the problem in Côte d'Ivoire is not mainly a lack of financing (although it is true that some projects are not helped by the entrepreneur's lack of savings or the absence of commercial banks willing to lend to small business). Any serious and competent promoters who have financially feasible projects can now find financing suited to their needs (their own funds, loans, lease–purchase arrangements) and their type of business (informal sector, micro- and small enterprise, SME, and so on).

On the other hand, this study identifies two real obstacles to the growth of micro- and small businesses:

- The first of these obstacles has to do with the business environment (economic, regulatory, taxation, and bureaucratic) and the discrepancy we see between the statements and the actions of the public authorities in this area.

- The second is the scarcity of bankable projects submitted for FIDI's consideration and the weak entrepreneurial abilities of the promoters we have seen.

It is going to take a long-term effort to change mentalities. This can be done through sensitization and training of promoters and young entrepreneurs and the creation of a new profession: the microenterprise adviser. The entrepreneurial spirit and the abilities that go with it do not invent themselves — they must be acquired and passed on. We need to promote a coherent and comprehensive national policy (tax incentives, appropriate regulations, simplified administrative procedures, and so on) and put a competent person in charge to see to its implementation.

For the short term, we need to establish a training and orientation centre, a sort of business promotion centre for SMEs. We should also make the banking law more flexible, so that private savings can be mobilized for micro- and small-enterprise development programs. Finally, we must make available technical assistance adapted to the needs of promoters and young entrepreneurs to give them the training they need and to help enterprises survive beyond their first year.

I will end by stressing a point that should be obvious: there is no way that an organization like FIDI can continue to expand its financing activities solely on the basis of direct investments. Loans and lease–purchase arrangements are much better suited to micro- and small enterprises. These are especially needed if we ever hope to see enough activity for an organization like FIDI to become self-financing. ❋

ADAPTING FINANCIAL SYSTEMS TO THE NEEDS OF SMALL-SCALE ENTERPRISES: SOME EXPERIENCES FROM NIGERIA

David B. Ekpenyong
Department of Economics, University of Ibadan,
Ibadan, Nigeria

A.T.T. Kebang
People's Bank, Ibadan, Nigeria

Introduction

Over the years, governments in Nigeria have developed regulations and guidelines to make credit facilities more accessible to small-scale enterprises (SSES). Some of these regulations and guidelines are directed at the establishment of more industrial development centres; the establishment of model industrial states to encourage prospective small-business entrepreneurs; full exploitation of existing World Bank programs for SSES; introduction of the National Economic Reconstruction Fund (NER-FUND); setting up of small and medium-scale enterprises (SMES) loan schemes; the establishment of a rural banking scheme and the requirement that the rural banks lend 50% of deposits generated in the local areas for investment in industrial projects in the same local areas; the requirement that banks lend 16% of their total loans and advances to SSES, and so on.

Despite these efforts by government, small-business owners continue to be denied access to credit. The banks insist on collateral that the small-business owners do not have. Unfortunately, high interest rates and lack of funds may have forced about 1 000 small and medium-scale industries nationwide to fold since the inception of NERFUND ("Small, medium-scale firms fold-up.... Association accuses NERFUND," *The Nigerian Guardian*, 6 April 1993). NERFUND is known to be granting loans to big industrialists. This has driven many SSES in Nigeria to rely mostly on personal funds and informal financial sources for their credit needs (Osoba 1986; Ekpenyong 1991).

Having realized this dilemma, government decided on 31 October 1989 to establish the People's Bank of Nigeria (PBN) to extend credit to SSES. The Bauchi Cooperative Financing Agency (BCFA), established in 1976 by a few farmers, has also made significant contributions to financing of SSES in Nigeria. The PBN is a governmental institution, whereas the BCFA is privately owned.

Because of the effectiveness of these two funding institutions in Nigeria, the objective of this paper is to examine their operational mechanisms and loan recovery rates.

The People's Bank of Nigeria

PBN is structured after the Grameen Bank in Bangladesh, India, with modifications to reflect the traditional nature of Nigerian society. Decree 22 (1990 People's Bank of Nigeria Decree) established PBN and gave it the following specific functions:

- Meeting the basic credit requirements of underprivileged Nigerians who are involved in legitimate economic activities in both urban and rural areas and who cannot normally benefit from the services of the orthodox banking system, owing to their inability to provide collateral.

- Accepting savings from this same group and paying interest on these savings after investing the money in short-term deposits with commercial and merchant banks.

This decree defines underprivileged Nigerians by their various trades and professions, including roadside mechanics, the self-employed, plumbers and electricians, small-scale traders, small-scale farmers and poultry and other livestock keepers, dressmakers, barbers and hairdressers, washermen and washerwomen, and other people throughout the country who need financial assistance to improve their trade and economic well-being.

As the managing director of the bank confirmed in 1993, PBN will not abandon its primary role of catering to these people to start soliciting deposits from the rich. The role of PBN is to ensure that the peasants and market men and women can obtain loans from PBN easily. PBN has been set up not necessarily to make profits but to give able-bodied and disabled Nigerians without access to commercial banks the necessary assistance to set up small-scale concerns.

Organization

Decree 22 provides for a board of directors for PBN. The Board of Directors is responsible for the overall policy and general management of the bank and has the Chairperson; the Managing Director; representatives of the Economic Affairs Department of the Presidency, the Ministry of Finance, and the Governor of the Central Bank of Nigeria; and four other people.

The Board of Directors is the highest policymaking body of PBN. The fact that government does not control policy-making explains the effectiveness of PBN's operations.

Operation

Decree 22 sets out conditions for PBN's operations:

1. *Funds* — Before August 1990, the maximum loan to a beneficiary was fixed at 2 000 NGN (in 1994, 22 Nigerian naira [NGN] = 1 United States dollar [USD]) and the minimum at 50 NGN. Since then the maximum loan has increased to 5 000 NGN. The size of loan provided to any one client is expected to increase over time.

2. *Service charges* — The service charge on a loan is not to exceed the bank's administrative costs for the loan. Initially, the service charge was fixed at 5%, but it was increased to 15% in August 1990 and has remained at that level. The commercial banks, in contrast, charge up to 80% and in many cases more.

3. *Repayment periods* — Every loan granted by PBN has to be repaid within 1 year, with a 2-week grace period. Repayment is in small, weekly instalments. New loans may be granted to people who have repaid their loans in full within the period specified.

4. *Procedures when a borrower dies* — If the loan recipient dies, the bank endeavours to retrieve as much as possible of the loan or its residue by whatever means it may consider appropriate, including the disposal of the assets or property purchased with the loan. This provision has been very effective because traditionally an outstanding debt is considered a disgrace and humiliation to the family. The borrower, therefore, tries not to leave such a legacy.

5. *Investments* — Decree 22 also requires the borrower to invest the loan from PBN within a short period, except in very extenuating circumstances, such as the death of a close relative or serious illness of the borrower. The borrower must use the loan only for the purpose PBN agreed to and cannot, under any circumstances, divert it or use it to pay staff salaries.

Procedures

It is PBN's policy that prospective borrowers be organized in groups, each consisting of about 13 people. Loans are granted to no more than five borrowers in the group at any one time. Each loan is jointly guaranteed by all the members of the group. This explains the success of the bank's operation. The repayment performance of the group determines the chances another batch of members has of receiving a loan. The group leader is the last to be considered for a loan. The group leader can only qualify for a loan if the bank is satisfied with the repayment performance of the group members.

Loan requests are received at the various centres by field officers. The field officers visit the loan seekers to ensure that they are actually low-income earners and require financial assistance in their trade or profession. The field officers then forward the loan requests to the appropriate branch managers. The branch managers evaluate the requests and send their recommendations to the respective zone managers for approval. The zone managers send the approvals to the head office for consolidation and control. The branches disburse the approved loans.

The field officers at the centres monitor the use and repayment of the loans, with the cooperation of the borrowing group leaders. The zone managers also send reports of the borrowing group's repayment performance to the head office.

The bank requires no collateral from any loan beneficiary — tight supervision by the the field officers and the joint responsibility of the group members replace the need for collateral. A default by a member of a group jeopardizes the chances of any member of that group qualifying for another loan.

Regular meetings between the bank staff and the members of the various groups ensure the cooperation of the loan beneficiaries. At such meetings, PBN informs the group members of the loan regulations and repeatedly emphasizes the importance of cooperation.

Performance of borrowers

A study conducted by Ekpenyong (1992) on the performance of PBN showed that as of 31 March 1991, PBN had established eight zones in the 30 states and Abuja and a total of 175 branches. The branches and loan beneficiaries were evenly spread among the states. The number of beneficiaries was estimated at 140 000, of which 60% were women.

Disbursements totalled 207 million NGN; 178.4 million NGN had been recovered, leaving a total outstanding of 28.6 million NGN. (Data from the Central Bank of Nigeria show that by 31 December 1991, 6.2 billion NGN had been granted in loans and advances by the entire banking sector to rural borrowers.)

Payback strategy

Long-term loans for cocoa or palm oil, for example, have a 1-year repayment period; seasonal loans for seasonal crops, poultry, and fishing have a 1-year repayment period, subject to a 3-month moratorium; and loans for other trades have a 1-year repayment period, subject to a 2-week moratorium.

Loans have so far been concentrated on agricultural projects. Recipients are given the option of repaying weekly or monthly (as they are able) within the 1-year repayment period. Recent data issued by PBN show a loan recovery rate of about 93%.

Factors contributing to the high loan recovery rate include the following:

- The loans are "soft loans" at concessional rates of interest.

- Because borrowers obtain the loans easily, they feel obliged to pay them back just as easily (compared with a situation where they might have to pay heavy fees to obtain the loans). Transaction costs are low.

- Rather than granting loans to individuals, the PBN grants loans to groups of traders or farmers, and so on, who come from the same locality and know each other very well.

- Loan recipients are always certified creditworthy.

- Repayments can be staggered. Loan recipients can pay any time they can afford to within the repayment period, instead of paying large sums at one haul.

- PBN staff effectively monitor the repayment of the loans.

Dimensions of the program

These findings reveal some important dimensions of this new program:

- There is an even spread of loan disbursements across the country — something the commercial banks have failed to accomplish, despite the government directive that they lend 50% of the deposits they collect in the rural areas for industrial projects in these areas.

- Some of the principal urban beneficiaries are in the local government areas in Lagos State, often referred to as the "slums," and inhabited by low-income earners. Modern financial institutions (the commercial banks) would not under any circumstances lend to these people.

- The sectoral distribution of the loans shows that they are meant for the core of the SSEs, that is, craftspeople, artisans, small-scale traders, mechanics, and so on.

- Women are not discriminated against, as is the practice of the orthodox banks. In the subsectors traditionally dominated by women (such as trading), women received as much as four times the number of loans granted to men in that subsector.

The Bauchi Cooperative Financing Agency

The BCFA was founded and registered as an apex cooperative society on 4 June 1976, under the *Cooperative Societies Law of Northern Nigeria*, with the objective of financing SSEs.

Organization

The agency has a board of directors consisting of 10 members — 7 elected and 3 seconded from the business or financial sector, as provided by the bylaws.

Operation

Activities are conducted at the zonal level, where the zone managers have direct contact with the members of the cooperative unions registered with BCFA. Each member of an affiliated union contributes a capital share of 5 000 NGN and is entitled to all the rights and privileges of a member, including attending and voting at the annual general meeting and receiving loans and advances from the agency.

Procedures

The applicant submits a loan request to the local Cooperative Society, which evaluates it and submits it to the zone manager for BCFA. The zone manager then evaluates the loan application, visiting the Cooperative Society and evaluating its records and also visiting and assessing the applicant. If the zone manager considers the application satisfactory, it is sent to headquarters. When the loans are finally approved at headquarters and the money is released, both the headquarter's staff and the zone manager undertake the disbursement.

The zone officers, together with the headquarters staff, also undertake the recovery of the loans when due. The zone officers provide support services (helping the cooperative unions to organize, plan, and produce bankable project documents, maintain adequate records, and so on), which have greatly enhanced the efficient use of the funds and recovery of the loans. Where a member of the cooperative defaults, the rest of the members are bound to pay back the defaulting member's share of the loan, which imposes on all members the responsibility of exerting pressure on each beneficiary to repay his or her loan.

Repayment strategy

The loan-recovery strategy adopted by BCFA is built around the planting and harvesting seasons — loans are granted during the planting season and recovered during harvest. The repayment periods are staggered to suit the different crops for which BCFA grants loans: maize, sorghum, millet, and beans. The maximum period granted for loan repayment is usually 9 months.

Performance of borrowers

The project is currently sponsored by the World Bank, but it was initially sponsored by the state government. Satisfied with the operations of BCFA, the World Bank disbursed $2.8 million USD for BCFA activities in the financial year 1990/91. When the activities of the agency were assessed for that year, the recovery rate was as high as 96%. The 1991/92 unpublished financial statement shows a similarly high recovery rate. The following year, the rate declined only slightly to 91.5%.

The following factors contribute to these high loan-recovery rates:

- The agency directly provides critical inputs (fertilizer, bull tractors, and so on) to the farmers. This enables the farmers to plant in time and to have a good yield.
- The agency awards a trophy to the society that pays up first.
- The structure of the cooperative unions is effective, coordinated, and built around the local members. These members know each other and encourage each other to pay up. There are known cases of the society collectively paying for a defaulting member and recovering the money from this member later.
- The agency screens the cooperative unions and registers only those that are well organized.
- The member unions strictly screen applications for loans.
- The zone officers and the headquarters personnel effectively monitor union activities.
- The agency disburses loans promptly, ensuring timely planting, which results in a good harvest.

- The agency considers the union's prompt payment as a factor increasing its loan eligibility.
- The agency uses effective education and training to inform the farmers of the benefits of prompt payment. Between September and December, the agency conducts education and training sessions for all its affiliated unions on the benefits of prompt loan repayment.
- The agency's organizational structure is simple and unbureaucratic, so things get done quicky.
- There is no government interference in the agency's operation.

Conclusion

The success of PBN and BCFA clarifies certain important facts:

- SSES in Nigeria, and in Africa as a whole, can be viable.
- It is possible to grant loans to SSES without collateral and still recover the loan. It is not collateral that guarantees recovery of a loan but the way the enterprise is managed and the way it is treated.
- Government bureaucracy or involvement in the financing of SSES is a serious hindrance to their growth and development. The management of PBN and BCFA is free from government interference.
- The operational framework of a lending institution needs to take account of social tradition. The operational frameworks of PBN and BCFA are built around the family and village, where there is loyalty to one's family and obedience to the elders. A borrower, for example, feels obligated to repay the loan to avoid the disgrace of being labeled "a borrower and debtor." The debtor is inclined to repay the loan before he or she dies, so that the surviving family will not have to suffer because of the unpaid debt.
- The terms of the loan agreement also motivate the borrowers to repay the loan. For example, no member of the society or group will obtain another loan if one isn't repaid, and this certainly puts pressure on everyone in the group to repay, if for no other reason than to escape the wrath of the other members.

- The tight administration and supervision of loan beneficiaries prevent their diverting the loans to other uses than those agreed to, a phenomenon very common among beneficiaries of loans from other financial institutions.

It is my view that informal financial institutions in Africa can be made to serve SSEs effectively. ❊

THE CHANGING ROLES OF KEY INSTITUTIONS IN THE IMPLEMENTATION OF CREDIT PROGRAMS FOR SMALL-SCALE ENTERPRISE DEVELOPMENT IN KENYA

C. Aleke-Dondo
Kenya Rural Enterprise Programme, Nairobi, Kenya

Introduction

In Kenya, as in many developing countries, policies for promotion of small-scale enterprises (SSEs) have been based on perceptions of SSE operators as poor and in need of cheap credit. Policies and credit programs based on this perception ignore the indigenous informal credit systems that for a long time have been the only source of credit for most SSE operators.

This paper looks at current and past credit schemes for SSEs and analyzes the changing roles of the key institutions. The paper also looks at the policies, programs, and activities of the major institutions providing credit for SSEs in Kenya, namely, a government direct-lending program, the Joint Loan Board Scheme (JLBS); an NGO, the Kenya Rural Enterprise Programme (K-REP); two commercial banks, Barclay's Bank of Kenya and the Kenya Commercial Bank (KCB); and, two development finance institutions (DFIs), the Kenya Industrial Estates (KIE) and the Small Enterprise Finance Company (SEFCO).

This paper has four sections. The first section discusses the consequences of past policies for the promotion of SSEs. The second examines the changing roles of the key institutions. The third discusses two issues that influence the demand for and supply of SSE credit — interest rates and the use of collateral and securities. The final section presents some conclusions concerning SSE credit policies.

This paper draws on the findings of studies of SSEs in Kenya by Mutua (1992) and Tomecko and Aleke-Dondo (1992).

Consequences of previous policies for SSE promotion

Policies for promoting SSEs in Kenya and many developing countries have been based on premises that ignore such informal credit systems as rotating savings and credit associations (ROSCAs). Some of these mistaken assumptions are the following:

- SSE operators are unable to organize themselves.
- They are too poor to save.
- They need cheap credit for their enterprises.

There were three major policy consequences of this misconception of SSE operators:

- Development banks and special credit programs set up to provide credit for SSEs neglected the role of savings mobilization in sustainable credit systems.
- Credit was subsidized.
- Credit guarantee schemes were set up by the government and donor organizations to cover anticipated losses.

These policy strategies had the following results:

- The scope of credit remained severely restricted, as there was no built-in growth factor that would have resulted from mobilizing internal resources.
- Few people received loans. The majority of SSE operators had no access to credit from the development banks or special credit programs implemented by the government or NGOs.
- Special credit programs were not managed professionally, which resulted in low repayment rates and decapitalization of the credit programs.
- Commercial banks, through which some of the credit guarantee schemes operated, had little motivation to screen their borrowers and recover their loans, which resulted in high default rates and continuous decapitalization.

In recent times, however, as a result of increasing shortages of external funds for credit programs for SSES and growing dissatisfaction with credit programs implemented by government and NGOS, there has been a reorientation of credit programs. New models have been introduced that are designed to help the lenders achieve financial sustainability and to reach many SSES. The focus is on promoting, not replacing, existing indigenous credit mechanisms, such as ROSCAS. These changes have become more pronounced in the 1990s.

The changing roles of the key institutions

Kenya has one of the longest histories of promoting SSES in Africa. The first real effort was made in 1967, when KIE was established. KIE was set up to provide credit, management assistance, and industrial estates to encourage Kenyan citizens of African origin to form enterprises in urban and rural areas. Today, there are 75 credit programs for SSES in Kenya, implemented by the government, DFIS, commercial banks, and NGOS. Table 1 provides an estimate of their relative contributions as of July 1992. Because commercial banks are not required to report the volume of credit they extend from their own resources, these estimates only include special programs that the commercial banks have implemented, usually in collaboration with donors or NGOS.

The significant increase in the number of institutions supporting this sector has not been matched by significant changes in policy, although many policy pronouncements have been made. However, significant operational changes have occurred among some implementing institutions. In the last 3 years, new lending methods and innovative strategies have been adopted for providing credit to this sector.

The government

The government has been a key actor in SSE development, directly implementing two credit programs: the JLBS and the Rural Enterprise Fund. The government is involved in four others through parastatal organizations.

The government, which has not been particularly successful in the credit and extension services programs it directly supports, is now, according to Sessional Paper No. 2 (Kenya

Table 1. Number of borrowers and portfolio outstanding by institution (July 1992).

Institution	Borrowers		Portfolio outstanding	
	No.	%	(KES)[a]	%
Kenya Industrial Estate				
Formal	1 544		612 000	
Informal	1 700		26 000	
Total	3 244	37	638 000	58
Small Enterprise Finance Company				
Formal	258		109 400	
Informal	204		3 000	
Total	462	5	112 400	10
Barclay's Bank	582	6	292 800	27
Kenya Commercial Bank				
Jua Kali 1	50		500	
Graduates	130		14 000	
Women	98		2 400	
Total	278	3	16 900	2
NGOS (K-REP)[b]	2 940		23 784	
NGOs (other)	1 470		11 892	
Total	4 410	49	35 676	3
Total	8 976	100	1 095 776	100

Source: Tomecko and Aleke-Dondo (1992).
[a] In 1993, 41 Kenyan shillings (KES) = 1 United States dollar (USD).
[b] K-REP, Kenya Rural Enterprise Program.

1992), expected to play a facilitative role in a number of vital areas, which could improve the overall climate for investment and expansion of SSEs.

The Treasury of Kenya has liberalized interest rates, which is expected to increase the availability of investment funds for SSEs. Price controls have been removed on a wide variety of goods, and import quotas have been replaced with selective tariffs. The Treasury is also pursuing a more market-oriented exchange-rate policy, which is making imported products more expensive than those locally produced.

The government, however, is uncomfortable with its new role as a facilitator of SSEs. This is clear from the contradictions apparent in the Sessional Paper. The most obvious of these is the inclusion of a newly created Rural Enterprise Fund with a loan capital of 400 million KES (in 1994, 41 Kenyan shillings [KES] = 1 United States dollar [USD]). The fund is interventionist, charges subsidized interest rates (8%), and ignores all the past failures of the government in implementing the JLBS, which is discussed below.

The Joint Loan Board Scheme

Started during the colonial period in 1955, the main objective of
the JLBS was to help indigenous African entrepreneurs start and
run small businesses. The main focus was and continues to be
on retail and wholesale trade, small hotels, restaurants, transport, and commission agencies. Tangible securities are replaced
with guarantors and in some cases chattels. Loan terms are
between 2 and 5 years, and the interest rate since the inception
of JLBS has been 6.5%. There is a board in every district and
major municipality. The boards are in charge of managing the
credit scheme. All these boards have substantial arrears, and
their continued support has on several occasions been questioned. The scheme continues to operate with direct subsidies
from the government, which in the fiscal year 1990/91
amounted to 4 million KES from the central government, with a
matching amount from local authorities, and also with what
JLBS receives from the borrowers who do repay. There have been
no rigorous evaluations done on JLBS, but even in the absence of
such studies, its large arrears categorize this program as a
failure.

The nongovernmental organizations

NGOS as a group of lenders are the newest and potentially most
interesting, as they are likely to bring about further growth and
sustainability of institutionalized credit for SSES. Although there
was some lending by NGOS in the late 1970s and early 1980s, it
was not until 1984, with the advent of K-REP, financed by the
United States Agency for International Development (USAID),
that any comprehensive approach to SSE credit emerged. K-REP
was established primarily as a subdonor of USAID. It channeled
loan funds to other NGOS, who either wished to extend their
lending operations but lacked funds or wanted to start their own
programs and needed technical assistance as much as they did
loan capital.

Experience reveals that the performance of the participating NGOS was mediocre, despite major efforts at institution
building, staff training, and the provision of funds for lending to
SSES.

Somewhat surprisingly, the first attempts were similar,
but on a more modest scale, to the "integrated approach" popular with DFIS in the 1970s. The program provided training to

individual borrowers before they received their loan and also provided them with postloan counseling. K-REP also supported the institution building of the NGO borrowers by giving a great deal of assistance for staff development, loan-monitoring systems, and conceptual planning.

After several years of trying this approach and recording recoveries averaging 78% and very low levels of disbursements, K-REP decided to alter course and adopt the minimalist model developed in Asia by the Grameen Bank of Bangladesh. Not only K-REP itself but all major NGOs operating credit schemes in Kenya today have adopted this model.

The main features of the model are the use of groups of five borrowers to secure the loans, the disbursement of small loans, high recovery rates, relatively low operational costs, and the mobilization of savings. Although this approach is still new in Kenya, it offers hope of cost-effectively providing small loans to a large number of SSE operators. This method has improved the cost-effectiveness of these programs to the extent that the ratio of credit administration costs to credit disbursed is 1:4.

Despite the fact that some of these NGOs are doing well, the long-term commitment of most of them to SSE lending is questionable. Many still have a social orientation and find it difficult to harmonize a tough-banking approach with their original goals of public welfare. The NGOs, however, that were set up specifically for lending to SSEs are less confused about their missions and offer some of the best prospects for sustainable programs for the SSE sector.

The Kenya Rural Enterprise Programme

K-REP was established in 1984 with funding from USAID. In the beginning, K-REP's strategy for developing microenterprises was to promote Kenyan NGO credit programs. The objective, then, was to build the institutional capacity of Kenyan NGOs. K-REP provided them with grants, training, and technical assistance. In a period of 4 years, K-REP supported a dozen credit programs. All these credit schemes were supplements to welfare programs. Eventually, it became clear that NGOs primarily involved in traditional social-welfare programs found the transition to sustainable lending difficult to make. It also became obvious that the "integrated" method of developing microenterprises — largely through grants or subsidized loans — had a limited impact on the beneficiaries, was costly, and could only be sustained or expanded through grant funding.

In light of this experience, the strategy was changed in 1989 in four ways.

* The program was redesigned to involve only four of the most promising NGOs.

* The method of credit delivery was changed from the integrated to minimalist approach.

* Financial assistance to assisted NGOs, which previously took the form of 100% grant but no loan, was changed to 70% loan and 30% grant.

* To address self-sufficiency concerns and put into practice what K-REP learned from experience, it broadened its program focus beyond the NGOs by launching its own direct-lending programs, the *Juhudi* and the *Chikola* credit schemes.

Some of the lessons learned

The change from the integrated to the minimalist approach in lending to small and microenterprises improved the impact and cost-effectiveness of the programs significantly.

Using the integrated method of credit delivery, seven K-REP-assisted NGOs lent only 15.7 million KES to 2 500 borrowers in 3 years (1985–1988). Start-up and operating costs totalled 15.05 million KES. On average, each loan cost the NGOs 5 976 KES, or 96 cents for every shilling, to disburse and administer. With repayment rates averaging 78%, the programs were losing 22 cents for every shilling disbursed. The only way they could continue operating was by acquiring more grant funds, which, in the face of dwindling donor resources, could not be sustained.

Results under the minimalist approach portray a brighter picture for the four K-REP-assisted NGOs and K-REP's own Juhudi Credit Scheme, which have adopted the minimalist group-based method of lending. In 3 years, the five programs lent a total of 132 million KES to 14 754 borrowers. The cost per shilling lent has declined, on average, from 96 cents to 25 cents, and repayment rates have improved from 78 to 94%. Revenues generated through credit activities now cover about 66% of operating costs. In addition, a total of 23 million KES, or 17% of the total amount lent, has been mobilized as savings.

- Can the current NGO welfare programs implement effective credit programs?

One major concern is whether microenterprise credit programs can succeed if they are run by traditional welfare NGOs. Although the Kenyan NGOs that have adopted the minimalist credit approach have made significant improvements, these NGOs are faced with the problem of balancing the objectives of welfare and the focus on sustainable credit programs. This conflict threatens the success of their schemes, as the attention of their management is split between credit and welfare objectives.

Welfare-oriented NGOs have traditionally approached the issue of development from a very broad perspective. Usually, the welfare programs focus on alleviating poverty by providing a number of free or subsidized services. Programs with a focus on sustainability, in contrast, are supposed to be providing a service poor people want and are willing to pay for. In the case of welfare NGOs, the focus is not on delivering credit efficiently but on providing another service to the poor. These differences in focus are largely responsible for the NGOs' slow transition to a financial-systems approach to lending to poor entrepreneurs. Part of the problem is probably lack of a common understanding among NGOs about who are or should be the beneficiaries of credit and who are or should be the beneficiaries of welfare services. Because NGO welfare programs focus on the poorest of the poor, their credit programs tend to serve the same constituency. When the criterion used to select clients for credit programs is poverty, the programs end up with borrowers who are not entrepreneurs. The poorest people in any community are not likely to be business operators. They are more concerned with the basic needs of survival and would likely divert loan money to serve needs more urgent than those of starting a business.

- Should NGOs pursue goals of financial self-sufficiency?

One issue that remains unclear to most welfare-oriented NGOs is whether the pursuit of financial self-sufficiency might subordinate the goals of broader community development. Emphasis on efficient access to credit and financial self-sufficiency is often misconstrued as a condemnation of the role of welfare services. Many argue that NGOs should not be satisfied merely with efficient disbursements of loans, high repayment rates, and maximum profit.

This argument contains some valid points. NGOs are development agencies and should not forget their development mission. The alternative, however, is not providing credit as a welfare service. This would not only waste resources but also work against broader development goals. It is possible for NGOs to provide credit to poor entrepreneurs efficiently without sacrificing the goals of broader development. This can be achieved by an NGO's specializing in credit and collaborating with NGOs that provide other services, such as training, promoting, and partly subsidizing SSEs.

Credit for microenterprise development has become a very specialized operation, which relies on sound credit-management principles. If these principles are compromised, efficiency is sacrificed.

- Do NGOs have the capacity to manage credit programs?

It is common for NGOs to start credit programs without being prepared. Often credit programs start before proper management information systems or qualified personnel are in place. Such programs are managed by staff who have no experience in the credit management field and are often unable to judge the quality of their portfolios.

Lack of capacity to manage credit is largely a result of remuneration policies that are not attractive compared with those in the commercial sector. Generally, welfare-oriented NGOs pay much lower salaries than the private sector. This limits their ability to recruit and retain qualified staff. Some organizations have a problem justifying a higher salary scale for credit staff and a lower one for welfare program staff. In some cases, staff implementing welfare programs are asked to double up as credit officers, even when the two roles conflict.

Chikolas (rotating savings and credit associations)

Like many countries the world over, Kenya has thousands of ROSCAS (chikola groups), which are a source of credit for thousands of people with SSEs. Many rural credit analysts are enthusiastic about the apparent success of such associations.

In Kenya, ROSCAS are found in rural and urban areas, either as registered social welfare groups (mostly women's groups) or as unregistered groups of friends and family members.

ROSCAs operate on simple principles. At regular meetings, each member contributes a fixed sum of money, which is given to one member, and each member gets a turn as a recipient.

The *chikolas* provide credit to those who would be ineligible to borrow from other sources. They also mobilize savings, serve a social function, and provide a form of insurance (from the group's savings). The *chikolas* offer a number of advantages to members. The main one of these is that their operations are simple and easily understood by even illiterate or semiliterate people, who form the bulk of their membership. Springing from local initiative, *chikolas* generate a sense of ownership and loyalty and embody truly participatory development. The *chikolas* are a promising approach to developing sustainable credit schemes for SSEs in Kenya.

One of the problems faced by these groups is their small capital base and thus a limited ability to meet the credit needs of the membership. With a larger capital base, a *chikola* could give more group members larger loans more often.

K-REP, beginning in 1991, recognized this need and began a loan program designed to meet it. K-REP prepares a contract with the *chikola*, which gives a loan to a group at market rates of interest for 1 to 2 years.

The *chikola* then lends a prespecified amount of the money received from K-REP to an individual at a rate of interest higher than that the *chikola* pays K-REP. Each member makes repayments to the *chikola*, which repays K-REP in monthly instalments. The money resulting from this rate spread is retained by the *chikola* as a way of building up its capital base. Benefits accrue to both the individual *chikola* member and the *chikola* itself.

This arrangement is a cost-effective way of extending credit because much of the administrative work, normally done by the loan officer, is done by the *chikola*. As many as 25–35 people may receive loans for the same amount of work as for one loan prepared by one loan officer. Because the groups that K-REP sponsors have been around for a number of years, they have achieved high levels of cohesiveness and thus avoid the interpersonal conflicts typical of new groups. In 2 years, K-REP made 62 loans to 55 groups. The loans, worth a total of 23 million KES, were made to 1 340 members. The repayment rate was 100%.

Commercial banks

Despite the fact that Kenya has a relatively sophisticated banking sector — 28 commercial banks with more than 400 branches, subbranches, agencies, and mobile units — most of the commercial banks are passive observers as far as lending to SSES is concerned. Until the 1980s, none of the commercial banks had a credit program specifically for SSES.

Although commercial banks have historically been the main deposit mobilizer and source of credit in the economy, their share of the economy has been declining as a result of the proliferation of financial institutions of other types. The system of commercial banks in Kenya is dominated by four major banks — KCB, Barclay's Bank of Kenya, Standard Chartered Bank, and the National Bank of Kenya — which together account for more than 60% of the deposits in and credit volume of commercial banks.

Although most bankers cite high risks and high transaction costs as justification for their reluctance to lend to SSES, many of the commercial banks admit that they have neither the technology nor the incentive to lend to the SSES. The few commercial banks that have SSE programs are servicing the sector more as a result of a donor or government initiative or as a public relations exercise than because they see the sector as a new and potentially growing market. Decisions to finance SSES are made in the boardrooms rather than at the operations level. Consequently, at the level of the branch, which is the entry point for most SSE operators, the tendency is to accept the applications only of those who can fully guarantee their repayment of the loans, regardless of the project's viability.

At one time, some bankers argued that the central bank's control of interest rates was the main factor preventing commercial banks from lending to the sector, because they could not charge the SSES the rates needed to account for the perceived risks. The central bank liberalized the interest rates, but there has been no change in attitude. Although one may argue that change is always slow and that it will take a while to see results, there has been no indication that the liberalization of interest rates will make credit from commercial banks more accessible to SSES.

Commercial banks make limited loans to SSES, based on projected cash flow, and this is usually to very well established customers. Otherwise, the bulk of their lending to SSES requires collateral in the form of land, buildings, or equipment. Discussions in Kenya seem to suggest that commercial banks will not be easily persuaded to grant collateral-free loans to SSEs, but the commercial banks seem willing to develop "functional equivalents," which would make conventional securities unnecessary.

Barclay's Bank of Kenya

Barclay's has been operating in Kenya for more than 75 years and has more than 90 branches and subbranches throughout the country. For the past 6 years, Barclay's has cooperated with a number of donors and local NGOs in the development of several schemes targeted at female entrepreneurs and graduates of Youth Polytechnic. These schemes are managed by the bank's Small Business Unit. Barclay's divides SSEs into two categories: those employing 1–9 workers and those employing 10–50.

At the other end of the spectrum, Barclay's manages a scheme (guaranteed by USAID) for projects worth as much as 4 million KES. Under this scheme the borrower is responsible for providing 50% of the securities, and the rest is covered by USAID. Barclay's assists the entrepreneur with a business plan, and the branch office monitors the loan to the SSE, just as any other loan. The USAID-funded Rural Private Enterprise (RPE) program was started by USAID in 1985 for the dual purpose of providing long-term credit to commercial banks to lend to SSEs and changing the attitude of commercial bankers toward small borrowers, de-emphasizing securities and placing more stress on the character of the borrowers and the potential of their projects. The RPE program is also being implemented by two other major commercial banks. Barclay's and the British Overseas Development Administration developed a scheme similar to the one Barclay's has with USAID but with targeted loan size ranging between 40 000 and 300 000 KES.

In collaboration with the Kenya Women's Finance Trust (KWFT), Barclay's runs a program for female entrepreneurs. Loans are fully secured by a guarantee fund, and KWFT provides management support to and monitoring of the borrowers. Barclay's supports, with its own funds, another NGO in a replication of the successful group-based lending scheme developed in Bangladesh. Barclay's also operates a scheme for graduates of Youth Polytechnic, guaranteed by the International Labour Office for loans worth between 10 000 and 60 000 KES.

With a growing network of branches, extending to many small towns, Barclay's considers small business one of its new markets, particularly for these recently opened branches.

RPE and the other programs run by Barclay's have three major objectives:

- to build up future clients;
- to enhance the image of the institution (with both the general public and the government); and
- to capitalize on the training opportunities these programs provide the bank's staff. Faced with significant problems in debt recovery, as all financial institutions in Kenya are today, Barclay's identified the need to expand the range of skills of its branch managers to include not only those needed to manage a branch and to evaluate securities, but also those needed to examine the cash flows, balance sheets, and business plans of their potential borrowers.

Kenya Commercial Bank

Another commercial bank that has been engaged in lending to the SSEs is KCB. KCB has the largest network of offices, with 69 full branches, 59 subbranches, and 117 mobile centres.

Although Barclay's is privately owned, KCB is predominantly owned by government, with only 30% of its shares owned by the public. Its interest in the SSE sector is due primarily to the government's direct involvement in setting the policy of the bank.

In addition to participating in the USAID-funded RPE program, KCB has a few other schemes aimed at the low end of the market. One of these is the *Jua Kali* Credit Scheme, also funded by USAID. This program started in 1987, operating only in Nairobi and giving 200 borrowers loans together worth 2.5 million KES. USAID provides an equal amount to cover administration costs. More recently, KCB started a graduate loan scheme, aimed at providing credit worth up to 300 000 KES to graduates to start new businesses. The total available under this scheme is 30 million KES, plus an additional 10 million KES for loans to female graduates.

The top managers of KCB appear committed to doing more than they are currently doing in the sector, and KCB is considering the appointment of one officer in each branch to handle this type of credit. KCB hopes to eventually merge its Special Loans Unit with its mainstream loans operation. The Special Loans Unit currently specializes in KCB's SSE schemes. As a step in this direction, KCB has begun looking for alternative forms of security, and in some of its branches KCB has started advancing loans against letters of allotment of land, rather than requiring full title deeds. KCB's experience in debt recovery on these loans has been similar to that with fully secured loans.

Development finance institutions

Two DFIS, KIE and SEFCO, are the main organizations in Kenya for enterprise promotion.

Kenya Industrial Estates

KIE was set up in 1967, mainly as a promotional agency for stimulating indigenous entrepreneurship, and is the oldest lending institution specifically aimed at SSEs. Its initial focus was on supplying industrial space, hence its name. In addition to providing entrepreneurs with sheds, KIE has also, at various stages, helped entrepreneurs by writing their feasibility studies, choosing their equipment and machinery, installing their equipment, and marketing their products. KIE also obtained import restrictions on foreign products, supplied raw materials, and so on. KIE has a model for providing technical assistance with credit, using what is called the integrated approach.

Kilby (1988) evaluated this approach in "Breaking the entrepreneur bottleneck in late developing countries: is there a useful role for government?" The main opponents of the integrated approach argue that by constantly spoon-feeding prospective entrepreneurs, the promotional organization only generates dependencies rather than self-reliance. Furthermore, when the roles of banker and promoter are combined, the banking side inevitably suffers, and poor repayment rates become common.

The cancellation in the past 2 years of large loans from two of KIE's main donors sharpens one's realization of the inadequacies of this approach. The donors were the World Bank and the German KfW (Kreditanstalt für Wiederaufbau). In the wake of Kenya's parastatal reform program, it is clear that KIE needs a more commercial approach to lending if it is to meet the audit requirements for its financial ratios. KIE secures its loans with land and buildings and some chattel mortgages.

In addition to KIE's making what it calls its formal-sector loans, it also has a scheme for lending to smaller enterprises (average loan is 22 500 KES). This program was launched in late 1988 with the assistance of the German government. The program's objective was to finance owners or managers of firms with an average of 2.5 employees.

This program secures its loans with rigorous selection procedures, chattel mortgages, and deeds of guarantee from two guarantors. An evaluation conducted in late 1991 indicated that the average growth in employment in these firms in 1 year of the program's financing was 50%.

KIE initiated an examination of itself to determine an appropriate plan for restructuring, although this was not in the government's immediate restructuring program. KIE redefined its mission statement to eliminate many of the subsidized elements. This was approved in principle by the government, but KIE has yet to demonstrate that it can do what is needed to achieve comprehensive reform, such as improving its recovery rate, reducing its branch offices, and increasing the productivity of its staff to generate a higher portfolio to staff member ratio.

The Small Enterprise Finance Company

SEFCO was established in 1983 with objectives like those of KIE. The main difference between the two organizations is that they have different shareholders. Whereas KIE is wholly government owned (99% by the Treasury and 1% by the Ministry of Industry), SEFCO is owned by the Development Finance Company of Kenya, the Netherlands Finance Company for Developing Countries, a German foundation called Friedrich Ebert Stiftung (FES), the Industrial Commercial Development Corporation, and the German Company for Investment in Developing Countries.

In 1979, with subsidies from FES, one of its shareholders, SEFCO started a revolving loan scheme for self-employment projects. The Double Credit Guarantee Scheme, as it came to be known, lends money to members of an association that guarantees its members' loans.

Each member of the association helps to guarantee every loan taken by a member of the association, as it is assumed that peer pressure will be strong enough to encourage the borrower to repay the loan. If the association should fail for some reason to honour the debt, then a guarantee fund comes into effect to pay SEFCO for the loan. The average loan is worth

10 000 KES. In December 1990, there were 16 associations with a total of 350 members, altogether employing 1 400 people. As of September 1992, the loans to these associations began to shrink. The approach was unsustainable in the long run, owing to the high cost of administering the program; furthermore, debt collection began to be problematic. SEFCO's management also felt that the image of an NGO was not appropriate for instilling the kind of respect it needed from its larger and more profitable clients.

Like KIE, SEFCO is seriously examining its future role as a financial institution. SEFCO is also anticipating a shortage of funds and has as a result applied for a banking licence as an alternative to permanently relying on increased shareholdings and concessional loans from donors. SEFCO may also change its shareholders, to include some of Kenya's larger institutional investors. SEFCO is gradually moving away from lending to those starting up businesses to lending to those expanding their businesses. The major constraint on SEFCO's operations is a lethargic legal system. Because of this, it is very difficult for SEFCO to foreclose on the loans that fail or go into heavy arrears. This fact alone forces SEFCO to make substantial provision for bad debts (between 5 and 10%).

The demand for and supply of SSE credit: what are the issues?

Tomecko and Aleke-Dondo (1992) estimated that the total effective demand for credit for SSEs in 1992 was 2.8 billion KES, not taking into account the influence of securities and interest rates. In the same paper, we suggested that the SSE sector, which is well known for mobilizing personal savings, could supply 65% of that demand and SSE lending institutions could finance the remaining 35%, approximately 1 billion KES. We pointed out that for the existing noncommercial banks to meet this demand, they would have to double their portfolios, necessitating an increase in their present institutional capacity. The portfolio is considered more of a constraint than disbursements because management of the portfolio means having additional trained staff to monitor the extra load. Because of managerial limitations, most institutions can only increase their current portfolios by up to 50%. The small NGOs have a greater ability to expand, but the larger organizations, such as development finance institutions, would have more difficulty. If funds were available, the maximum growth in portfolio of the current institutions is not likely to be greater than 20%. The obvious conclusion is that there will continue to be an unmet demand for credit for SSEs for the foreseeable future unless commercial banks radically change their policies, enough to accommodate more SSEs in their lending operations.

How to match supply and demand

Given the serious gap between the demand for credit from the sector and what can feasibly be supplied by the established institutions, there are only two options: to further increase the capacity of these institutions or to try to maximize the impact of lending by making credit available to the SSEs with the greatest potential for growth. KIE and SEFCO manage about 68% of the portfolio, but they are rethinking their long-term strategies and, therefore, are not in a position to expand significantly. There can be no increase in institutional capacity without the major participation of the private-finance sector. The other option, that of targeting the SSEs capable of growing, is far more realistic. This can be done by increasing the price of credit (the interest rate) and by alternative use of collateral against loans.

Interest rates

In recent years, with the growing recognition of the strategic role that SSEs play in the economy of every nation and the necessity of credit in SSEs' survival and growth, much more attention has been placed on how credit programs can be sustained without subsidies. During the 1960s and much of the 1970s, SSE credit was synonymous with subsidized interest rates. This was also the case for many rural agricultural credit schemes. What has happened to development banks is the most obvious example of the negative consequences of subsidized interest rates. In Africa, most development banks are insolvent and cannot survive without injections of additional share capital or concessional loans from overseas.

What matters to the SSE borrower is that credit is available and that processing time and transaction costs are reduced to a minimum. Higher interest rates are of little significance to the entrepreneur, compared with the time, energy, and transportation costs required to obtain subsidized credit. Easy access to credit is the single most overriding consideration for an SSE entrepreneur constrained by lack of credit (Mutua and Aleke-Dondo 1991). This is why money lenders can charge annual interest rates as high as 240%.

It is expected that as an SSE grows, it will graduate from such informal forms of credit to cheaper commercial bank loans. The borrowing history of many SSEs traces progress from the informal money lenders to NGOs, which, although they require no tangible collateral, charge interest rates as high as 35%. As the SSE entrepreneur acquires more assets, he or she can obtain credit from DFIS, which charge about 30% interest. The next step is credit from commercial banks' special loans units, whose interest rates are about 25%. With assets for collateral, the entrepreneur may finally obtain access to regular commercial loans at perhaps a 20% rate of interest. This continuum of financing sources is shown in Table 2.

Small enterprises may enter the more formal financial system at the same time as lending institutions achieve sustainability if these institutions make the correct use of market interest rates in all their credit programs. The high interest rates charged by NGOs for small loans and the lower rates charged by the commercial banks for larger loans give the entrepreneur an incentive to graduate to commercial bank loans. When the enterprise has grown as a result of an NGO loan, with its easier security terms, the entrepreneur will have more securities and be in a position to obtain cheaper credit from the commercial banks.

How much interest are SSEs currently willing to pay? Most of the programs offering credit to small borrowers are not completely open about their interest rates. Many have administration charges, forced savings or insurance funds, and other

Table 2. Comparative advantages of institutional lenders.

	Annual interest rate (%)	Average size of loan (KES)
Money lenders	50[a]	NA
NGOS	35	5 000
DFIS	30	20 000
Commercial banks' special loans units	25	150 000
Commercial banks' regular loans units	20	500 000

Source: J. Tomecko (unpublished data).
[a]Can be as high as 240%.

similar fees in addition to the interest. Sometimes the interest is calculated on a "flat" basis, meaning that if a client pays off the loan before scheduled there is no difference in the interest payment charged. This effectively raises the interest rate and means that most of the NGOs who list 27% as their interest rate are in effect charging 35%.

The 35% interest rate is very close to that charged by other sustainable programs in other parts of the world, that is, commercial bank rate (22%) plus 10–15%. This means that it should be possible for a well-managed financial institution to lend to SSEs and still be sustainable.

The main conclusion, therefore, is that if the market interest rates for SSEs (currently 35%) are charged, institutional capacities will be strengthened by additional revenues, demand will be limited to the borrowers who have the higher incomes needed to pay these rates, and the profitability of the businesses being served will not be significantly affected.

The result of adopting market interest rates will be more money directed at growing businesses. Can credit institutions for SSEs be sustainable? Although this has yet to be seen in Africa, there is plenty of evidence from Latin America and Asia to conclude that these institutions can be sustainable. Examples of successful programs are cited by Jackelen and Rhyne (1991). The common elements of success in these programs are that the poor are treated as commercial clients rather than beneficiaries; interest rates are 10–15% above the commercial bank rates; there are a large number of borrowers; and a substantial proportion of clients' savings is mobilized, thereby reducing the programs' dependence on external sources of funding.

The use of collateral and securities

The need for collateral and securities is one of the critical bottlenecks in lending to the SSE sector. This issue is often addressed with more emotion than reason. In Kenya, where land titling has gone further than it has in most African countries, it has not been difficult for commercial as well as development bankers to restrict disbursement of loans to those who can secure them with land and buildings. Consequently, there has not been much need to consider other sources of collateral.

Recently, however, even commercial banks are beginning to look for alternatives. In Kenya today, a branch manager is far more likely to be asking serious questions about the project's viability than about the land and buildings needed to back up the loan.

In many respects, collateral is a substitute for information about the borrower. Someone who is well known usually is more acceptable than someone who just comes in "off the street." We shall look at four ways lending institutions in Kenya are substituting better information about the borrower for tangible collateral.

Group securities

Using group securities as a form of collateral has been popular in many countries of Asia but was never effective on a large scale until the Grameen Bank in Bangladesh made it famous. With the exception of four small programs, all of the NGOs that are lending to small enterprises in Kenya are using group securities. With a few exceptions, recovery rates under these schemes are remarkable, sometimes more than 90%, demonstrating that peer pressure effectively secures small loans.

Self-selection

Another program that completely circumvents the land-and-building route is the KIE Informal Sector Project (KIE/ISP). To obtain the information that is required to make a decision on the viability of a business and on the character of the applicant, the lending institution makes the candidate perform a series of tests. (1) The candidate keeps a record of all raw materials purchased and all sales for 4 weeks. Information is then available on the basic gross margin of the business and the commitment of the entrepreneur to the enterprise. (2) One of the program's field officers confirms this information with a visit to the businesses of the 50% who make it this far.

The officer compiles a simple balance sheet to compare the sales with the capital employed and verify that the entrepreneur meets the criterion of being in business for at least 1 year. (3) The candidate has to prepare a business plan. Although candidates receive classroom instruction on preparing a business plan, they must do it themselves, and about 10% drop out at this point. (4) The final test is to provide some movable asset, such as a sewing or welding machine, even if it is from a friend or guarantor, that can be used for a chattel mortgage, and 15% drop out here. This program is usually left with about 25% of its original applicants.

Very good recovery rates (92%) are also recorded with this scheme, showing that self-selection combined with a chattel mortgage to secure a small-business loan is a feasible alternative to the more traditional collateral of land and buildings. The maximum loan under KIE/ISP for second-time borrowers is 100 000 KES.

Business support services

Another way of substituting information for collateral is the Barclay's–K-MAP Credit Scheme. The Kenya Management Assistance Programme (K-MAP) is a Kenyan NGO set up in 1986 to establish better links between small and large firms in Kenya. The program accepts the voluntary contribution of management personnel from large firms to assist small enterprises with specific technical and managerial problems. K-MAP has a few hundred small businesses under its umbrella and conducts regular management training courses in addition to an average of 3.5 counseling sessions for each business.

To qualify for the scheme with Barclay's, the applicant must have been registered with K-MAP for at least 18 months and have received training and counseling on a regular basis. The feedback on this to the bank must of course be positive. The scheme is partly supported by the USAID loan guarantee fund, but Barclay's is willing to reduce the collateral requirements on these loans by 50% because of the 18-month history of good performance with K-MAP.

Credit referencing

One of the main complaints from formal financing institutions is that small businesses lack a track record. Again, the absence of information is a significant block to extending credit to the sector. Because the larger banks would like to have this information and the smaller organizations are the ones that have it, the two groups have come together to establish the Small Enterprise Credit Association (SECA).

SECA performs an advocacy role for the institutions that provide SSEs with credit. SECA is establishing, with United Nations Development Programme assistance, a credit reference system with two objectives: (1) to run duplication checks on all loan applicants to make sure that no discredited borrower from one program receives a loan from a second; and (2) to provide credit histories for borrowers with a good repayment history so that these may be used as track records with the larger banks.

Conclusions

These trends in lending to SSEs clearly indicate that most of the institutions moving in a positive direction are in the private sector. The commercial banks are taking an increasing interest in the SSE sector, and the NGOs are filling an important gap at the lower end of the market by encouraging SSEs to graduate to commercial bank loans.

The government has investments in both KIE and SEFCO. KIE has been labeled as strategic and is, therefore, not for sale to the private sector. It is, however, badly in need of restructuring if it is to play a prominent role in future SSE financing. This restructuring process will require a firm orientation toward commercialization, elimination of political interference with its management and project selection, and an injection of new equity. SEFCO already has significant shareholders in the private sector and should be wholly privatized. Privatization would be in line with government policy and could only have a positive effect on the sustainability of this important financial institution. Some fledgling NGOs still operate at the fringe of sustainability because their portfolios are not large enough. The government should pass on, through the concessionary funds it receives from donors, soft loans to NGOs that have demonstrated the ability to disburse and recover loans and to encourage SSE borrowers to graduate to loans from mainstream financial institutions. These NGOs may be the new generation of private-sector DFIS and should have recognition and support from the government.

The commercial banks are interested in having their managers screen loan applications on the basis of the applicants' business prospects. This fits in with the banks' need to ensure that as few as possible of their loans fall into arrears or fail. Branch managers will need some training when they are attached to donor-funded SSE projects. The College of Banking should be encouraged to offer this type of training to commercial-bank staff on a regular basis.

Despite new attitudes and fewer risks, there are few tangible incentives for branch managers to aggressively expand business in the SSE sector. Because the interest rates offered under schemes targeted at small business do not vary more than a few percentage points from the rates offered by commercial banks, the overall profitability of a branch would not be significantly affected by increased lending in this sector. Although interest rates were liberalized in June 1991 and inflation is 36% (according to the Central Bureau of Statistics cost of living index), there is still a reluctance among commercial banks to charge higher interest rates to SSEs. Until there are incentives for banking staff to expand business in this sector, commercial banks are likely to continue treating SSEs as a novelty rather than as a prospective market.

All of the major lenders complain about local political impediments to debt recovery in (1) the sale of repossessed land or (2) the legal system, where cases are reportedly dragged out interminably. The banks are unwilling to lend because of the effect of these impediments on their cash flows for disbursement. The main culprits are said to be the district commissioners, who have no *de jure* role in these matters. At the very least, the government should circulate instructions prohibiting district commissioners from engaging in such activities. ✳

Part V

Innovations for Increasing Competitiveness

IMPROVING ACCESS OF SMALL AND MEDIUM-SIZE ENTERPRISES TO NEW TECHNOLOGIES

Alan Kyerematen
Director, Empretec Ghana, Accra, Ghana

Introduction

Technology has emerged in recent times as one of the key strategic variables in economic development. In Africa, technology as an instrument of change is now receiving special attention in national planning. However, there are still many issues requiring urgent attention before access to new technologies improves in Africa.

Technology has been defined as "knowledge required to produce goods or services" and, alternatively, as "the application of practical or mechanical sciences to industry or commerce and the methods, theory and practices governing such applications." Whichever definition is applied, the advantages of technology are no longer a contentious issue, either in developed or in developing economies. What is at issue is the lack of policies that enhance access to it.

This paper examines a number of factors that influence the transfer of technology and provides some guidelines on facilitating the transfer of technology to small and medium-size enterprises (SMEs) in African countries. It also examines the approach adopted by Empretec, a business development agency in Ghana that works with SMEs to improve their access to technology.

Background and context

One of the phenomena of recent times has been the role played by technology in the development of many countries. Technological innovations have had a major effect on the global pattern of trade and industry. These innovations have taken place primarily in industrialized, developed economies and more recently in what are referred to as the newly industrialized countries.

In manufacturing, improved technology is rapidly changing products and processes. The result is that the competitive advantage of cheap labour in most developing countries is disappearing. For example, the textile and clothing industry, which provides considerable export potential for African SMEs, is facing major competition from the increased use of computer-aided design and computer-aided manufacturing in industrialized countries. Several developing countries in Southeast Asia and Latin America have, however, considerably improved production. They use new technologies to manufacture a wide range of new products for export.

African countries need to review their situation in relation to new and emerging technologies and then design policies and programs that will help reduce the technology gap between themselves and developed countries. The critical role that African SMEs will have to play in closing this gap cannot be overemphasized — they constitute more than 90% of the enterprises in Africa.

Factors influencing technology transfer and access in Africa

A number of factors limit or facilitate technology transfer and access to new technologies in African countries. These factors may be considered both at the macro level and at the enterprise (micro) level.

Technology culture and the promotion of science and technology

Although many African countries were technological pioneers centuries ago, this is no longer true. The importance of technology in improving quality of life is not fully appreciated or adequately demonstrated in most African countries. The development of science and technology (S&T) is often hindered by a lack of clear policy and vision.

Perhaps the greatest service that a government can perform is to champion new technology. Most African governments have only paid lip service to S&T development, instead of creating an environment in which small business can choose what technologies it needs and determine how best to acquire them. To build such an environment, African governments need trade, tax, legislative, and regulatory policies that promote effective technology transfer. These governments should be committed to creating an educated populus that has the knowledge and the will to master new technologies as they evolve.

At the community and family levels, the promotion of S&T requires a new look at restrictive child-rearing practices that stifle exploration, experimentation, risk-taking, and questioning of the status quo.

Infrastructure and physical facilities

Another critical factor limiting access to and transfer of new technologies in African countries is the state of existing physical facilities and local infrastructure: power and water supply, telecommunications, availability of spare parts and servicing facilities, etc.

- The unreliable power supply prevents the effective use of much of the sophisticated equipment imported into Africa.

- The poor state of the telecommunication infrastructure limits the introduction and effective use of "high-tech" communication facilities and equipment.

- The lack of spare parts and servicing facilities in many African countries constrains the introduction of useful equipment and machinery.

- The lack of any adequate maintenance service in Africa also limits the development and use of new technologies. New machines and equipment are prematurely put out of service by the lack of proper maintenance.

Institutional support

Technology transfer can be enhanced by efficient and effective operations of public-sector research and development (R&D) institutions. However, in African countries, there are problems associated with R&D institutions:

- Research activities are not demand driven. R&D institutions set their research goals without assessing or analyzing what is required for socioeconomic development. The needs of the private sector, in particular, are often ignored.

- R&D institutions attempt to generate new technologies while paying little attention to the crucial need for assimilating and adapting imported technologies.

- R&D institutions pay inadequate attention to contract research and other income-generating opportunities that would ensure their survival.

- Research institutes lack autonomy and adequate funding.

- Most research activities do not result in any product development.

As a result of some of these problems, R&D institutions in Africa have not helped to make foreign technologies more accessible, nor have they developed a wide range of indigenous technologies.

Technological service capability

Technological capabilities consist of the information and skills — technical, managerial, and institutional — that allow productive enterprises to use equipment and technology efficiently. The successful transfer of new technologies to African countries has been limited by a low level of technological capability. Simply providing equipment and operating instructions, designs, or blueprints in most instances does not ensure the transfer of technology.

The required technological services range from macro-level industrial planning to micro-level project identification, feasibility studies, plant specifications, engineering and plant design, civil construction, machinery installation, plant commissioning, and so on. In most African countries, there is a considerable range in capabilities among local consultants providing these services.

Technology as a marketable commodity

One special characteristic of technology is that it is a marketable commodity. Ownership is protected by proprietary rights in the form of patents, copyrights, and trademarks. Because its development costs money and involves risks, technology is marketed with the objective of making a profit.

With reference to African countries, however, the term technology transfer suggests a donor and a recipient, instead of a seller and buyer. The cost of buying technology is actually one of the most crucial elements influencing access to new technology; in general, the cost of technology is proportional to its level of application.

Many SMEs in Africa cannot afford to tap into technological opportunities on their own, and they do not have the resources to participate in R&D programs that will provide new technologies or link them with suitable partners.

A national technology information system

The international technology market is imperfect. For most standard technologies, several alternative sources can be identified. Knowledge of such sources, therefore, constitutes an essential aspect of technology transfer and acquisition and requires the development of a national information system on S&T in selected areas of priority. Such a system would have linkages with external databases and sources of information about alternative technologies.

Many technologies and much scientific knowledge are in the public domain and readily available. Information in books, journals, and reports can be acquired at minimal cost. Many useful technologies (tools and how-to books on their use and maintenance) can be bought off the shelf in the international market. African SMEs should not have to reinvent the wheel.

Other competing factors at the enterprise level

In many instances in Africa, new or enhanced technology may have a role to play in an enterprise, but there are likely to be other more critical issues limiting efficiency and profitability for a particular enterprise: limited financial resources, poor information management, lack of skilled staff, inadequate market size, and so on. New technology, therefore, may be of secondary importance to many entrepreneurs and to the survival of their enterprises. This limits the motivation to acquire new improved technologies.

Improving access to new technology — strategic considerations

There is no standard approach or universal system for technology transfer any more than there is agreement among experts on a structure for a successful individual transfer of technology. However, some strategic considerations will help improve access to new technologies.

Transnational corporations

Transnational corporations (TNCs) are generally considered the primary source of new production technologies. TNCs transfer technologies through a variety of linkages with local companies, including joint ventures, licencing and contractual arrangements for technology and technical services, subcontracting agreements, and franchises. TNCs also provide technology upgrades and supply equipment. These are all means that increase access to new technologies and enable the rapid endogenous growth in technological capability. In some of the most successful cases of technology transfer, TNCs have set up a special department to collaborate with SMEs.

Subcontracting and inter-firm linkages

Large local companies often subcontract the provision of component products and services out to small companies. As well, some small companies form interfirm linkages for flexible specialization and collective efficiency. Both of these approaches play an important role in technology transfer.

A major spur to the technological modernization of SMEs comes from large firms that want to create and maintain an efficient network of suppliers. The large firms do this by providing extensive technical support and quality control to enable SMEs to meet standards. The large firms also support their subcontractors by giving them fairly stable employment. This relationship has helped the SMEs to become innovative and efficient.

Flexible specialization provides firms with multipurpose equipment and multiskilled workers to manufacture a variety of products. The small-firm variant of the concept of flexible specialization is based on the understanding that small firms not only compete with each other but also complement each other through vertical links and horizontal collaboration. As a result, there is a collective ability to deal with changes in the market and to innovate. The clustering of small firms provides a seedbed for the exchange of new technologies.

Intermediary institutions

African countries require active intermediary structures to bridge three kinds of gaps: gaps between the suppliers (academic and R&D institutions) and the users (production sectors); gaps between the traditional (old) and modern (emerging) technologies; and gaps between the local (generated) and foreign (imported) technologies.

In the Republic of Korea, the government established the Korea Institute of Science and Technology (KIST) as an active intermediary between the S&T community and the industrial community. KIST was able to attract high-calibre people from abroad, receive constant patronage from the head of the government, and gain credibility by concentrating on a few activities determined by a needs survey. KIST was soon successful at making the private sector appreciate the competitive value of technology and research.

In Japan, concerted efforts on the part of government, industry, R&D institutions, and the general public, under the umbrella of the Ministry of International Trade and Industry (MITI), ensured the formulation and implementation of mutually beneficial strategies. For example, through these efforts, imported basic technologies and indigenous peripheral technologies were spread to many local firms to promote use and competition. This resulted in step-by-step building of national capability, starting from repair and leading to imitation and improvement of imported technology. Whenever necessary, Japan hired foreigners to transfer knowledge.

The Empretec Ghana approach

Empretec is a business development agency sponsored by the United Nations Development Programme (UNDP), the Overseas Development Administration (ODA) of the United Kingdom, the United Nations Centre on Transnational Corporations, Barclay's Bank of Ghana Limited, and the National Board for Small-Scale Industries. The main objective of Empretec is to act as a catalyst for private-sector development by providing a comprehensive range of support services for SMEs. This includes helping SMEs get access to new technologies.

Before Empretec introduces the SME to a technology, it prepares the entrepreneur and the enterprise to absorb and to make effective use of technology. This approach prevents any unplanned quantum leap when the new technology is then introduced. Empretec also strives to improve the general operational efficiency of the SME. Empretec starts with company analysis, assessing its strengths and weaknesses. If the assessment points to a need for technology, then Empretec proceeds with any of a number of options.

Training and awareness programs

A series of intensive training sessions introduces entrepreneurs to alternative forms and sources of technology and ways to obtain them. Contractual obligations are explained, and the participants learn how to negotiate contracts.

Diagnostic studies and extension support

Local consultants with expertise in technology transfer may be hired to diagnose the problem and assess the technological requirements of a particular firm. The consultants then provide a practical hands-on program to help solve the problems. Often, all that a company needs to improve its competitiveness is to have an expert visit the site and suggest new plant layout, new training, or readily available technologies. The expert may also help the company implement a quality-assurance program to increase productivity and eliminate waste. The extension support program helps SMEs develop, acquire, install, and make use of technology.

The consultants engaged to work with the SMEs may be from R&D institutions, or they may be corporate executives.

Subcontracting

Subcontracting may be used to promote links between SMEs and large private companies in the region, as well as government agencies interested in subcontracting to the SMEs the production of component goods or the delivery of services. The large companies may provide technical assistance to the subcontractors in the form of training, product development, quality control, or product packaging. In other instances, the large companies provide raw materials and finance the purchase of equipment.

Subcontracting links have helped some SMEs refine their products and also upgrade their machinery and equipment to deal with large contracts.

Empretec is working to establish a subcontracting exchange, which involves

- identifying the subcontracting needs of larger companies that could be met by SMEs;
- assessing the supply potential and capacity of selected SMEs to fulfil specific orders;
- matching requirements and capacities in a database;
- organizing meetings between buyers and sellers and providing assistance in negotiating terms of contracts; and
- organizing seminars and training sessions on fulfilling subcontracting obligations.

Linkages with foreign companies

One of the objectives of the Empretec program is to link local entrepreneurs with foreign companies in a variety of arrangements, including joint ventures, franchises, licencing agreements, technology upgrading, and equipment supply. Empretec provides assistance in negotiating the exact terms of such linkages. The first step in this process is helping the entrepreneurs prepare investment profiles. Then Empretec helps entrepreneurs look for foreign partners.

In one instance, a British company was linked to a Ghanaian company to manufacture crop-spraying equipment in Ghana. The technology developed by the British company was transferred to the Ghanaian company.

In another instance, a local computer software-engineering company was linked to a British company in the same field to create new software.

Experience has shown that one of the most effective ways to transfer technology from foreign companies to local SMEs is through intermediary organizations such as Empretec.

Providing technological information

Empretec provides information on alternative sources of technology. Such information is available in some detail in various technical bulletins subscribed to by Empretec, as well as in foreign databases to which Empretec is linked. There is, however, still a large gap in Empretec's technological information base.

Industrial attachments

Empretec also provides technical assistance to local industries through the British Executive Service Overseas (BESO) scheme. Under this scheme, which is sponsored by the ODA, retired industrial experts from the United Kingdom volunteer to come to Ghana to work hands-on with local industries to diagnose and solve various technological problems. All cases of BESO assistance so far have resulted in significant transfer of technical skills and knowledge to local staff, greatly improving production capabilities.

In one case, a British expert helped a local company to become the leading tire-retreading company in Ghana. The expert assisted the company in production planning, quality control, maintenance of plant and equipment, and marketing.

In another instance, a fish-processing expert helped a local company set up a fish-processing plant.

Procurement service

Empretec runs a procurement service as one means of improving access to new technologies. The objectives of the Empretec procurement service are to

- help client companies to identify the most suitable and competitive equipment to meet their requirements for technology and to arrange for the purchase, insurance, and delivery of specific equipment; and

- provide assurance to financial institutions that the company is getting the appropriate equipment at the best price and that the institutions' funds are being used properly, with appropriate contractual, freight, and insurance arrangements.

The procurement service is being implemented in collaboration with Crown agents in the United Kingdom.

Industrial fairs, seminars, and conferences

Empretec promotes client companies' participation in local and international fairs, seminars, and conferences. Such participation provides a unique opportunity for local entrepreneurs to learn about new technologies and sources of equipment and raw materials. These venues also provide a forum for the exchange of ideas and offer the client company an opportunity to test its own product technology in a competitive global market.

Other Empretec services

Technology is only one of many factors in the running of a business. Other factors influence the value and performance of technology. Empretec, therefore, provides other complementary services to enhance the capacity of SMEs to make effective use of technology. These include:

- *Entrepreneurial training* — Empretec offers a 2-week skills-development workshop intended to enhance the entrepreneurial competencies of participants and to help them adopt the attitudes and skills necessary to run a business successfully. Follow-up seminars deal with specific functional areas in management.

- *Business plan preparation* — Empretec assesses the technological requirements of enterprises and helps them prepare business plans.

- *Credit sourcing* — On the basis of the business plans prepared, Empretec is able to help the entrepreneurs negotiate loans from banks and other financial institutions.

- *Loan-monitoring service* — Empretec's Loan Monitoring Service encourages lending by Ghanaian financial institutions to SMEs by providing regular and accurate financial information to the banks on the performance of loan beneficiaries.

- *Business advisory services* — Empretec provides general business advisory services and consultancy support to help client companies manage their businesses efficiently.

Although Empretec's program to help SMEs gain access to new technologies is still in its early stages, evaluation of specific projects and activities already implemented has been positive. The number and quality of pipeline projects and related enterprises already participating in various Empretec schemes are an indication of the feasibility of the Empretec approach.

Target beneficiaries

The Empretec program is targeted at SMEs that already operate in the formal sector, employ between 10 to 100 people, and have sales ranging between 50 000 and 500 000 USD per annum. They are normally high-growth-oriented companies started and run by young, dynamic entrepreneurs with a reasonably high level of education. Currently, more than 300 entrepreneurs are participating in the program. They represent a diverse range of businesses, mainly value-added manufacturing or service activities, particularly those with an export orientation.

Fees and charges

All Empretec support services earn fees. Generally, Empretec aims at recovering 60% of the cost of undertaking any particular assisgnment. It is projected that over the next 5 years, Empretec will become self-sustaining. Against this background, Empretec is to be incorporated as a nonprofit foundation, guaranteeing it an independent corporate identity.

The level of success

Although the Empretec program is still in its early stages, it has succeeded in generating considerable enthusiasm among SMEs in Ghana by establishing an effective entrepreneurial and management training capacity and providing a comprehensive range of business support services. The competitive advantage of Empretec has been its integrated hands-on approach to problems encountered by SMEs, as can be seen from the variety of support activities it undertakes.

Since its inception in October 1990, Empretec has provided training and a variety of services, including financing, to more than 350 Ghanaian entrpreneurs:

- Ten entrepreneurship workshops were conducted in the major centres of industry, namely, Accra, Kumasi, and Takoradi.

- Twenty management seminars were given on various management topics.

- More than 300 entrepreneurs participated in workshops on developing linkages with foreign companies.

- Working relations have been established between SMEs and local and foreign banks and financial institutions.

- More than 190 entrepreneurs are benefiting from the follow-up business diagnosis and extension services nationwide.

- Offices have been established in Accra, Kumasi, and Takoradi to support local enterprises.

The second phase of the project, currently being implemented, focuses primarily on helping the SMEs establish more business linkages with access to technology.

Lessons learned from the Empretec experience

A number of lessons have been learned from the design and implementation of Empretec projects:

- For the entrepreneurship development program to be effective, its activities must be demand driven. They must also be designed in a way that will address the specific needs of the target beneficiaries, using an integrated approach.

- SME support organizations must have an entrepreneurial outlook and be dynamic and able to respond quickly to the needs of the target beneficiaries. Implementation arrangements should avoid bureaucratic procedures.

- A hands-on approach is required at the initial stages of a project, and considerable resources are required to effectively monitor the performance of SMEs.

- The selection of beneficiaries ultimately determines the success of a project. The ultimate goal of the Empretec approach is to develop linkages between local SMEs and foreign companies and requires that only SMEs with a clear potential for growth be selected.

- Technology transfer and access for SMEs are more likely to occur in growth-oriented, innovative companies than in survival-oriented enterprises.

- The supporting or facilitating role played by intermediary organizations such as Empretec is critical to helping SMEs gain access to new technologies.

- A prerequisite for technology transfer and access is a solid technological information base, which will provide vital information on alternative sources of technology.

- A more general approach to enterprise building, including training, financing, and institutional support, will enhance the value of technology for SMEs and improve its accessibility.

- A major impediment is that inadequate funds prevent Empretec from extending its support to a wider range of entrepreneurs.

- SME support programs are likely to remain inefficient as long as the macroeconomic, legal, and political environment is not supportive of private-sector development in general and SME development in particular. ✳

THE ROLE OF BUSINESS ASSOCIATIONS IN INCREASING THE COMPETITIVENESS OF SMALL-SCALE ENTERPRISES

Elias Dewah
Botswana Confederation of Commerce, Industry and Manpower,
Gaborone, Botswana

Introduction

In Botswana, the entrepreneur with a small-scale enterprise (SSE) is almost synonymous with the indigenous entrepreneur. Out of about 40 000 enterprises in Botswana, only about 2% are medium- and large-scale enterprises, that is, enterprises employing more than 25 people. Although there are far more SSEs, the majority are very much marginalized. SSEs will remain powerless until they are organized and encouraged to participate actively in dialogue with the government, for their own economic benefit. It is, however, comforting to note that politicians, especially politicians in multiparty democracies, are becoming more sensitive to the needs of organized SSEs.

SSEs employ a lot of workers, particularly unskilled and less educated workers. SSEs can be established in any part of the country because of their minimal demands for power, transportation, and so on. SSEs can to some extent arrest the migration of the rural population to urban areas, which is a problem in Botswana. SSEs are a training ground for new entrants into the modern economy.

The large enterprises in Botswana formed the Botswana Confederation of Commerce, Industry and Manpower (BOCCIM) in 1971 and soon found that without the inclusion of the SSEs in its fold, its power as a national private-sector organization would be incomplete.

People accused the organization of being an elitist, urban-based organization that only served the interests of the large and mostly foreign-owned companies. In 1988, therefore, BOCCIM extended its membership to SSEs, and now about 60% of BOCCIM's membership is made up of SSEs.

There is also a growing feeling among the medium- and large-scale enterprises that they have a social and economic responsibility for helping SSEs. BOCCIM is exploiting this feeling to the fullest extent. The strengthening SSE sector is integral to the success of large-scale enterprise. A dynamic SSE sector increases the demand for the goods and services of medium- and large-scale companies. The combined power of a strong SSE sector and the medium- and large-scale enterprises can more easily influence government policy, for the benefit of the whole private sector.

BOCCIM has a well-established program of management assistance for the SSEs. Called the Botswana Management Assistance Programme (B-MAP), it coordinates the business counselling services offered on a voluntary basis by successful medium- and large-scale companies. Large companies also finance the salary of the B-MAP manager and his official transportation, office rental, utilities, and so on.

As a united private sector, represented by a strong national association, the business community in Botswana has found it easier to present its views to the government on all issues affecting the management of the economy. BOCCIM has discussed with government the quality of the education system in the country, health issues, the problem of AIDS, utility costs, licencing, price controls, the exchange control regime, the availability of land for productive use, labour laws, gender issues, the immigration law, the investment climate in the country, tax issues, official corruption, and ways the country can become more competitive. Through this dialogue, SSEs have gained more than the cooperation of the large enterprises. They have been exempted from licencing requirements in the manufacturing sector and are receiving generous support from both the government and NGOs. This support includes management advice, training assistance, and direct financial assistance for manufacturing, agricultural projects in the horticultural and small stock division, and small mining ventures. There is now a proposal to extend this assistance to the tourism sector so that SSEs can play a meaningful role in this important sector of the economy.

The promotion of small-scale enterprises

The promotion of SSEs develops in three phases. The first phase requires mainly direct government intervention, in which the Ministry of Commerce and Industry goes all out to promote new SSEs, whether they are sole proprietorships or cooperative ventures. The second phase comes with the joint effort of the government, financial intermediaries, business associations, and NGOs to provide financial and management assistance. The third phase builds the SSEs' competitiveness, which relies heavily on the creative and productive power of the SSEs themselves and the assistance of business associations.

The role of business associations

It is in the third phase that business associations help the SSEs contribute to the economic development of the country. Business associations speak the same language as all business people, whether they have a large or a small business.

Everyone knows that the SSEs are marginalized, but when business associations tell SSEs that this is not conspiracy but a problem to be overcome, the SSEs listen. Governments have discussed this problem for a long time now, but the position of SSEs is still fragile, and rural poverty continues to haunt many countries in Africa even after three decades of independence.

To serve the SSEs, business associations must constantly scan the internal and external business environment and help identify business problems for the SSEs. Business associations should help SSEs prepare their annual budgets, taking into consideration the likely increases in wages, inflation, taxes, fuel costs, interest rates, costs of utilities, and so on. Without the assistance of business associations in all these aspects of SSE business, SSEs would find it very difficult to compete or even to survive.

It is worth noting that there is a general tendency for business associations to concentrate their services in urban areas. Business associations must reach out to the rural areas, as well, and establish an outreach program, committed to rural development and staffed by well-trained, experienced personnel.

In southern Africa, the leading political players supported the liberation of Zimbabwe, Angola, and Mozambique and, more recently, the democratization of South Africa. However, the business players in the region still have their part to play. The inevitable relaxation of trade barriers between countries in the region will bring its own problems. SSEs will face stiff competition, and some may not survive. Their products will have to compete with imports at home and with products of other countries abroad. Business associations in the region collaborate, with the aim of avoiding trade conflicts. Politicians may be drawn into these conflicts and pressured to support one side or the other. This should not be allowed to develop in southern Africa or elsewhere in Africa. Business associations should help develop intraregional skills-training programs for SSEs, intraregional trade missions, and an effective information exchange system.

Business associations should accept the help of the large-scale enterprises and multinational conglomerates willing to provide a free business counselling service to the SSEs. This free technology transfer could enhance the ability of the SSEs to compete and face the difficulties ahead.

In Botswana, large-scale enterprises do not regret having small-scale enterprises as competitors but look to them as potential clients, and large-scale enterprises are, therefore, willing to help SSEs develop. There is also very little evidence to suggest that SSEs will individually grow to challenge the larger enterprises. Large-scale enterprises and SSEs are linked by trade relations, generally through subcontracting. Business associations provide a forum where the large and small businesses can together challenge government regulations that block private-sector development and growth. Business associations help convince the SSEs to look to large-scale enterprises as potential sources of assistance. B-MAP, which is similar to K-MAP in Kenya, now has close to 100 volunteer business counsellors from large companies and professional organizations. These volunteers provide business management guidance and advice to more than 150 SSEs.

SSEs in Botswana are gradually becoming aware of the need to raise productivity as a way to gain a competitive edge. Together with large-scale enterprises, SSEs are pressuring the government to establish a Bureau of Standards, which will raise the quality of Botswana's products and increase their acceptance abroad.

Together with large-scale enterprises, SSEs have been invited to participate in several BOCCIM seminars and workshops to discuss ways to gain a competitive advantage nationally and internationally. Together with large-scale enterprises, SSEs are engaging in a series of dialogues with top government officials on the state of the economy, the interpretation of free-market enterprise in a less industrialized economy, the liberalization of exchange control, inflation and recession, gaining a competitive advantage, and so on.

To increase the competitiveness of SSEs, business associations provide education and training. This takes many forms: on-the-job training, off-the-job training, attachments, educational tours, seminars and workshops, talks by guest speakers invited to address special topics, information dissemination, and so on. BOCCIM does all these things and is beginning to see a change in attitude among entrepreneurs — rather than asking government to step in and help them out, they are starting to regard competition as a survival test for a business. Entrepreneurs with this attitude oppose any form of subsidization.

Recently, BOCCIM sponsored a series of 1-day seminars for chief executives of businesses of all sizes. The common theme was how to survive in a competitive business environment. Executives were told that to compete does not mean to sell at lower prices but to produce good-quality products at a lower cost, provide efficient service, and maintain a well-trained, highly motivated staff and high productivity.

Business associations, together with labour associations, play a pivotal role in the development and empowerment of the private sector in Africa. Business and labour associations have, in a number of cases, tried to undermine the bureaucracies that have delayed the advancement of the private sector and its competitiveness for many decades.

Conclusion

The task and challenge of business associations are to make the private sector, especially the SSEs, appreciate that they are partners of governments and not just passive observers or victims of business laws and regulations formulated without their consent. Business associations have to show entrepreneurs with

SSES that rather than asking the spirit of an ancestor to make a business successful, they need to acquire management skills. Competitors have to be confronted in the marketplace with high-quality goods and services. ✽

TRAINING FOR ENTREPRENEURSHIP AND BUSINESS SUCCESS IN WEST AFRICA

R. Kouessi
*African Centre for Advanced Management Studies,
Dakar, Senegal*

Introduction

Senegalese schools and universities have recorded some success with programs designed to prepare management personnel for medium- and large-scale enterprises, but they have not done as well with programs for small-business managers and still less in developing new entrepreneurs. This indicates a serious gap in our training programs — small business plays an important role in developing countries, and their governments are always looking for magic solutions from newly created enterprises, especially the jobs and incomes they produce.

In Africa, small-scale enterprises (SSES) represent the class of industrial and commercial business that is most important to job creation and income distribution. In Senegal, large-scale industry accounts for less than 10% of all industries, and the remainder is dominated by small- and medium-scale enterprises (SMES). Admittedly, SSES produce less than 50% of industrial output, but they still generate more than 60% of employment. Furthermore, these data do not fully reflect the value of enterprises in the informal (nonstructured) sector, so we can say that small businesses and small-scale industries are the very engine of the economy.

Senegal has made every effort in the last 10 years to promote the private sector and developing SMES. We have created industrial parks equipped with counselling and training facilities for SMES, a program to improve the business climate, a one-stop window to expedite the process of forming a company, lines of credit to help entrepreneurs finance their start-up, and so on.

Despite these efforts to create a class of dynamic entrepreneurs who can to rise to the challenge of development, we can do more to make private-sector development policies effective. What is missing is a spirit of enterprise among the Senegalese, and, if we can go by US and Canadian experience, we can acquire this spirit through training.

This research will highlight the impact that training programs have on potential entrepreneurs, an area where knowledge is still very sketchy or nonexistent. We will examine cases where entrepreneurs who received training have nevertheless failed to get their business off the ground. We will suggest improvements, such as a system for providing continuing guidance and counselling during start-up and a system of credit suitable for small-enterprise managers.

The purpose of this study is to assess the Program for Enterprise Creation and Small Business Development (Création d'entreprises et développement de la petite entreprise, CEPE), set up by the African Centre for Advanced Management Studies (Centre africain d'études supérieures en gestion, CESAG). The paper will (1) introduce and explain the program; (2) assess how this program has changed the attitudes and behaviour of participants, 9 months after it was launched; and (3) offer some thoughts on the theory and practice of training for entrepreneurs.

Background to the study

Professionals and academics alike are paying more and more attention to entrepreneurship. Universities, training schools, and research centres are developing research and training programs to support economic development programs in Africa. CESAG is part of this movement and has in fact developed some highly original programs for training entrepreneurs. In 1987, the Consultation and Enterprise Creation department in cooperation with institutions in North America — principally the Faculty of Management Sciences at Laval University in Quebec, Canada, and a private US firm, Management Systems International, based in Washington — set up a research program to identify and select entrepreneurs. The objectives of these programs were to (1) develop assessment tools for identifying features characteristic of African entrepreneurs; (2) develop programs and courses on enterprise creation and SME management; and (3) offer training programs to students, as well as to current and potential entrepreneurs.

The assessments we made at the end of each training course showed that all the participants were satisfied. The program has also been very successful in attracting participants and in producing tangible results: enterprises were created; various documents have been published; and a professional association, the Senegalese Association of Enterprise Creators (Association sénégalaise des créateurs d'entreprises, ASCE), was formed. From 1989 to 1993, CESAG managed to train a much-needed number of entrepreneurs in Senegal and across West Africa. So far there have been more than 20 program cycles, involving about 500 entrepreneurs.

Program structure

The general structure of the program is shown in Table 1. The program is spread out in stages over a 5-month period in what virtually amounts to an enterprise incubator.

The seminars take the form of workshops for 20–25 participants, each taking 2 weeks. The main modules of this session are (1) seeking out opportunities and taking the initiative; (2) taking risks; (3) respecting commitments; (4) persisting; (5) striving for efficiency and quality; (6) setting goals; (7) seeking information; (8) planning and systematically following up; (9) using persuasion and building a network of contacts; and (10) developing independence and self-confidence.

The training method is based on case studies, role playing, and the exchange of experiences so that participants can

Table 1. Program structure.

Components	Duration	Interval[a]
Identification, interview, and selection of participants	2 weeks	2 weeks
Developing the spirit of enterprise	2 weeks	2 weeks
Market analysis	1–2 days	1 month
Technical, economic, and financial studies	1–2 days	1 month
Legal and administrative aspects	1–2 days	1 month
Small-business management; personnel and human resources	1–2 days	1 month

[a]The program is given in stages to allow participants to make progress with their projects.

learn what lies behind the success of the best entrepreneurs. Throughout the workshop, the participants have a chance to put these lessons into practice in a controlled environment (set up like a microenterprise), where they can find out what their strong and weak points are and discover whether they have what it takes to succeed in business.

Participants spend 4 or 5 months working under supervision, attending 1-day workshops covering topics that will help them finalize their projects (market, technical, economic, and financial studies, legal and administrative matters, small-business management, and so on). They also receive training and support from the program instructors.

Review of the literature

The economist defines an entrepreneur as someone who combines financial resources, labour, raw materials, and other inputs to give consumers greater value than they had before. The psychologist says that such people are usually motivated by a need to gain or accomplish something, to experiment, to fulfil themself, or even to escape from someone else's control. Vesper (1982) tells us that entrepreneurship is

> The dynamic process by which new wealth is created. Wealth is created by individuals who take the major risks in terms of capital, time or professional commitment, so as to give value to a good or service. However new or exclusive the product itself may be, its value must be instilled in part by the entrepreneur, to the extent he assembles and allocates the necessary abilities and resources.

This view is based on ideas in political economy, such as wealth creation, risk capital, and the value of a good or service. The political economist places the entrepreneur front and centre in economic and social life and in economic policy debates. On all sides, during any widespread economic crisis, we hear it said that salvation will come from business and entrepreneurs. Yet, according to Ronsdadt (1984), "For anyone trying to launch his own business, the experience is one of enthusiasm, frustration, anxiety and hard work: insufficient business, intense competition, lack of capital or credit, etc." Why would anyone volunteer to run such risks? The best way to answer this question is to examine the process by which a person decides to become an entrepreneur.

The CEPE program is urgently in need of assessment, as it is supposed to be a machine for turning out entrepreneurs. We should point out here that some authors criticize traditional business courses that lump together entrepreneurship and small-business management. Can we ponder these types of decisions, systematize them, and instill them in people to make them into entrepreneurs? McClelland (1961) gave a lot of thought to this question, and through his research he identified the desire to succeed as the critical psychological characteristic of the successful entrepreneur. McClelland and his associates developed a training approach called Motivational Training for Success, which attempts to develop and enhance this critical characteristic. His theory was that if people know how to recognize the success motive in their daily life, they will be able to apply it consciously and learn to use it to greater effect in their business. Following McClelland, other authors developed a teaching system for strengthening the character traits of future entrepreneurs. Gasse et al. (1992) arrived at virtually the same conclusion as McClelland in their study of the entrepreneurial potential of Senegalese entrepreneurs.

Ronsdadt (1984), later supported by Hirsch and Candida (1985), determined that entrepreneurship is the process of creating something of value that is unique by taking the necessary financial, psychological, and social risks and being rewarded with money and personal satisfaction. Ronsdadt, like McClelland (1961), insisted that entrepreneurship can and must be taught and that the characteristics of an entrepreneur have to be developed through a proper training program. Starting from this basis, Ronsdadt suggested that entrepreneurship training emphasizes the skills needed to perceive and assess business opportunities. The training should also enhance the entrepreneurs' ability to set goals and should aim to build self-confidence. According to Ronsdadt, programs must be structured, with courses and case studies, and at the same time unstructured, to allow participants to develop a network of acquaintances.

Chusimir (1988) remarked that the framework used in management courses is inappropriate for a program in entrepreneurship. He commented that the Master's of Business Administration (MBA) program is better suited to training managers than producing entrepreneurs, who must have a taste for risks and be able to put up with ambiguity. Sexton and Bowman

(1984) thought that the entrepreneurial traits of the participants should be taken into account when the course material is being designed and teaching methods are being developed. Entrepreneurship courses must rely substantially on practical experience and, in particular, on what has led to the success of the best entrepreneurs. Creativity and innovation, risk taking, and self-confidence are the keys to entrepreneurship. Teaching methods must take these into account.

Studies on the effectiveness of training programs are rather out of date, and research is lacking, especially dealing with entrepreneurship training. Our assessment of the CEPE–CESAG program tries to go beyond the simple, conventional evaluations of training courses, which are limited to measuring the degree of participant satisfaction with the knowledge and skills acquired.

Most authors who have addressed the question have not gone beyond the students' own perceptions of programs and training objectives. Kirkpatrick (1979, 1984), however, in his model for evaluating training programs, suggested four levels of analysis: reactions, learning, behaviour, and results. The first evaluation level (reactions) focuses on how participants reacted to the program and their degree of satisfaction with the course content, the teaching tools used, the length of the program, and so on. The second level (learning) evaluates the degree of retention of information. The third level (behaviour) is of special interest to us because it assesses the effect of the program on participants' behaviour. The fourth level (results) tries to evaluate the impact of the training on the entrepreneurs' results (increased business volume, profits, etc.). In our study, we used the last two analytical levels of Kirkpatrick's model to assess the responses of participants to a questionnaire.

Method

Questionnaire

The CEPE program has three main elements: an introduction to the personal characteristics of successful entrepreneurs; the development of a business plan; and an enterprise start-up project (financing, legal and administrative aspects). These elements were summarized in a questionnaire administered 9 months after the program began. The questionnaire had four sets of questions covering (1) the personal characteristics of entrepreneurs; (2) the business plan; (3) the project; and (4) follow-up and program continuity.

The first series of questions sought to identify which entrepreneurial characteristics the participants realized they would have to strengthen to become entrepreneurs and the behavioural changes that resulted when the entrepreneurial characteristics were applied and translated into new enterprises or new activities in existing enterprises.

The second part of the questionnaire was designed to discover whether the participant was sufficiently motivated to draw up a business plan during the course and finalize it afterwards.

The third part assessed the development of the participant's project after the course ended and gauged the program's impact on the fate of this project. It asked such questions as, What stage was your project at during the training program? What stage is it at now (on 30 June 1990, when the data were collected)? How has the workshop helped with the progress of your project? Other questions dealt with obstacles or problems the participants faced in carrying out their projects.

The final series of questions assessed complementary courses on managing the start-up of an SME, taken after the basic entrepreneurship module, and sought participants' opinions on the kinds of support and counselling they needed for their projects at this stage. The questionnaire helped us discover what financial contribution the participants themselves might make toward the continuation of the program, which the United States Agency for International Development (USAID) and the Canadian International Development Agency (CIDA) now subsidize.

Sample selection and data collection

The questionnaire was given in June 1990 to 65 entrepreneurs or prospective entrepreneurs from the first three cycles of the program, who were invited for a day of reflection and discussion about the CESAG experiment. The 31 questionnaires that were completed and returned by the participants who actually took part in the discussion day represented 50% of the total survey population and are sufficiently representative of the whole population for this kind of survey.

The data were collected by three of our course instructors. After filling out the questionnaire, participants in the discussion day were divided into three workshop groups with the
following themes: (1) a diagnostic assessment of the entrepreneurship training offered by CESAG; (2) supervisory and training
help for the promoters finalizing their business plans and
launching their projects; and (3) the institutional environment
and the emergence of small businesses.

After wide-ranging and productive discussions in the
plenary session, it was apparent that participants appreciated
this research and evaluation exercise. We feel confident that the
data we collected are reliable.

Results

The purpose of this survey was to measure the impact of the
course on the behaviour of the participants 9 months after the
launch of the program. According to the survey, 35% of those
interviewed took the workshop in October 1989, and 52% took
the one in February 1990. Only three people in the sample, or
10%, participated in the April 1990 program. The low representation from this last cycle reflects the fact that that particular
group consisted of doctors and dentists, who received funding
immediately after the training course from an SME assistance
program. Most of them were unable to accept the invitation to
take part in the discussion day because they had already taken
up duties in various towns in the interior.

Enterprise creation and behaviour changes

The study results show that 12 out of the 31 people interviewed
in our sample, or 39%, reported that they had created an enterprise after the workshop, and 7 people, or 23%, had developed
new activities for their already established businesses. When
asked how much time had elapsed between the end of the workshop and the launch of the enterprise, 77% did not reply, indicating that entrepreneurs have trouble determining exactly
when their enterprise is launched — the take-off period is
usually rather long. Nevertheless, 16% replied that launching
their business took 1–3 months; 3% launched their enterprise
within 1 month after the workshop; and 3% did not do so until
after 6 months. The average for this variable, ignoring the

nonresponses, was 2 months and 14 days, or 64 days, which suggests that participants moved quickly to transform their dream into reality. This figure, however, is probably biased by the very high rate of nonresponses (77%).

As Tables 2 and 3 show, participants generally said that their behaviour did change (97%) and that friends and family members remarked on this change (77% of responses). These research results confirm our basic theory. Participants unanimously (with 6% nonresponse) agreed that the CEPE program had been of great use to them and had helped them discover the characteristics and behaviour that make an entrepreneur (65%) and the ways and means of strengthening these in their own case (68%).

Sixty-eight percent of respondents found no areas that had been missed or insufficiently developed in the workshop. One participant in four gave no opinion (26% nonresponse) on this point. They thus implicitly agreed that the overall teaching goals of the program were achieved.

Table 2. Responses to the question: After the workshop, would you say that your behaviour changed?

	Number of responses	Frequency (%)
No response	0	0
Yes	30	97
No	1	3
Total	31	100

Table 3. Responses to the question: Did family and friends remark on the changes in your behaviour?

	Number of responses	Frequency (%)
No response	8	26
Spouse	9	29
Family member	13	26
Business acquaintances	17	42
Friends	2	55
Fellow workers	1	6
Domestics	1	3
Associates	1	3
Total	52[a]	

[a]The total number of responses (52) exceeds the number of respondents (31) because respondents could give multiple responses (5 maximum).

Before enroling in the program (application, preliminary screening, interview, final selection) and during the workshop, the most cited entrepreneurial characteristics and behavioural traits that respondents felt the need to strengthen were using persuasion and building networks of contacts (55% of responses), planning and carrying through (48%), taking risks (42%), and persisting (39%) (Table 4).

After the workshop, the most cited entrepreneurial characteristics and behavioural traits that respondents felt the workshop had strengthened in them were seeking opportunities and taking initiative (52% of responses), persisting (48%), using persuasion and building a network of contacts (48%), and seeking information (42%).

The participants learned (and remembered) that any business begins with the identification of a commercial opportunity, and to seize it demands initiative, talent, energy, and creativity. They gave up trying to go it alone, and they pooled their efforts with other entrepreneurs and worked together on the enterprise projects. Contact networks, persuasiveness, and the need for resolve and perseverance to achieve results — all these were clearly appreciated, thanks to the program method and the exercises included in the workbook. On the other hand, some participants felt they had failed to strengthen some entrepreneurial characteristics, either because of a lack of opportunity (39%) or because of a lack of effective means (19%).

Table 4. Responses to the question: What are the personal characteristics of entrepreneurs that you felt needed strengthening before or during the workshop?

	Number of responses	Frequency (%)
No response	0	0
Seeking opportunities	10	32
Persisting	12	39
Taking risks	13	42
Demanding efficiency and quality	8	26
Keeping commitments	6	19
Setting goals	9	29
Seeking out information	15	48
Planning and systematically following up	17	55
Having self-confidence	5	16
Total	95[a]	

[a]The total number of responses (95) exceeds the number of respondents (31) because respondents could give multiple responses (5 maximum).

To keep the spirit of entrepreneurship alive among the participants after the course, the program ends with a personal contract — the participant promises to work at strengthening at least three personal characteristics and behavioural traits of entrepreneurs and describes the steps planned to meet this commitment.

According to the survey, 29% of respondents felt that they lived up to their personal contract entirely; 42%, moderately; 19%, barely; and 6%, not at all. Respondents gave various reasons for not living up to the terms of their contract: lack of time (32%), inappropriate contract (3%), or lack of financial means (3%).

The business plan (feasibility study)

Preparing a business plan, often called a feasibility study or project plan, is far from being a futile exercise. Whatever one may think of it, its main purpose is to outline the course that the planned business should take during its first 3–5 years. An entrepreneur who is going to invest much or all of his resources is surely eager to know in advance whether the project is likely to achieve its objectives. Mistakes that are caught when a business plan is being prepared will be less costly and painful than if they are not discovered until the project is under way.

Nineteen percent of respondents cited planning and systematic follow-up and 29% cited taking risks as weak points in their entrepreneurial characteristics and behaviourial traits. To help strengthen these, the CEPE program included exercises on business-plan development throughout the entrepreneurship workshop. Under the supervision of their instructors, participants drew up a business plan for their microenterprise (52%) or actual business project (35%). After the training, 65% of respondents continued to work on the business plan started during the workshop, and 29% started fresh with a new business plan for a different project concept. The feasibility study designed for the CEPE program proved useful, as 6 participants out of 10 followed this as a model for their business plan.

Our instructors were deluged with requests for advice and assistance of all kinds after the initial workshop and during the in-depth sessions, which leads one to think that the program achieved its purpose in introducing the business-plan notion and having the participants take part in developing their own plan. However, some participants gave up on the exercise, because they could see no chance of getting financing for their projects. Nevertheless, the business plan has an important role as a guide for the entrepreneur, even before it becomes part of a request for credit. The search for financing for a new enterprise is a long process, and entrepreneurs must always have a project plan ready to submit to a banker or potential partner. Bankers and investors are constantly on the lookout for bankable ideas and feasible projects.

From planning to launching the enterprise

Of course, there's more to becoming an entrepreneur than attending a workshop, changing behaviour, and developing a business plan. There will be many hurdles to clear before an entrepreneur can actually get a project off the ground. CEPE also had an impact on this aspect of participants' projects.

According to the survey, 32% of respondents' projects were at the concept stage during the workshop (Table 5). After the workshop, this proportion fell to 19% (Table 6). During the workshop, 39% of participants were seeking financing and 3% were in the start-up phase (Table 5). After the workshop, about

Table 5. Responses to the question: At what stage was your project at the time of the workshop?

	Number of responses	Frequency (%)
No response	0	0
Project is a concept	10	32
Project is being planned	8	26
Financing is being sought	12	39
Project is ready for start-up	1	3
Total	31	100

Table 6. Responses to the question: What stage is your project at now?

	Number of responses	Frequency (%)
No response	1	3
Project is a concept	6	19
Project is being planned	3	10
Financing is being sought	9	29
Project is ready for start-up	8	25
Project is under way	4	13
Total	31	100

40% had launched their own business (25% were in the start-up phase, and 13% had their projects already under way) (Table 6). According to the survey, as Table 7 shows, 45% of respondents saw the seminar as having advanced their project, in part by helping them assess and recognize their own strengths and weaknesses but mainly by helping them in the practical aspects of getting started. Thus, 32% felt that, thanks to the program, they could now set clear and specific goals, and 17% related the progress they had made to the business plan they had developed.

Participants who already had a business before enroling in the program said that the program improved the way they treated employees, customers, and suppliers (26% of responses) and that they had made progress in their planning (19%) and their organizational and control (23%) methods.

Yet besides the one significant gap — lack of entrepreneurial spirit — which the CEPE program is trying to fill, there are other equally important obstacles to the success of entrepreneurial projects.

A poor environment for enterprise creation

The socioeconomic environment in Senegal has undergone profound changes in recent years, and the employment situation reflects these changes. The public authorities have adopted a new policy for putting young school graduates to work by steering them toward nonsalaried jobs. This already disruptive situation is exacerbated by the government's own problems, as it is trying to reestablish macroeconomic stability and respond to pressure from development agencies to reduce the size of the public service. The government has instituted a policy of inducing state employees to take "voluntary departure" and early retirement and to become entrepreneurs.

Table 7. Responses to the question: How did the workshop help advance your project?

	Number of responses	Frequency (%)
No response	2	6
Planning	5	17
Setting goals	10	32
Putting capital to work	14	45
Total	31	100

Problems persist, despite the government's attempts to create a favourable environment for the birth of SMEs (upgrading skills, creating a job placement office, directing some NGOs to finance individual or group projects, creating the one-stop window, and so on). Participants who met during the discussion-day workshops found the state's incentives too theoretical. For example, the participants noted the inefficient management in some support programs for SSEs, which led to administrative delays in approving projects. These administrative delays mean higher costs, because of inflation. According to the final report of the workshop on the institutional environment, "administrative formalities are too slow and cumbersome as far as notary fees and access to the one-stop window are concerned." The eligibility conditions are sometimes inappropriate and inconsistent, and access to credit is difficult.

There is little information on the taxation of new businesses. The participants recommended that the state develop a comprehensive communication and information policy for entrepreneurs and that it amend legal provisions to bring them up to date. Fifty-two percent of respondents cited bureaucratic delays as a major obstacle to carrying out their project.

If these obstacles are not overcome and the CEPE program does not manage to develop an institutional link with the banks and other funding bodies and the assistance programs for SMEs, new businesses will not become a reality. Forty-five percent of respondents mentioned trying to get access to credit as a difficult step in the process of enterprise creation. Generally, a promoter does not have personal wealth and cannot offer a bank guarantee. This situation, combined with lack of business experience, means that the would-be entrepreneur is disqualified from financing for a project. Some promoters were faced with problems in finalizing their business plan (29% of responses) and reaching partnership agreements with foreign firms (19% of responses). It was pleasing to note that for lines of credit at certain banks, the finance analysts were increasingly prepared to put more weight on the project's profitability than on guarantees.

Follow-up — individual and group counselling

When we asked participants their opinion of the in-depth modules on SME management, 61% answered that the ideas for market studies and marketing were very useful. Some participants found the financial aspects and the profitability studies of projects fairly useful (16%) or very useful (48%), and the majority found the principles of human-resource management for SMEs very useful (55%).

The entrepreneurial process is a long one, and the basic module of the entrepreneurship program is not enough by itself to transform an aspiring entrepreneur's dream into reality. This is why we introduced the complementary modules on SME management in the program and reinforced these with individual and group counseling for promoters. What this amounts to is a complete program for guiding the entrepreneur toward the creation of an enterprise.

Generally, participants responded very positively to the continuing support program (55% of respondents were very satisfied and 18% were satisfied). At the same time, they deplored the lack of information about program content and dates for the in-depth sessions (some participants received no invitations to these sessions or received them late), and the participants felt that they needed more time to study and develop many of the topics. This helps to explain the small number of participants (35%) who came back to CESAG after the workshop. Each participant had agreed to stay in touch with one or two other participants after the basic training workshop and to keep the instructors informed about their progress. If participants had kept this commitment, there would have not been a communication problem.

Participants recommended (1) making the topics for the in-depth sessions more practical and less theoretical, like the basic workshop; (2) handing out supporting material for the courses; (3) ensuring regular follow-up of promoters and providing some concrete and specific supervision for each group of promoters when they were developing and finalizing their business plans; (4) setting a deadline for finishing the business plan and setting up an effective follow-up system; (5) providing help finding financing and partners; (6) arranging for regular meetings with specialists on each topic; and (7) computerizing the program.

These recommendations entail a whole set of complementary programs. We agree that they are necessary for supporting the creation of enterprise, but they would be costly.

Program financing and continuity

The CEPE program was set up with the support of CIDA, which helps select and develop training modules, and USAID, which pays for the training program and finances training bursaries for participants.

Participants cannot be expected to pay the true cost of the program, which is estimated at 300 000 XOF (in 1994, 570 CFA francs [XOF] = 1 United States dollar [USD]) for each participant. Because of the contribution of CESAG, participants pay only the modest sum of 25 000 XOF. This means in effect that if funding bodies stop giving priority to private-sector promotion and small-business development, the program is going to lack resources for its operations.

It is from this perspective that we envisage having to set a fee for program participants. When asked to estimate what it would cost to take this type of training, participants replied that the price might be between 25 000 and 50 000 XOF (32%), between 50 000 and 100 000 XOF (10%), or between 100 000 and 200 000 XOF (19%).

Most of the participants were willing to pay up to 50 000 XOF, or one sixth of the actual cost. This suggests that the program is going to have to be supported by governments and development agencies if it is to continue to draw its participants from the ranks of unemployed school graduates, laid-off public servants, and others who have little money.

Because of the program's valuable objectives and the value participants claim to have derived from it, the appropriate thing might be to organize a proper publicity campaign about the program and its accomplishments to generate increased demand for it from institutions (governments, NGOs, and development partners, in general) and to attract other participants, such as solvent business operators who want to assess their entrepreneurial skills and enhance their own prospects. The impact of the program, then, would be felt more in the growth of established businesses than in the creation of new enterprises. The program could easily be turned into a course on personal effectiveness for business managers. The present make-up of the target group (current entrepreneurs in the start-up phase and would-be creators of an enterprise) seems to be a good formula because the program creates a kind of multiplier effect, with current entrepreneurs serving as models for others. If for financial reasons we had to eliminate the aspiring entrepreneurs as a subgroup, the program would lose something of its essence. The people in charge would have to be rigorous at the selection stage and keep testing ever higher fees to approach or reach the break-even point.

Conclusion

The program is intended to sensitize Senegalese people to the importance of entrepreneurship in meeting the new challenges of development; to support creators of enterprise as they develop their business plans and seek financing; and to help these entrepreneurs so that they don't have to "go it alone." Ninety-seven percent (or 30) of the respondents felt that the program sensitized them and changed behaviour, and most of them felt that their family members, colleagues, associates, and friends had noted this effect.

The CEPE program has actually encouraged the emergence of entrepreneurs. In the first 9 months after the course began, 39% created their own enterprise, and four of these enterprises were already up and running; 23% of respondents developed new activities in their established businesses. Among the remaining participants, 25% were at the start-up stage and another 29% were seeking financing, which shows the remarkable impact of the program. The program puts its main emphasis on skills needed to discover business opportunities and to assess their feasibility (business plan) and on the need for the promoter to follow through. But preparing a business plan is not enough. An entrepreneur also has to be able to mobilize resources and find start-up funding if his or her dream is to become reality.

These results have both practical and theoretical implications. At the practical level, they allow us to assess development policies for the SME sector in Senegal. At the theoretical level, the results represent a contribution to our understanding of the factors that make some entrepreneurs models of performance and efficiency. In particular, the results tend to confirm that the psychological element is a basic determinant for becoming an entrepreneur. Environmental factors and the lack or inadequacy of financial resources are real enough, but they can be circumvented by true entrepreneurs. Nevertheless, the state must improve the business environment.

The purpose of our research was to assess experience with the CESAG program for enterprise creation and the growth of small business, and the reader should thus keep in mind a few considerations qualifying our conclusions. The study was conducted 9 months after the program started. If the interval had been longer, more enterprises would have been created and the results more reliable. But because the program is spread out over 5 months, it seemed advisable to use the data at hand. If the questionnaire had covered such variables as age, sex, level of education, and type of project, it might have helped us clarify the findings and steer us toward a look at enterprise creation according to sector of activity or basic education level of the entrepreneurs and so on. Also, this was the first study of its kind in the Senegalese economic environment, and there are no points of reference with which to judge the value of the results.

Finally, the data were taken entirely from the participants' own perceptions of the impact of the program on their projects. This is common practice for this type of study, but it means that the validity of our results depends in part on the mood of the respondents at the time of the survey. The results need to be expanded, perhaps through full-scale studies 5 years after entrepreneurs complete the program to determine how many launch their own businesses, how many jobs are created, what the level of earnings is — in short, the impact of the program on the Senegalese economy. ✶

EFFECTIVE DEVELOPMENT OF A NATIONAL APEX INSTITUTION: THE CASE OF THE MALAWIAN ENTREPRENEURS DEVELOPMENT INSTITUTE

Mark Havers
Overseas Development Group, Durham University Business School, Durham City, UK

Sosten M.C. Nyoni
Malawian Entrepreneurs Development Institute, Mponela, Malawi

Introduction

The development of institutions that have a key role in the promotion of small-scale enterprises (SSES) is important for donor-funded projects that promote SSES. The creation of effective domestic institutions to support business development on a sustained basis without the continuing input of expatriate managers is vital for the future of African and other developing countries. Anecdote and experience suggest that an appropriately designed project for developing an institution has a good chance of achieving this aim. Furthermore, this is more effective than other interventions, such as piecemeal overseas training.

A common mechanism for developing an institution is a partnership between that institution and a similar one (often from the donor's country in the case of a project supported through bilateral funds). This relationship could take a number of forms, such as a series of short-term consultancies or a long-term, continuous and comprehensive arrangement, which is referred to as a "twinning" partnership.

This paper describes a twinning project that both parties consider successful so far. The paper focuses on the concept of the relationship and the process by which it was established and is being developed, rather than on its content. It looks at the institutional framework for the project, the control and management of the project, and its likely future. The authors believe that these are the most significant factors in the project's success and will be of interest to those undertaking similar projects in Africa or elsewhere, and not just in the area of SSE development.

The Malawian context

Economic and social

Lying close to the bottom of the global rankings (see Table 1 for comparisons) of both gross national product (GNP) per capita and human development index, Malawi's economy is based largely on agriculture, which provides the main source of income and employment for about 90% of the population. However, with annual population growth estimated at more than 3%, there is increasing pressure on the country's land; there has been a drop in average landholding from 1.6 ha to 1.1 ha in just a decade, and 30% of the people now cultivate less than 0.5 ha each. Taken together, these factors have meant that there is a grave need to increase the employment opportunities available to the 100 000 or more people who enter the labour market every year without a realistic prospect of finding work. The Malawi government has responded to this problem in many ways; one of these is offering entrepreneurship development programs under the Malawian Entrepreneurs Development Institute (MEDI).

Table 1. Comparison of Malawi with some neighbouring countries.

Country	GNP per capita, 1990 (USD)	Human development index
Malawi	200	0.166
Tanzania	110	0.268
Zambia	420	0.315
Zimbabwe	640	0.397

Source: World Bank (1992), UNDP (1992).

Small enterprise

Daniels and Ngwira (1993) recently estimated that in Malawi there are approximately 570 000 micro- , small- , and medium-scale enterprises (MSMEs), employing more than 1 million people. The average Malawian MSME employs 1.8 workers, including the proprietor. However, more than 60% of the enterprises have just one worker, and 975 have one to three. One-fifth of the population older than 15 is engaged in the MSME sector, and 90% of MSMEs are located in rural areas.

In terms of industrial structure, the Malawian MSME sector consists mainly of trade (52%) (97% of the traders are retailers) and manufacturing (43%). Daniels and Ngwira (1993) commented that the predominance of trade in Malawi is striking, compared with other countries in the region, where manufacturing is typically the dominant sector.

The most frequently reported constraints on MSMEs in Malawi are input problems; marketing and working capital are also frequently cited. The amount of training and assistance proprietors receive is low throughout Malawi: 92% of all proprietors have never received training in areas such as management, bookkeeping, or marketing; only 6% have received assistance during operation from a government or donor organization.

The partners

The Malawian Entrepreneurs Development Institute

In the late 1970s, the Malawi government set up the Vocational Training Institute (VTI) to train disadvantaged groups in the technical skills needed to secure employment. However, it still proved difficult for the institution's graduates to obtain employment, and so it was decided to reorient the program to provide training for self-employment rather than employment — "to develop job-makers rather than job-seekers."

Thus, in 1985, VTI became MEDI, with the key emphasis still on artisanal-skills training but with a new entrepreneurship component.

Time and experience showed that this change was insufficient and that the whole emphasis of the institution needed to move from technical-skills training with an entrepreneurship component to entrepreneurship training with technical elements; so in 1989 a substantial United Nations Development Programme (UNDP) and International Labour Office (ILO) project (No. MLW/88/022) was put in place. This project, entitled Strengthening of the Malawian Entrepreneurs Development Institute, had a number of components, including new equipment and buildings; technical assistance from a chief technical adviser and UN volunteers; and overseas training for key MEDI staff. However, the most significant component — indeed, the central strategy of the project — was to be a twinning partnership with one or more overseas institutions with capability in the field of small-enterprise development. Following a selection process, which is described below, Durham University Business School (DUBS) became MEDI's only partner.

MEDI's main aim is to create employment opportunities by developing self-employed entrepreneurs and those who will become the employers of others. Only those candidates who show some entrepreneurial qualities are invited to join one of MEDI's programs to increase the likelihood of the graduate's creating a business.

MEDI's target groups are the following:

- *Women* — Women participate in special programs that take into account the particular constraints of their family responsibilities and commitments.

- *Those who already have technical skills* — Those who already have technical skills receive training in entrepreneurship development leading to sustainable SSEs.

- *Established entrepreneurs, either self-employed or running small enterprises* — Established entrepreneurs receive training to allow them to expand their activities and (or) make their businesses more sustainable.

- *Technical instructors and field operators* — Technical instructors and field operators benefit from the trainers' programs, which help them introduce entrepreneurship into their own activities so they may help develop an enterprise culture in Malawi.

MEDI provides a series of entrepreneurship development programs with technical components covering production, construction, and service management and planning and with workshop practice sessions and industry assignments. Participants in these programs can choose their own business ideas, and MEDI responds with the most appropriate program, including training in the choice and use of technology, processes, tools, and equipment. MEDI focuses on broad industrial groupings, and through programs of market research it identifies nontraditional business ideas with potential.

Durham University Business School

DUBS, founded in 1965, offers a variety of MBA and executive-level education and training programs in business and management. However, about half of the school's activities are in the Small Business Centre (SBC), Europe's largest and oldest institute for the study of enterprise, entrepreneurship, and small-business development.

SBC is totally self-funding, which is unusual for a British university institute, and operates as a federation of small businesses with a central mission, or set of objectives.

> The mission of the Small Business Centre is to be a leader in the understanding and development of enterprise, entrepreneurship, and small and medium business, through research, innovation, and dissemination of relevant knowledge, models, and approaches.

It was with SBC that MEDI established its twinning relationship. DUBS was a suitable partner for MEDI because of the following factors:

- its comprehensive coverage and experience in all issues relating to enterprise, entrepreneurship, and small-business development;

- the businesslike way DUBS organizes itself into a group of small businesses, each responsible for its own performance and each covering a specific area, such as business development, enterprise and industry education, or network development;

- DUBS's considerable experience in Africa and other parts of the developing world, reflected in the fact that one of its small businesses is the Overseas Development Group (which now manages the twinning partnership with MEDI, as well as SBC's other activities in developing countries);

- DUBS's commitment to the continuous development of new products and programs through a cycle of research,

innovation, testing, and dissemination; and last, but by
no means least,

• DUBS's family-like and informal way of doing things.

The key success factors

The key success factors in the twinning of MEDI and DUBS derive
primarily from the partnership's initiation and implementation.
These success factors should be of interest to other institutions
considering embarking on or supporting a similar arrangement.

MEDI's legal status

Evidence from the literature on enterprise development (such as
Gibb and Manu 1989; Stearns and Otero 1990) suggests that an
enterprise development agency may be effective if it is as much
as possible like the enterprises it is seeking to serve; that is, it
should be entrepreneurial rather than bureaucratic; dynamic
rather than static; invulnerable to political or government interference; and, above all, independent.

VTI was first established as a department under the Ministry of Labour in Malawi. It kept this status when it became
MEDI in 1985. However, in April 1990, its status changed, and it
is considered very significant that the project as a whole and the
twinning in particular took place in the context of MEDI's changing its legal status from that of government department to a
nominally autonomous trust. Mainly as a result of its continuing need for subvention by government and donors, the trust is
still officially under the Ministry of Labour (which has employment creation within its mandate), but the idea and goal of real
independence have a vital impact on the organization's culture
and attitudes.

The twinning gave support to and was supported by the
change in legal status; particularly, the change of status neces-
sitated and facilitated the transformation from a bureaucratic to
an entrepreneurial organization. As MEDI makes further progress
toward financial self-sufficiency and as the government feels
able to give it more freedom, the organization will begin to
show the beneficial effects of its independence.

The ownership and nature of the twinning of MEDI and DUBS

There was minimal external involvement either by the donor or the Malawi government in setting up the twinning arrangement, in sharp contrast to normal international practice. A team of senior MEDI staff visited a number of relevant institutions in both Europe and Asia and chose a partner institution, which they then invited to Malawi to plan the detailed activities under the partnership and to negotiate an agreement. Of course, an important contribution was made by ILO's technical advisor, and approval was sought from UNDP and the Malawi government, but ownership of the whole agreement was firmly in the hands of MEDI and DUBS.

Equally important was the nature of the relationship they developed. The word *twinning*, which is used to describe this relationship, was very carefully chosen to reflect what was really happening. This was to be no mere collaboration or link but a twinning that would bind the two organizations together in a variety of ways. For example, this twinning does not just involve a few elite individuals from each institution but many of DUBS's and all of MEDI's teaching and other professional staff. Nor is the relationship confined to work and professional matters; great emphasis has been placed on building personal contacts between the two institutions around a variety of social and cultural activities. As one staff member said, "We care both professionally and personally for each other."

The wide-ranging nature of the twinning arrangement

The partnership covers all aspects of MEDI. The partnership does not concern itself narrowly with particular programs or activities but looks much more broadly at the full range of the organization's needs. Thus, its coverage includes such diverse areas as

- selection processes;
- teaching styles;
- curriculum and materials development;
- internal organization; and
- the ways MEDI markets itself.

Table 2 outlines some examples of activities under the twinning.

Table 2. Examples of activities under the twinning.

Number of programs	Activity	Duration	Objective
3	Teaching and Learning Styles Workshop	2 weeks	To further develop the teaching abilities of all MEDI teaching staff and enable them to identify and apply appropriate teaching and learning techniques to different types of learners
5	Supervised materials development at DUBS	10 weeks	To research and develop in finished form a new set of core materials for use at MEDI
7	Study of income generation for MEDI	2 weeks	To identify income generation mechanisms appropriate to MEDI and recommend ways to introduce them

There is an underlying view that the projects and the twinning have to involve all aspects of MEDI. Otherwise, strengthening one part would just serve to expose the weaknesses of the others, without doing anything to correct them. In addition, the flexible nature of the twinning (see below) allows the organizations to formulate other interventions where needed.

Control of the twinning arrangement

Many development projects (in particular, those with a foreign partner) use expatriate staff (generally, from the foreign institution) in ostensibly advisory positions on a full-time basis at the domestic institution. The most common result is that these employees take on an increasing number of responsibilities at the institution during their time there, leaving a vacuum when the time comes for them to leave.

Under the UNDP project, an ILO chief technical adviser (not from DUBS) was attached to MEDI. He was there in the early part of the twinning partnership, but his input to the organization decreased over time so that his departure coincided with the twinning's moving into full swing. There have been no DUBS staff actually resident at MEDI at any time during the twinning partnership. This has reinforced MEDI's ownership and control of the scheme.

Thus, although a wide range of staff from each institution have moved in both directions, MEDI has at all times retained full control (and its agents felt that they were maintaining that control) of their own organization and activities. As a result, MEDI not only has been able to take on a role more than equal to that of DUBS in determining the direction of the twinning but should suffer no particular shock from the sudden loss of DUBS as a management resource when the project is complete.

Equally significant is the leap of faith taken by the donor institution and the Malawi government. By giving MEDI both the responsibility and the power to control its own destiny, the government and the donor created genuine opportunities for development of the most meaningful kind. MEDI has responded to the trust the government and DUBS have shown and made major progress toward an independent future.

Achievements and flexibility under the twinning

When representatives from DUBS first visited MEDI, detailed plans were made for a series of movements of staff between MEDI and DUBS. The purpose of each movement was to complete a very clearly defined activity with a very clearly defined objective designed to increase the capability of MEDI, according to the overall plan. This approach has ensured a steady progression of achievements under the agreement, which have both stood as valid in their own right and built on each other in a powerful, cumulative way.

There has been visible progress under the twinning, and this has been important in maintaining commitment to and enthusiasm for the partnership on both sides. However, the need for a clear plan has not obviated the need for flexibility to address issues that have only become apparent along the way. At the start of the twinning, not all the monies available were allocated to specific activities: some were held back. This proved to be an extremely wise move — at the midpoint of the twinning project, MEDI was able to specify a short list of supplementary activities it wished to undertake to address needs that had become apparent as the twinning progressed.

Top-level commitment within the institutions

At all levels in both organizations, but particularly at the top, there has been commitment to and involvement in the twinning. Right from the start, the directors of both institutions have shown a considerable personal interest in and commitment to the partnership, and this has been reflected in all the partnership's activities. This commitment has filtered down to the managers and staff, and their enthusiasm has helped to strengthen the partnership at the operational level.

Lessons from a successful twinning

The lessons of this successful partnership are clear and have implications for the use of change agents in policy implementation and development elsewhere.

The nature of the process is all important and must be underpinned by an appropriate organizational structure and status; it must give the institutions control of the change they are undergoing, and that change must be all-embracing but at the same time tightly focused; it must be based on a program encompassing a range of activities to achieve well-defined goals; and it must be led from the front.

The dynamic, changing needs of the SME sector must guide the partnership; it should not be rigidly pushed along by external interventions designed to meet needs perceived at the time of the initial agreement. The external imposition of piecemeal change, with lukewarm internal support in an inappropriate organizational structure, is bound to fail, regardless of how right its programmatic prescriptions may be. ✿

INCREASING SMALL-ENTERPRISE COMPETITIVENESS IN EXPORT MARKETS THROUGH CONSORTIUM MARKETING: AN EXPLORATORY STUDY

J.T. Muzamani
*Faculty of Commerce, University of Zimbabwe,
Harare, Zimbabwe*

Introduction

In some developed countries, small enterprises have used export consortia in their export entry and expansion strategies. The main reason small enterprises form export consortia has been to increase their competitiveness on the international market. However, the success rate of most consortia has been dismal.

In this article we derive success factors for export groups from international marketing literature. We test these success factors on the horticultural industry in Zimbabwe to see whether grouping for export can increase international marketing competitiveness for small growers. We then discuss the benefits of consortium marketing as a vehicle for grouping for export.

The literature on consortium export marketing

International marketing literature has tended to use the terms "grouping for export" and "consortium marketing" interchangeably. However, in this paper we define *grouping for export* as any form of collective exporting that might be achieved through one of the following mechanisms:

- the export of products by several firms through one large company that has the resources to form an export organization;

- the use of an intermediary or a merchant to group a number of exporters; or
- the formation of an export organization owned by several exporters.

An export organization owned by several exporters is how we define *consortium.*

Consortium exporting occurs, therefore, when a number of firms in a given industry cooperate in exporting or form an association to penetrate the export market. The main difference between a consortium and other export groups is that a consortium is owned by all the exporters using it. The literature has looked at four aspects of consortium marketing: stimuli, benefits, role, and problems.

Research has shown that the main stimulus to forming a consortium is the realization that a firm cannot enter the international market on its own. This might be because entry would be too costly or too risky.

In a Norwegian study, Welch and Joynt (1984) found that an external change agent, unconnected with the firms in the consortium, is an important stimulus in consortium marketing. The external change agent, for example, can identify the potential for group exports.

Welch and Joynt (1987) summarized some of the important benefits that firms can derive from consortium marketing (see Table 1).

Many problems can arise in consortium exporting, however. The OECD (1964), for example, showed that export consortia had a very low success rate.

Savitt (1977) pointed out several potential problems: an unwilligness to share information on the part of firms that

Table 1. Benefits of consortium marketing.

Consortium marketing has the following benefits:
- It makes the group more visible in the marketplace
- It makes the group more attractive to potential foreign agents and distributors
- It makes the group more interesting to domestic support organizations
- It mobilizes the disparate export-relevant skills of the group members
- It produces economies through the joint use of export facilities at home and abroad
- It spreads the risks and costs of exporting
- It combines the resources of the group to support the export operations

Source: Welch and Joynt (1987, p. 58).

might be competing domestically; concerns about patents and copyrights; discrepancies because the firms are different sizes; and loss of market share when the product offering of the firms changes.

However, a statement by Welch and Joynt (1987, p. 58) summarizes the need for consortium marketing, even though there might be operational problems:

> Nevertheless, export grouping does represent a feasible means of overcoming the resource deficiencies and risk concerns often expressed about the exporting step: by combining with other small firms it is possible to create a more powerful export entry vehicle, capable of mounting a stronger foreign market entry effort.

The horticultural industry in Zimbabwe

One of the most important nontraditional success stories in the export drive in Zimbabwe has been the horticultural industry. By 1991, 1% of all the flowers sold in Europe were of Zimbabwean origin. With exports of 15.8 million USD, Zimbabwe was the sixth largest exporter of floriculture products into Europe.

In 1993 the industry expected to export $300 million ZWD worth of horticultural products (in 1994, 8.06 Zimbabwe dollars [ZWD] = 1 United States dollar [USD]). This has made the horticultural industry the second largest agricultural exporter in the country after the tobacco industry.

The horticultural products can be divided into those that are targeted toward the domestic market and those that are targeted toward the export market:

Export market	Local market
Fine vegetables	Vegetables
Citrus fruit	Deciduous fruit
Passion fruit	Subtropicals
Subtropicals	Bananas
Mangoes	Pineapples
Cut flowers	Grapes
Fresh herbs	Table
Essential oils	Wine
Tree nuts	Mushrooms
	Tree nuts

There are several important differences between horticultural products that are produced for the local market and those that are produced for the export market:

- Produce in demand locally is usually not in demand for the export markets.
- Generally, produce sold in the local market is grown by organizations that are not major exporters.
- Most of the produce destined for the export market is grown deliberately for that market by exporting firms.
- The produce that is exported is of a much higher quality than produce that is sold locally.

Problems faced by exporters

To understand what stimulates grouping for export within the horticultural industry in Zimbabwe, we must first look at the problems facing exporters of horticultural products.

- There is stiff competition on the international market, and Zimbabwean firms have been at a disadvantage because they lack export experience — Zimbabwe did not begin full-scale exporting until the mid-1980s, and most of the growers are new to the industry.
- Zimbabwe is farther from export markets than most other exporting countries, so its freight costs are higher. In addition, freight space is not guaranteed, given the shortage of south-bound freight carriers.
- The exporting of horticultural products is highly complex because high-quality but perishable products require excellent freight-handling facilities and packaging.
- Foreign markets want large consignments and a complete product offering.

Because of these problems, firms participating in the horticultural industry in the early 1980s found themselves highly uncompetitive. They had a reputation as desultory suppliers of mixed-quality produce in poor packaging. Delivery was unreliable.

The Horticultural Promotion Council

The Horticultural Promotion Council (HPC) was formed to create an enabling environment for those growing and exporting horticultural produce. The organization represents the interests of growers and exporters of flowers, vegetables, fruit, herbs, essential oils, spices, and tree nuts.

The HPC works to increase the competitiveness of horticultural exporters. It does this in the following ways:

- The HPC acts as the mouthpiece of the horticultural industry. The HPC is, therefore, the link between the industry and the government, various embassies, and aid organizations.

- The HPC organizes freight space. Before the formation of the HPC, booking of freight space was haphazard. Speculative booking by some growers complicated matters. The HPC's role is to try to ensure that adequate freight space and export facilities are available to the growers.

- The HPC helps its members to obtain foreign currency by negotiating for foreign currency facilities and making sure that funds from the export retention scheme are available to producers.

- The HPC provides producers with technical data. The HPC has provided data from the studies of the effects of biological controls and pesticides on the ecology of major pests and on the growing of horticultural produce in Zimbabwe.

- The HPC organizes and participates in horticultural exhibitions.

- The HPC provides statistical data to the Reserve Bank and other interested parties.

The exporting of horticultural products

The handling and freighting of flowers are two aspects that are well developed in Zimbabwe because they are critical to the marketing and distribution of flowers.

Most of the flower growers market their products through importers' agents, many of whom have representatives in Zimbabwe, and through local export agents (Chidzawo 1990). These flowers are then sold directly to wholesalers in Europe or indirectly through the flower auction system.

A firm can distribute its flowers to the foreign market through its own distribution channels, through an export management company (Brasch 1978), or through an export consortium.

Both the export management company and the export consortium export the products of several firms. The export management companies discussed in the international marketing literature, on the other hand, emphasize service to individual exporters. With an export management company, the grouping is done by a single, large grower or by an independent company involved in the freighting and marketing of horticultural products. With an export consortium, the grouping is done by the growers themselves.

Within the horticultural industry, the export management company provides many of the same services and benefits as the export consortia discussed in the international marketing literature (Rabino 1983, p. 22).

In this paper we look at whether growers within the horticultural industry must group for export. In addition, we look at a question that has not been addressed by the international marketing literature: why firms should use consortium marketing instead of export management companies.

Research method and design

We used two methods to gather data on the need for export grouping and the need for export consortia. (1) We sent a questionnaire to 19 flower export groups identified by the HPC. Of the 19 questionnaires sent to the growers, 10 were returned correctly filled in with usable data. (2) We conducted follow-up interviews with four export groups, Produco (Pvt) Ltd (a consortium), and the HPC.

Before we designed the questionnaire, we identified several success factors in the international marketing literature on grouping for export. These success factors are listed in Table 2.

We then designed a questionnaire, which grouped the success factors into the following five factors:

- *Factor 1* — There must be tangible and significant benefits that individual growers can derive from exporting.

    To determine whether this success factor pertains to the Zimbabwe horticultural industry, we needed to find out to what extent the growers depend on the export market. Our hypothesis was that a high level of

Table 2. Success factors in grouping export.

The following factors contribute to the success of grouping for exports:

- There is a strong commitment to a joint opportunity or problem; in exporting, the opportunity is market penetration

- There is an external change agent, who fosters the grouping

- Export marketing by oneself would be infeasible, costly, or risky

- The number of members in the group is small

- The group members must be able to create both "people fit" and an "organizational fit"

- A common, external threat draws the group members together

- The member firms represent the same industry, and they produce standardized products

- Members produce complementary rather than similar products if there is a possibility that their products would compete with each other in external markets

- A trade association or another group that can carry out more general objectives already exists

- The organization and interrelationships of those in the group are established before export activity begins

- The members need resources, which might be finances or know-how

- The risk is spread and economies of scale are achieved

- The members develop new products and are searching for growth; the government offers incentives

- Some of the firms have previously failed in their export efforts

Source: OECD (1964), Pate (1969), van de Ven (1976), Stenburg (1982), Rabino (1983), Welch and Joynt (1984, 1987), Rosson and Blunden (1985).

dependence on the export market leads to a high level of commitment to exporting.

- *Factor 2* — It should be necessary or advantageous for firms to export through an export group.

To determine whether this success factor pertains to the Zimbabwe horticultural industry, we needed to find out if firms had ever failed in their solo export efforts and what advantages consortium exporting offers. Our hypothesis was that if firms have failed in a solo effort but need to export, then they are more likely to join an export grouping. In addition, benefits from export groups can stimulate firms to join an export group.

- *Factor 3* — It should be possibile for the consortium members to create both a people fit and and organizational fit.

  To determine whether this success factor pertains to the Zimbabwe horticultural industry, we needed to ask the export groups if they felt firms had a choice of export groups to join, what important factors determined the choice of export groups and whether there were long-standing conflicts in export groups. Our hypothesis was that a good organizational fit and people fit increased the chances of success of the export group.

- *Factor 4* — There must be very strong external influences to stimulate firms in the industry to form an export consortium.

  To determine whether this success factor pertains to the Zimbabwe horticultural industry, we needed to find out whether external change agents, incentives, or the existence of the HPC had stimulated the formation of export consortia.

- *Factor 5* — The product mix of the members of a consortium must be complementary and together must provide synergy.

  To determine whether this success factor pertains to the Zimbabwe horticultural industry, we needed to find out whether there was competition among different companies in a consortium for the local or export market and whether their products were complementary or similar. Our hypothesis was that decreased competition among companies in an export consortium for the same market increased the chances of the success of the consortium.

Findings

Factor 1

We found that, on average, the growers using export groups exported 90% of their produce. All growers represented by the export groups began growing flowers for the sole purpose of exporting and would not survive in floriculture without the export market. The local market was basically seen as too small and as having a very low rate of return.

What these results show is that the growers have to export to survive in the horticultural industry and that for an export group to be successful there must be, as we supposed, tangible and significant benefits from exporting for the individual grower.

Factor 2

Within the export groups, 60% of the respondents stated they began exporting on their own and then joined an export group. The reasons for the termination of the solo effort were mainly problems with freight coordination, logistics, competition, prices, and export financing. The advantages that consortium exporting offers are freight coordination, economies of scale, product mix, and trade financing.

What these results show is that there are benefits to being part of an export group. Solo marketing can have serious disadvantages: a sole exporter may be unable to offer competitive prices and efficient delivery.

Factor 3

All the export groups that responded to the questionnaire were private limited companies. Of these, 80% exportated only horticultural products. The number of members in each export group varied from 15 to 84. About half of the groups did not start exporting immediately. Most export groups felt that growers chose a group on the basis of service, efficiency and price. All of the groups reported no conflicts among members.

What these results show is that a private limited company can be an effective export group and that there seems to be very little conflict among members of export groups.

Factor 4

Only one export consortium reported a strong influence from an external change agent, a shipping company. Unlike the external change agents mentioned in the international marketing literature, however, this external change agent did eventually join the consortium. What these results show is that external change agents, incentives, and the existence of the HPC generally did not stimulate the formation of export consortia. No nonmarket incentives or outside threats had stimulated them to form an export group.

All the respondents felt that the existence of the HPC had no effect on their entering into an export group.

Factor 5

Most of the horticultural products exported by the export groups competed with each other on the international market but not on the domestic market: 50% of the products were similar, and the other 50% were complementary.

What these results show is that there are not enough complementary products to prevent conflict among members. If their consortium markets the similar products in the foreign market, the products would be in competition. However, consortia are advantageous in the most critical aspects of horticultural exporting, which are freight and handling.

The case for a consortium as an export group

The results of the survey mainly show that there is a need for grouping of horticultural produce for the export market because there are tangible benefits to be derived from grouping. The export groups in the horticultural industry provide many services (see Table 3).

Grouping for export solves the following problems faced by small-scale exporters in developing countries:

- The group can provide the knowledge and expertise required by exporters.

Table 3. Services provided by export group.

Export groups provide the following services:

- They group the produce of different growers into one product offering. This allows growers to concentrate on producing one or two varieties instead of a whole product range as required by the foreign market.
- They can offer producers lower freight rates because of the economies that result from higher tonnages being exported.
- They improve the quality of the produce by freighting it as soon as possible.
- They have the expertise to freight their members' produce.
- They provide the members with efficient cold-storage facilities to improve the competitiveness of the produce.
- They find foreign representatives or marketing agents for all the growers in the consortium.
- They are effective in negotiating lower freight rates for their members.
- They provide their members with short-term export financing whenever this is necessary.

- The group provides the financial and human resources required by the small-scale exporter.
- The group can monitor the international market for the small-scale exporter.
- The group can collect information required by the small-scale exporter.

However, using an export management company raises a number of problems for the small-scale grower:

- Some of the export management companies export dry cargo also. This may result in suboptimal services for the horticultural producers.
- The independent companies sometimes lack the level of expertise in horticultural products required by the growers.
- Some independent companies are too small to have the human and financial resources required for the export of horticultural products.
- The export management companies often charge high rates for their services.

A solution to these problems is for the growers themselves to form and own a consortium. An example of such a consortium is Produco (Pvt) Ltd.

Produco (Pvt) Ltd — a consortium

Produco (Pvt) Ltd was officially launched in February 1993 exclusively for handling and freighting horticultural products. It is the only export group in the horticultural industry that meets the definition used for consortia in this paper.

The company was formed by horticultural growers who were unsatisfied with the service provided by existing freight channels. Produco (Pvt) Ltd is, therefore, a real consortium in terms of its ownership by growers, but also includes freight companies. At present, 34 producers of horticultural produce own 56% of the company; two freight companies, Walford Meadows and Freight International, own the rest.

The group is structured as a private limited company with a board of directors and professional managers. The organization is not run as a cooperative. The owners of the company only participate in its affairs through the board of directors and by voting at annual general meetings. The cooperative form of organization was rejected because of their high failure rate.

To reduce the possibility of conflict among growers or the dominance of one grower, each of the members is restricted to owning only one share in the company. This ensures that all the growers have an equal voice in the running of the consortium.

Another important point is that although Produco (Pvt) Ltd was mainly formed by growers and freight companies to provide a more efficient and cost-effective freight service, the consortium is a profit-making company. The company offers its services not only to shareholding growers but also to other growers who are not shareholders. There is no preferential treatment for either the shareholding growers or the nonshareholding growers.

Produco (Pvt) Ltd provides the following unique services to exporters of horticultural products:

- It owns some of the country's largest cold rooms, exclusively designed for horticultural products.
- It keeps its cold rooms open 24 hours per day, 365 days per year to give growers flexibility in the delivery of their produce.
- It keeps its offices open 13 hours per day, 7 days per week to maintain constant communication with the growers and the freight industry.
- It has an efficient communication system and keeps in radio contact with both growers and the freight industry.
- It offers highly competitive rates to the growers because it concentrates on the export of horticulture.
- It shares its profits with the shareholding growers.
- It makes bulk purchases of inputs such as fertilizers for the growers.
- It can more easily solicit the help of consultants than individual growers can.

Produco (Pvt) Ltd enhances the growers' competitiveness in the international market by offering more competitive rates; air-freighting the flowers to ensure that they are fresh as possible when they arrive in the foreign markets; and providing better customer service.

Problems like those causing the failure of many consortia discussed in the international marketing literature have not affected Produco (Pvt) Ltd because of its structure:

1. The inclusion in the consortium of profit-making shipping companies has been instrumental in the success of Produco (Pvt) Ltd. The shipping companies provide special expertise in shipping and ensure that the consortium is run as a professional business venture.

2. Giving the growers the status only of shareholders circumvents problems arising from having growers with conflicting agendas all trying to influence the day-to-day operation of the consortium. Growers are not business people, they are farmers. If they were left to run the business, they would probably cause the failure of the consortium.

3. The provision in the articles of the consortium that each grower have only one share prevents conflict and the dominance of any grower.

4. Although the consortium could have been involved in all facets of marketing horticultural products, the consortium's affairs are simplified because its articles specify that it be involved only in freight. This is important because the consortium performs only the duties that are critical to the growers' competitive advantage, generating none of the conflicts of interest that might arise from the marketing of one grower's specialty over another's. Thus, simplifying the objectives of the company avoids conflict and provides tangible benefits to the consortium members.

Conclusion

The literature clearly indicates that exporters in developing countries have difficulties competing in the international market. Although consortium marketing offers a solution to some of the difficulties, many export consortia have failed to increase the competitiveness of the small exporter. The literature on consortium marketing also reveals some of the important determinants of the success of export marketing groups. Our survey results indicate that most of these success factors apply in the Zimbabwe horticultural industry. A case study of Produco (Pvt) Ltd, a new consortium of horticultural producers, shows that consortia can be used by firms to increase their competitive advantage in international markets.

Although this study as a whole concentrated on the horticultural industry, it may be possible to extrapolate the findings and predict that export consortia could be successful in other industries in which competitive advantages could be obtained from grouping for export. To determine whether such consortia could succeed, the researcher in this area should determine whether exporting is of critical importance in the industry, whether benefits can be derived from grouping for export, and whether additional benefits can be obtained by grouping through a consortium. ✻

The Private Sector as a Change Agent in the Development of Small-Scale Enterprises: Large Firm–Small Firm Linkages in Kenya

Catherine K. Masinde
Faculty of Commerce, University of Nairobi,
Nairobi, Kenya

Introduction

Attention has recently become centred on the role of the private sector in Kenya and many other developing countries as these countries face increasing international pressure to rely on market forces for economic regeneration. Yet, the private sectors of these countries are not themselves healthy. One of their main weaknesses is a poorly developed small- to medium-scale enterprise (SME) sector. (In this paper, SME means a firm employing fewer than 50 people; the term *jua kali* refers specifically to small, technology-based firms with fewer than 20 employees.)

Some initiatives for SME development have emerged from the private sector itself as strategies not only to stimulate general demand in the economy but also to develop an adequate supply and distribution network for the private sector's own production requirements. The private sector in Kenya has developed a specific policy for the SME sector, in addition to providing some direct assistance (marketing, training, and work space). However, this paper suggests that business relationships developed through contracts and strategic alliances help build the capabilities of SMEs to complement the requirements of large firms and are, therefore, more desirable.

Considerable effort has already gone into developing SMEs, but the strategies for this have focused on assistance to SMEs in isolation. Yet, it is clear that there are benefits to be derived from the way large and small firms can complement each other. The Japanese have built their industrialization strategy on such complementarity (Sato 1989). There is also a growing realization in European countries that the value of SMEs is in their relationship to large firms (Becattini 1990). In developing countries, however, the relationship between large and small firms is somewhat adversarial. Owing to the continued dominance of large firms, it is difficult to develop SMEs without the cooperation or involvement of these large firms. In proposing a linkage strategy, this paper explores the contributions of large firms as change agents in SME development.

After some brief background on the relevant literature and the Kenyan context, this paper explores three case studies from Kenya, to illustrate the various forms of links already in Kenya: assistance and support (British American Tobacco Co. Ltd [BAT]); mentoring and counseling (Kenya Management Assistance Programme [K-MAP]); and alliances and contractual relationships (General Motors Kenya Ltd [GMK]). This is followed by an analysis of the cases and their implications and some recommendations for policy.

Background

Links between large and small firms have been in the industrial sector many years, chiefly through the mechanism of subcontracting, or "farming out," as a strategy for smoothing production. Some of these relationships are strategic alliances and collaborations (Kogut 1988) in which the firms have a symbiotic relationship. Others result from the fragmentation of existing firms that find it necessary to concentrate on core activities while farming out those activities they consider subsidiary (Poire and Sabel 1984); this has come to be known as flexible specialization or lean production. The small firms benefit because they can collectively (Brusco 1986) or individually enter markets hitherto only served by large firms because of their economies of scale. The large firms benefit because they can reorient themselves from mass production to small-batch production and from vertically integrated organizations to decentralized or disembodied organizations. In turn, this reorientation means a division of labour between firms in an industry.

Current management theory in the west argues that more flexible systems are required to meet the increasing global demand for customization of goods and services. Hence, industry is moving away from Fordist modes of production. If Kenya is going to be competitive in international markets, it will have to rethink its philosophy of favouring mass production and large, vertically integrated organizations.

Links between large and small firms could help Kenya achieve several development and industrialization goals, not only by disseminating the accumulated knowledge of the large firms but also by mitigating the effects of their dominance. The goals of development and industrialization include restructuring of industry ownership; development and transfer of technology; reduction of monopolies and deconcentration of industry; privatization of state corporations; and full use of capacity and resources.

A high priority is to increase the share of indigenous capital in the economy. Large firms are a major source of more advanced technology and technological expertise. The privatization of state corporations and the restructuring of firms to reduce monopolies can be facilitated through SME promotion. Finally, as firms concentrate on core activities and procure from external sources those inputs and services they consider subsidiary, a greater use of capacity will result. The question is how to motivate large firms to contract with small firms for products and services.

Because of the dominant role of large firms in Kenya, the development of SMEs is partly a function of the willingness of large firms to accommodate them. A linkage strategy would help promote SMEs without antagonizing the large firms.

Historically, firms in Kenya have had incentives to integrate and internalize activities: to protect against resource and market volatility and to compensate for the weaknesses in the supplier structure. The slow technological progress of small, local firms and, hence, the low quality of their products made them seem useless to large firms. A link strategy must address both these issues.

The search for an SME linkage strategy in Kenya

The government has tried to "encourage partnership between Kenyan and non-Kenyan entrepreneurs" for the transfer of management and technical skills (Kenya 1989b, p. 224) through joint ventures and subcontracting. Sessional Paper No. 2 of 1992 on the *jua kali* sector reiterates the need for local indigenous businesses to interact with larger businesses (Kenya 1992). However, Kenya had not taken deliberate steps to encourage such links until the establishment in 1991 of the Kenya Sub-Contracting and Partnership Exchange (KSPX), which aims to promote industrial subcontracting in the country.

The KSPX was set up under the auspices of the United Nations Development Programme (UNDP), the International Labour Office (ILO), and the Government of Kenya to oversee the formalization of links between large and small firms and to offer a forum for these firms to meet and explore subcontracting and licencing possibilities. A data bank has been started to supply detailed information on the capabilities of suppliers (SMEs) and the requirements of buyers (large firms), with a view to helping them team up. Although this has not yet resulted in any subcontracting relationships, there have been several seminars and workshops on quality standards to prepare small firms for subcontracting relationships with large buyers. About half of the small firms represented at these seminars already supply large buyers.

Still in its infancy, KSPX has had little apparent impact, and there is considerable doubt within some sections of the business community that KSPX will be successful. One of the main problems is apparently its lack of specific knowledge about SMEs and what they can supply to large buyers and its lack of understanding of the organizational framework for subcontracting.

The Government of Kenya recognizes the potential of KSPX to promote external sourcing and subcontracting, to do for Kenya what these did for industrial development in Europe and Japan. So, in consultation with KSPX, the government selected the motor industry as a pilot subsector for the initial KSPX promotion of links among firms. The strategy was to streamline the motor-vehicle industry and encourage local procurement of components. This strategy was expected to develop a local capacity to supply the automobile-assembly industry and other industries. KSPX has since extended its operations to the metal industry, with plans to progressively cover most sectors in manufacturing.

Although the KSPX needs more time to prove itself, one of its weaknesses is its limited understanding of how to motivate large firms to subcontract to local SMEs and what conditions are necessary for this to occur. Hence, the KSPX does not yet reach a wide range of firms. Without a policy that encourages large firms to participate, a subcontracting exchange will have limited effect.

There are, however, examples in Kenya of links between small firms and large firms — some large firms directly assist SMEs by providing training, counseling, promotion, marketing, work space, and so on. The following case studies outline large firm–small firm links ranging from direct assistance to contractual relationships.

Case studies

The first case is a direct assistance program initiated by BAT in Kenya to help SMEs and microenterprises market their products. The second case is the training and business counseling initiative of K-MAP. The third case is the subcontracting relationship between GMK and its various suppliers. The first two initiatives were based on the findings of a government survey, which highlighted the problems of the SME sector (emphasizing training, financing, and marketing) and possible strategies to ameliorate these difficulties (Kenya 1989b). The third of these initiatives was based on the need to build a local supply base for the activities of GMK and the automobile-assembly industry.

British American Tobacco (Kenya) Ltd — direct assistance programs for marketing SMEs

BAT is a multinational company in Kenya's tobacco industry. Aside from its contribution to the economy, BAT has taken various corporate initiatives to help SMEs. Based on the government's conclusion that small enterprises face a major difficulty because of lack of exposure for themselves and their products (Kenya 1989b), BAT has since 1989 cosponsored the marketing and promotion of the small-enterprise sector and its products through annual exhibitions and symposia organized in collaboration with the *jua kali* associations and the government. BAT exhibits various products and promotes a positive image of the informal and small-enterprise sector as a prerequisite to stimulating demand for the sector.

BAT officials report that the four exhibitions already held (one prototype exhibition and three full-fledged exhibitions) have had a reasonably positive impact on the sector, with more than 700 artisans exhibiting more than 2 000 items. Although the artisans probably benefited from the opportunity to expose their products to a wider market, there has been no formal survey to assess the full impact of the exhibitions. Nevertheless, the publicity given to the exhibition has improved the general image of the sector and its products. More important, the exhibitions gave the participants a valuable opportunity to network with other *jua kali* operations from around the country.

The objectives of the exhibitions are "to offer marketing, promotion and opportunities for diffusion of innovations to *jua kali* producers." There are four key players in this relationship:

- BAT coordinates the organization of events and provides about 60% of the budget.

- The Ministry of Technical Training and Applied Technology (MTTAT) coordinates the activities of the *jua kali* participants, their exhibits, and their transportation and accommodation needs and also manages the information requirements for the exhibition, thus financing about 40% of the budget, mainly in kind.

- The Ministerial Committee is made up of representatives from various government institutions.

- The Provincial *Jua Kali* Exhibition Committee handles the overall coordination of the exhibits. This committee has various representatives from BAT, MTTAT, the provincial administration, the Ministry of Culture and Social Services, and the local *Jua Kali* Association. The Provincial Commissioner is a patron.

In addition to participating in the exhibits, various researchers and academics gather in symposia to examine policy and operational issues pertinent to the sector.

Merits

1. The BAT initiative came at a time when there was no specific marketing assistance given to small enterprises, particularly very small enterprises and microenterprises. This neglect could have stemmed from the

entrepreneurs' belief that small firms serve only local markets and that displaying their wares at the doorstep of their workshops was enough to attract customers. BAT realized that there was a provincial, if not national, demand for many of the *jua kali* products, which therefore needed to be more widely exposed. The BAT initiative thus filled a critical gap in SME services.

2. The various supporters of and participants in the BAT initiative see it as having a positive impact on employment (owing to increased sales) in their localities, which leads to increased purchasing power in the local community.

3. Through the wider exposure of artisans and their products, there are opportunities for the exchange of ideas. According to one of the organizers, the general ambience of the exhibitions is that of "curiosity, eagerness to find out what others are up to and to learn new ways of doing what they were already doing."

Demerits

1. MTTAT formed the *jua kali* associations to bring together *jua kali* artisans in specific geographical locations, but the role of these associations should be more specifically and clearly defined. They should have a more prominent role in the organization and management of the exhibitions.

2. Because the BAT initiative targets the *jua kali* (technology-based) sector, the initiative has tended to alienate other SMEs that do not fall under the government's definition of the applied technology sector. Yet, these other SMEs would also likely benefit from the promotional and marketing assistance offered by this program.

3. Although the symposia are a significant component of the BAT initiative, their full value to the sector is not clear. For example, the exhibitions themselves offer a rich environment for active research on the diffusion and adoption of innovations (from academics and innovators to *jua kali* artisans, and from artisans back to the academics and innovators). However, the academic

contributions of the symposia are inaccessible to most of the major players in the program. In addition, the symposia could contribute more by providing a forum for debate among the participants about the value of the exhibitions.

4. Both the sponsors and the participants need feedback. Although there has been a one-off evaluation of the impact of the program, there is no specific evaluation built into its framework. Hence, neither of its sponsors has been able to assess its contribution to the SME sector. No one addresses the important question, What happens after the exhibitions?

Kenya Management Assistance Programme — mentoring and business counseling

K-MAP is a Kenyan company limited by guarantee, initiated in 1987 by a Kenyan businessman in collaboration with the large-scale business community. In 1993, it was registering as an NGO. K-MAP brought together large- and medium-sized companies to assist small businesses by providing training and business counseling with the voluntary time and the skills of its member companies. To quote its mission statement, K-MAP is the result of the desire of the large-scale enterprises in Kenya to

> Share their skills with small, less experienced entrepreneurs, even at the risk of nurturing competition.... They [the large-scale enterprises] saw the need for positive linkages between large and small businesses; linkages that are bound to yield high dividends and benefit the society as a whole.

Although K-MAP's financial base has recently expanded to include other donors such as the Overseas Development Association (ODA) and The Netherlands government, the initial funding for this project came from the United States Agency for International Development (USAID). K-MAP's Strategic Five-Year Development Plan — 1992 is a plan to generate the bulk of K-MAP's budget (92%) from internal sources, particularly membership fees and other activities. Currently, member companies contribute a small amount of the budget through fees, as do the clients. Various fundraising projects have also been launched. Although the skills bank (executive skills and time) remains the most vital resource of the project, K-MAP continues to rely heavily on donor funding. It is hoped that eventually clients will be able to pay for the full cost of counseling.

K-MAP offers the following services to its clients:

- One-on-one business counseling of small-business clients, either on their own premises or at the K-MAP offices — This is K-MAP's core service, and it includes pre-investment counselling to assist clients in business planning, proposal preparation, business development, and business rehabilitation.

- Training of clients and prospective clients, through open workshops and seminars — To date, these workshops have been general, sectoral (for specific business sectors), or custom designed for specific organizations. In most cases, the custom-designed workshops are regarded as consultations, as there is no open invitation to participants.

- Publication of simple booklets on basic business topics.

- A quarterly newsletter (*Small Business Forum*) to update members, counselors, and clients on K-MAP activities and other relevant issues in business — Currently, this newsletter has a circulation of 7 000.

- The production of audio cassettes on business topics of interest to SMEs or to promoters of SMEs.

- A consulting service for recruiting personnel for small firms, motivating employees, and reviewing business strategies.

- Annual promotional exhibitions to provide a forum for small firms to expose themselves and their products and to exchange ideas about product improvement and better customer relations.

- A credit guarantee program in collaboration with Barclay's Bank (Kenya) and supported by ODA.

K-MAP offers these services to small businesses located mainly within the Nairobi metropolitan area. K-MAP intends to apply the lessons learned from these pilot activities in Nairobi elsewhere in the country.

K-MAP's target group is the small, formal-business sector rather than the microenterprise sector. An unpublished impact study of K-MAP's activities found that its clients were engaged in small-scale manufacturing (48%), trade (28%), and services

(24%). Although there are no rigid rules, the scarcity of resources has forced K-MAP to adopt a stringent selection process. The beneficiaries initially seek out K-MAP, and the very small businesses are not among them beause they are not likely to have heard of K-MAP. However, as K-MAP expands its outreach program, it is expected that this will change.

Key players

The key players in the K-MAP project include the member companies (from all industries), who pledge management time and skills; the counselors, who are highly motivated by a sense of social responsibility and the challenge of running a business; and the secretariat staff, who coordinate all activities. At this juncture, it is important to note that the initial impetus for K-MAP's activities came from its founders. Their personal networks and those of individuals in member companies have been invaluable in stimulating interest in K-MAP's activities. The zeal and vision of these champions have transformed ideas into successful projects.

K-MAP's assistance works in three distinct stages:

1. K-MAP advertises its activities (for client and counselor recruitment) through its newsletter, exhibitions, and daily newspaper advertisements. To a large extent, K-MAP also relies on the word-of-mouth advertising of its clients and member companies.

2. When an SME approaches K-MAP, the K-MAP seretariat staff arrange a diagnostic counseling session to identify the client's needs. In a second phase of this stage, the secretariat staff match the client with a counselor on the basis of the client's needs and the availability of relevant skills.

3. The secretariat staff evaluate the counseling sessions, considering the perceptions of the client and the counselor, and file the results of this evaluation for future reference or communicate them directly to the counselors at the regular counselors' meetings.

Performance

In 1992, K-MAP had 412 clients, 228 volunteer counselors, and 121 member companies. In 1991, K-MAP reported more than 980 counseling sessions (including any contacts, irrespective of duration) involving SMEs and both the secretariat staff and the volunteer counselors. In 1992, K-MAP organized 35 workshops, with altogether more than 1 660 participants from various sectors of the economy. Most of these workshops were general, but some were sectoral, and others were designed for specific clients.

All of K-MAP's clients participated in an external evaluation of its counseling service. Most of the clients felt that K-MAP had helped them make changes in their business (76% of respondents) and that their staff members had gained new skills because of this service (86% of the respondents) (unpublished impact study report, 1992).

In 5 years, K-MAP has established its reputation as a unique organization, with a unique method of assistance. One of the most outstanding merits of the K-MAP initiative is, of course, the deliberate use of the capacity, experience, and expertise of the large-scale business community to help SMEs develop. Because of the favourable environment for K-MAP in Kenya and the tremendous goodwill of the business community, this initiative provides an example of how the private sector can assist SMEs. Because of the efficiency and devotion of its staff, K-MAP has a good future as an assistance institution.

The counseling program provides opportunities for the counselors to establish their own businesses on the basis of the experience they gain working closely with SMEs. The international literature suggests that people working in small firms are more likely to establish their own firms than those working in large firms.

There are opportunities for cross-fertilization of the ideas of people from large- and small-scale firms in the course of counselors' and clients' seeking solutions to problems. When large firms seek to rationalize activities in response to fragmenting markets, such counselors are likely to be able to bring into large firms useful experience gathered from dealing with small firms.

K-MAP's Strategic Five-Year Development Plan — 1992 envisages the expansion of services, to include the KSPX, currently housed in K-MAP but operating semiautonomously; a technical counseling service; and a credit referencing service, in collaboration with various financial institutions, particularly Barclay's Bank (Kenya) [this program was established in late 1993].

General Motors (Kenya) — strategic alliances and contractual relationships

GMK is an American multinational corporation operating in Kenya's automobile-assembly industry. GMK's main contribution to SME development is its use of SMEs as suppliers. But GMK has embarked on a program to provide work space to *jua kali* artisans within Nairobi, with plans to expand into other areas. GMK is also involved in a program to develop a supplier base of local motor-vehicle parts and components suppliers. Although the contribution of work space is critical for very small firms in Kenya, the supplier base is a more important contribution, as it encourages formal small firms to operate alongside large firms.

GMK and two other assemblers, Associated Motor Vehicle Assemblers and Kenya Vehicle Manufacturers, constitute the automobile-assembly sector in Kenya. This sector needs a lot of suppliers because one firm cannot supply all the parts and components that go into a vehicle. However, there has been a tendency to rely on imports because the sector operates on a completely knocked down (CKD) kit system — various firms import kits from manufacturers around the world (under franchise) and then contract the assembly process to any of the three assemblers. Consequently, local suppliers have not broken into the parts and components market, except for some of the 31 items that before 1993 were required by legislation to come from local sources. In June 1993, the old legislation was revoked by the government and imports were liberalized. Consequently, both the assemblers and their suppliers were expected to compete with imports. However, accompanying this change was a higher duty on directly imported commercial vehicles, meaning that locally assembled cars would be able to compete even at higher prices. But because the market for cars in Kenya is small and fragmented, large firms have found it difficult to operate in the parts and components sectors. Hence, small, local firms dominate both the new and replacement parts and components markets. At the same time, because of the inadequacy of this supplier base, assemblers have had to import many of the parts and components they require.

Other legislation requires that firms in the automobile-assembly sector procure at least 40% of their inputs locally, but this legislation is unsuccessful — importers of CKD kits continue to import a large part of the vehicle. The industry (importers and assemblers) argue that "there are few incentives to source locally" and that "the poor quality and high price of the locally produced parts and components preclude them from consideration." In Kenya, the automobile-assembly sector can meet about 60% of its requirements from local sources, yet according to its chief executive officers, it has been constrained by poor incentives, an unreliable supplier base (particularly poor quality and poor delivery standards), and ongoing agreements on sourcing policies with principal suppliers of CKDs. This combination of a poor incentive structure and a poor supplier base makes it necessary for the government to remove the policy impediments preventing local assemblers from using local parts, components, and services.

Table 1 shows what is sourced locally by the various importers and assemblers. More than 60% of the domestic suppliers of these items are categorized as SMEs. Because, in addition to services, an average of 25 000 parts and components go into the production of a car, this proportion is negligible.

Although the automobile-assembly industry in Kenya is reluctant to source locally, particularly from local SMEs, GMK has

Table 1. Aggregate estimated proportions of locally sourced automobile parts and components.

Parts or components	Proportion locally sourced (%)
Tires and tubes	100
Shock absorbers	80–90
Paints	100
Seat frames	100
Leaf springs	60–70
Cushions and auto trims	70–80
Exhaust and silencer systems	100
Bulbs	65–70
Wiring harnesses	50–60
Metal parts (such as battery carriers)	10
Glass	90
Oils, fuels, and lubricants	100
Batteries	90–100
Radiators	95

Source: Field notes (1992/93).

a corporate policy of progressively increasing their local sourcing. To this end, it has developed a program to improve their
suppliers' organization, quality standards, and delivery time to
match specific supplier-selection and development criteria. GMK
currently has more than 80 suppliers of inputs (components,
parts, and services), mostly firms employing 5–19 people.
Although GMK plans to reduce its supplier base (currently, it
maintains at least two suppliers for each item), the impact on
the SME sector is likely to improve, as GMK will continue to concentrate on improving the standards of a few suppliers.

Although GMK demands that the suppliers meet their
basic selection criteria, its program progressively improves the
quality, delivery, and organizational capacity of the supplier. It
is important to note here that such suppliers are not obligated
to supply exclusively to GMK. Other importers who do not have
similar development programs have benefited from GMK's quality standards for SMEs.

The impact of import and trade liberalization

Import and trade liberalization have had the greatest impact on
subcontracting and partnerships. Lower levels of real income in
Kenya have lowered demand for cars, and the automobile-
assembly industry has suffered considerably from competition
with imported secondhand and new cars, which are usually not
properly taxed and often do not enter the country legally.

Between 1990 and 1992, the sector was hard hit by the
scarcity of foreign currency for the purchase of imported CKD
kits. Total production in the sector fell by 45%, from 14 056 in
1990 to 7 770 in 1991 (Kenya 1992). Then the liberalization of
imports meant parts and components could be imported, apparently more cheaply because of the alleged inefficiency of local
suppliers. However, a substantial duty (40%) was at the same
time levied on imported commercial vehicles (the duty is only
10% on parts and components imported for automobiles assembled locally). Thus, assemblers have access to imported inputs,
and they can compete with imported vehicles on price.

At the moment, there is still considerable worry about
the fate of the small suppliers. Competition with imports
should make their production more competitive and the quality
of their products more internationally acceptable. To some
extent SMEs also use imported inputs, and the SMEs can now

procure these inputs more easily, whereas they were hitherto inaccessible because of restrictions on foreign exchange. On the other hand, because this sector has not had time to establish itself, it may collapse in the face of this competition. It is still too early to assess the full impact of import and trade liberalization on this subsector.

Conclusion

Although the private-sector initiatives to provide assistance to SMEs are good and timely, strengthening contractual relationships between large and small firms is also desirable. The following are some suggestions for improving the value of these relationships.

Requisite conditions for links between large and small firms

The BAT initiative and K-MAP are largely based on the social responsibility of the large firms. Although this approach to assistance is useful (even critical in the development of SMEs where large firms predominate), it depends on the extent to which large firms perceive a need to put something back into society. Consequently, it is not easy to anticipate the form and level of assistance that this approach can make available to SMEs. To a large extent, this is up to those who are running the large firms and depends on their good intentions.

The relationship between GMK and its local suppliers suggests that this type of link may be in line with the development strategies of both the small and large firms. A large firm's perception of an SME as being capable of meeting its input or distribution requirements is a function of the incentives (for both parties) in the market. This type of link also depends on the ability and willingness of the small firms to link up with large firms.

The role of government

The government should encourage harmonious and supportive relationships between large and small firms and improve the economic incentive for large firms, rather than legislating to ensure linkage. For example, if there is dismantling of the incentives to integrate vertically, there should be a concomitant dismantling of the policy impediments to the development of SMEs, particularly those that create monopolistic tendencies in some industries. At the same time, there should be a systematic withdrawal of the state from direct involvement in SME activities (both assistance programs and commercial activities) that could be better performed by the private sector.

The role of SMEs

The SME sector has contributed to its own weakness by perpetuating its dependence on government support. Although it can also be argued that recent SME growth is due to government intervention, the current shift from government "interference" in the private sector means that the SMEs must learn to rely on themselves and other players in the private sector. This suggests a shift in emphasis from government support to self-help or large-scale sector support. Hence, SMEs will have to play an active role in determining what "assistance" they need and want from the government and the private sector.

First, the SMEs must develop the capacity to bargain with large firms (on the basis of the quality and availability of SMEs' goods and services), as well as with the government through associations. Experience in Japan and Italy suggests that SMEs increase their collective bargaining power by clustering and (or) networking. SMEs must then develop a framework for bargaining (develop clusters and networks) (Kaplinksy 1991). Currently, the *jai kali* associations offer some form of network, but their activities have not yet expanded to include advocacy and representation. Nor do these associations offer an organized forum for commercial activities, such as a subcontracting exchange facility. Other forms of networking and clustering for procurement and equipment use are also possible (Sverrisson 1992).

SMEs will have to improve their standards to meet the demands of large firms and to counter the criticisms that their products are of poor quality and their performance is less than adequate. SMEs will have to tap into the various resources available for quality improvement. If relations with large firms are collaborative, there is an opportunity for SMEs to improve to meet the standards imposed by these firms. The GMK program offers one promising model. ❋

Part VI

Conclusion

THE OTHER TWO THIRDS: A SUMMARY OF PAPERS, DISCUSSIONS, AND CLOSING REMARKS

Philip English
Social Sciences Division, International Development
Research Centre, Ottawa, Canada

Jacob Levitsky
Independant Consultant, London, UK

The papers published in this volume are only a small part of the work that went into the conference and the ideas that came from it. Another 23 papers were written, presented, and circulated. Most sessions were supplemented by a vigorous discussion that benefited from the depth of experience represented by the participants. The conference closed with a panel of five speakers from five different sectors, followed by a valiant attempt by the two chief rapporteurs to summarize the entire conference.

Not willing to see this wealth of information slip away, we have tried in this chapter to capture the essence of the presentations and discussions that could not be reproduced in full because of the constraints on the length of this volume. For this, we have been greatly assisted by the reports of the various rapporteurs who covered each session (see Appendix 1).

National policy frameworks and processes

One plenary session was devoted to the experience of other developing regions, in the belief that their successes may provide useful lessons, even for different socioeconomic settings.

The first speaker was Chee Peng Lim of the Economic Commission for Asia and the Pacific, in Bangkok, who reviewed the relevance of east Asia's experience to Africa. He stressed that the most successful efforts to promote small- to medium-scale enterprise (SME) in Asia focused on the overall efficiency of the economy, instead of trying to serve multiple, social, and economic objectives.

The Korean case was offered as a good example. The Korean efforts concentrated on developing technology, raising competitive capacity, and promoting cooperative links between large and small enterprises.

In Taiwan, promotion of SMEs was effective because one unit of government provided an integrated package. In Malaysia, on the other hand, more than 30 public agencies offered various forms of assistance to SMEs.

Chee also emphasized that help for SMEs was more effective if the public agency responsible worked closely with the private sector. Chee gave the examples of Japan and, again, Korea, where public SME agencies work through SME associations. In Korea, the Federation of Small Business, with 16 000 members, coordinates subcontracting, bulk purchasing and selling, information services, and technology transfer. In most other Asian countries, SME associations are still weak and have only limited membership. He noted, too, that organizations that also cater to large enterprise rarely serve the interests of SMEs. In Taiwan, foreign trading companies help by providing designs and quality specifications — small-scale enterprises (SSEs) that are able to meet these standards can participate in the boom in labour-intensive exports.

Turning to the critical role of conducive policies, Chee cited the Philippines and India as examples of countries where vast resources are directed to this SME sector but the results are limited because of inappropriate policies. Zoning policies have proven restrictive to the development of SMEs in Malaysia. In some countries, heavy taxes and import tariffs have also hurt, as have overvalued exchange rates. Tax concessions, such as those for importing new machinery, have tended to favour larger enterprises. Governments also discriminate against SMEs at times by purchasing mainly from larger suppliers.

Although Chee recognized that conditions in Africa are different, he believed some lessons could be learned from Asia. He stressed the importance of promoting export-oriented SMEs, mobilizing private-sector support to complement government efforts, encouraging the linkage of SSEs and large-scale firms, and avoiding the fragmentation of assistance programs.

The paper from Latin America dealt with the financing of microenterprise and is summarized below in the Financial Services section.

The dramatic policy changes in one eastern European country, Hungary, were examined by Eva Bakonyi, Managing Director of the B'nai B'rith there. SMEs play a major role in Hungary by providing a means of shifting from a socialist to a market economy; a vehicle for privatization; and service and trade after a long emphasis on industrialization.

The SME environment in Hungary evolved through three stages: from prohibition, to patience, to promotion. The dominance of state-owned enterprise was so complete that, by the end of the 1970s, craftspeople and private traders accounted for less than 2% of the working population. Toward the end of this period, the government took a more relaxed approach to the activities of the private sector, which were still officially illegal.

The promotion phase began in 1980 with the renting out of state trading and catering outlets to private entrepreneurs. This was followed by the legalization of a wide range of private enterprises. This process accelerated after 1988 with political pluralism and the growing acceptance of private ownership. In the last 5 years, there has been an entrepreneurial boom involving some 240 000 companies and partnerships and about 650 000 self-employed people.

Although the legal barriers have disappeared, there are still many gaps in the institutional environment for SMEs, especially in the financial sector. Many commercial banks have been created, but their lack of experience has hurt the SMEs in particular. The heavy burden of taxes and social security charges is another common complaint. Finally, the macroeconomic context, with recession, high inflation and government debt, and hence high interest rates, is not conducive to investment.

Salah Brik Hannachi, Tunisia's Secretary of State for International Cooperation and Foreign Investment, shared some of the lessons from his country's recent experience. Even though entrepreneurs may not be in short supply, they still need training; for this, such mechanisms as incubators have proven helpful. Structural adjustment programs are not enough, as they do not deal with the particular problems of individual sectors or activities. He described a program to assist automobile-parts producers that is supported by the German Agency for Technical Cooperation (GTZ).

Hannachi also emphasized the importance of subcontracting as a way of promoting SSE development. Trade shows and other fora in Europe and the Middle East have been used as opportunities to set up such arrangements with foreign companies.

In a presentation rich with metaphors, Hannachi concluded by comparing the role of government to that of a coach. The government should not attempt to be an economic agent (or player); nor should it be content simply to set the rules and enforce them (as a referee). Rather, the government has the responsibility for training entrepreneurs, promoting teamwork, providing information, and developing strategies.

The views of Enoch Moyo on the Zimbabwean case (this volume) were supplemented by those of a government official, Edgar Chigudu, of the National Economic Planning Commission. He stressed the need for the collaboration of government, business organizations, donors, NGOs, and researchers, noting that there has been a tendency for these groups to develop their own conclusions independently. Even within government, different ministries take initiatives to promote SMEs without coordinating their efforts.

Studies in Zimbabwe have identified major constraints on SME development — a scarcity of foreign exchange, material shortages, and transport problems, which affect the whole economy, and some laws and regulations that impede SSEs in particular. These include complex licencing laws and labour and tax laws that discourage informal businesses from formalizing themselves. In general, the government has neglected or even discriminated against SMEs, such as in its procurement activities. The government-supported Small Enterprise Development Corporation (SEDCO) only lent to formal registered businesses, and it demanded collateral.

Chigudu expressed some concern over the impact of structural adjustment programs on small businesses. To mitigate the effects of high interest rates and cheap imports, the Zimbabwe government introduced a limited credit guarantee scheme; the government was also considering special tax incentives. The central bank encouraged a new venture capital organization.

A government official from Mauritius painted a more optimistic picture. Jairaz Pochun, Acting Director of the Small and Medium Industries Development Organization (SMIDO), described the development of SME policy in Mauritius. In 1983, the Small Industries Development Organization (SIDO) was set up to promote SMEs. By the following year, SMEs could obtain loans at preferential rates of interest. Next, schemes were introduced that offered young Mauritians opportunities to start businesses. In 1988, registered small-scale industries were exempted from paying duties on imported production equipment.

In 1993, SMIDO replaced SIDO as an autonomous body. Its mandate is to

• conduct entrepreneur and management training;

• provide extension and information services;

• set up common facilities for maintenance and parts fabrication;

• promote subcontracting linkages and cooperation among enterprises; and

• assist in marketing.

The Development Bank of Mauritius plays a complementary role by financing SME projects through its Small Scale Industries Scheme (for industries employing fewer than 25 persons) and its Small Rural Enterprise Scheme (for new small activities undertaken by the unemployed and by people with an annual income of less than 1 200 USD). In addition, various private-sector organizations have been active. The Mauritius Employers' Federation, the Mauritius Chamber of Commerce and Industry, the Centre de promotion des petites enterprises, and the Association des petites entrepreneurs de Maurice have all helped SME operators by training them, helping them prepare feasibility studies, and disseminating information among them.

Pochun concluded that as a result of this active support, there is a new spirit of entrepreneurship in the country — three out of every five employed persons have a second job or co-own an SSE. The Mauritius government appears to have played a relatively successful, interventionist role. By developing a new public agency to coordinate and implement support programs for SMEs, Mauritius is to some extent running counter to moves in other countries, where these activities are being handed over to private-sector organizations and NGOs.

Théophile Capo-Chichi, Director General of the Centre for the Promotion of Employment and Small and Medium Enterprise (CEPEPE), described the process by which Benin developed its approach to SSEs. By the mid-1980s, the policy of concentrating on large, state-owned enterprises was clearly not working. The ILO and UNIDO funded two studies in 1987 on the role of SMEs, and these studies led to the creation of CEPEPE. This is a completely private venture, created by the Benin Chamber of Commerce and Industry and the National Employers Association.

Three seminars, funded by the United Nations Development Programme (UNDP) in 1988, strengthened the dialogue between the public and private sectors and led to the creation of several other structures. A joint commission was set up to look at the complaints of the private sector. This was followed by the creation of the permanent Consultative Industrial Council, made up of both industry and government representatives, to maintain contact between the Ministry of Industry and the private sector.

Various actions have improved the policy environment and directly promoted SSEs. Benin provides training, helps entrepreneurs prepare project dossiers and obtain financing, and monitors enterprise development. Although Benin is still in the early stages of its reforms, it has already succeeded in giving SSEs more confidence. The private sector, which at one time was actively discouraged, is now accepted as a partner in the country's development.

Discussion

The question period at the end of this plenary session on non-African experiences focused on the Asian paper by Chee. It was pointed out that African governments are encouraged not to be interventionist, whereas Asian success seems to derive from direct state involvement. Chee had recommended that support agencies provide a comprehensive set of services, and this seemed to contradict the emphasis in the literature on specialized institutions. An African speaker argued that what was really needed in Africa was advice on implementing policy rather than on designing it, and he wondered to what extent anything could be learned from Asia in this regard. Chee responded by emphasizing that the involvement of the private sector was needed for both policy formulation and policy implementation.

Chee created a stir when he said that economic development should take priority over social objectives, even gender equity. This theme was picked up again the next day, when several participants questioned the degree to which SME policy reforms were addressing the needs of women — that is, in legislation, access to information, training, and resources, and in dealing with social and religious beliefs and behaviour patterns. There was an obvious sentiment that there is still much to be done in Africa. Nonetheless, a woman from Mauritius offered some grounds for optimism, saying that there were relatively few disadvantages for women in her country, probably owing to the multiculturalism of its society.

Again, in the break-out sessions, there was a scepticism about the relevance to Africa of the Asian model of policy reform. It was suggested that more lessons could be drawn from the progress being made in Mauritius, Kenya, and Zimbabwe. Focused discussions in smaller groups would clarify the strengths and weaknesses of different approaches. Organizing such opportunities was seen as a useful follow-up to the conference.

Regulatory reforms

One of the key addresses on reforming the regulatory environment was given by Louise Tager, Executive Director of the Law Review Project, in South Africa. She emphasized that deregulation was crucial in her country because, historically, South Africa has had a legal framework designed to protect a privileged class of white people, to the exclusion of the black majority.

To create an appropriate legal environment for South Africa, some basic principles would have to be followed:

- There must be one set of laws for all kinds of business, formal and informal, whoever owns or manages them.
- Laws should be enforceable through civil rather than criminal action.
- Laws and regulations are needed to ensure public health and safety and to protect human rights and the environment; they should not go beyond that.

- Most standards should be left to the market to safe-guard.
- Laws must not be used as a means of oppression — as they once were in South Africa.
- Consultation with all relevant groups, particularly with groups representing the informal sector, is vital in designing the new legal environment.

Of course, there are some vested interest groups, such as established businesses (many of which have enjoyed years of protection), trade unions, and some government officials, who are opposed to deregulation because they fear the loss of jobs and power. There are also more widely held concerns that dereg-ulation may lead to lower standards, or even chaos. These con-cerns must be addressed, but they will not be major problems if the laws are well designed. Likewise, approaches such as benign neglect or a system of exceptions are sometimes proposed as alternatives to deregulation, but neither approach would be sat-isfactory.

One break-out session on regulatory reform further explored the special case of South Africa, particularly the activ-ities of the Sunnyside Group (SSG). The Executive Director, Chris Darroll, explained that the SSG was formed in 1987 to lobby for an enabling environment for small business. This coalition of 72 groups has been able to maintain a narrow focus on deregulation; thus far, more than 200 pieces of inappropriate legislation have been removed. In addition, specific focus groups generate coherent policy proposals. These groups of experts focus, for example, on deregulating the Red Meat Marketing Board, on access to finance, or on the liquor industry.

Darroll ascribed the SSG's success to six factors:

- acting collectively;
- providing consistent evaluation of policy priorities;
- setting up expert focus teams;
- monitoring and evaluating the implementation process;
- educating and raising the awareness of the public; and
- identifying a champion.

She explained how the policy process is being played out in South Africa. She described the National Economic Forum (NEF) structures and the various regional development funds, all of which are consensus-seeking structures focusing on developing a coherent policy for promoting small firms. However, small firms are not directly represented at the NEF. She concluded by expressing the hope that the new democratic government would institute appropriate minimal legislation for the development of small firms.

David Moshapalo, also associated with the SSG, then discussed the kombi-taxis (or minivans) used for public transport in South Africa. He provided a detailed account of how heavy regulation effectively wiped out any indigenous black transport entrepreneurs. In addition, government subsidization of bus transport services created a further barrier. Because of a loophole in the Transport Act of 1977, a black taxi industry developed, but it was only after 1987 that government accepted its legitimacy.

This industry continues to face the following problems:

- excessive saturation of the market caused by uncontrolled deregulation, which hampers profitability and creates feuds among taxi owners;

- recession in the South Africa economy, reducing demand;

- lack of facilities; and

- a very poor image.

Various policy suggestions were made, including the possible extension of the "buxi" project in Johannesburg, where taxis cooperate with buses, bringing customers from the suburbs to main bus arteries. Another idea was that instead of the government subsidizing the providers of public transport, consumers should be given some form of financial assistance, allowing them to choose their own means of transport. Some form of subsidization was considered essential because of the long distances imposed on nonwhite commuters under apartheid by the Group Areas Act.

The development of black contractors in South Africa's construction industry was the topic of a paper by Teddy Mtshali. A combination of factors allowed black contractors to emerge again by the 1980s — job reservation was scrapped, allowing blacks to train as artisans; and blacks were given the right to live on land in urban areas, thus increasing the demand for housing construction and renovations, much of which was met by black contractors.

However, two main constraints inhibit small-scale contractors from growing; management problems and inadequate finance. The organization of which Mtshali is director, Entrepreneurial Development (Southern Africa) (EDSA), introduced training and credit programs to address these problems. This organization has given 83 introductory courses and 37 intermediate courses since 1989, and an advanced course is being developed. EDSA took over a loan scheme in 1990, in cooperation with two commercial banks.

Alliances within the informal construction sector have had mixed success. Two black builders' associations have been established, generating some competition. On the other hand, EDSA brought representatives of development organizations, builders' associations, financial institutions, and professional bodies together to establish the Small Contractor Action Forum. This forum has enhanced communication and cooperation and started to influence policy. The members have been active in the Construction Industry Forum of the SSG.

Following the presentations, questions were raised about the financing arrangements for small firms in South Africa. It was explained that credit unions (*stokvels*) based in black townships are a major source of finance, and NGOs are also important. A new Community Bank, formed in 1994, was expected to play a role. Commercial banks are present, but their high collateral requirements tend to be a major constraint.

Moshapalo fielded a question about progress being made toward the formation of a nonracial association of employers. He explained that problems rooted in the poorly developed capacity of black business organizations were impeding efforts.

A final point was made by a conference participant from South Africa. She argued that deregulation was not the only or even the key issue for small-business development in that country. According to her, research clearly showed that entrepreneurs find other constraints more significant, such as access to markets, finance, and training. Although regulation is one instrument that can create an enabling environment, many others (for example, budgeting, macroeconomic policy, institution building) may prove even more effective.

Clement Ngwasiri, of the University of Buea in Cameroon, maintained that entrepreneurs trying to start up new businesses in his country still face substantial barriers, even though structural adjustment was initiated in 1989.

Interviews with traders in the major commercial city of Douala in July 1993 revealed that more than 80% of them found it difficult to meet the requirements for formally registering their businesses. Private-sector reforms, enacted in 1990, left bureaucrats with too much discretionary power, so they were imposing restrictions and introducing their own interpretations of the precise meaning of some legislation.

Ngwasiri also held that property rights are poorly defined in Cameroon. The enforcement of these rights in the law courts is inadequate, creating a lack of confidence in the legal system. Compliance with regulations is still too costly in time and money for SSEs. The speaker also criticized the Cameroon government for closing down two major institutions supporting SMEs: the Banque camerounaise de développement, the main development bank, which had special credit lines for SMEs; and the Centre d'assistance aux petites et moyennes enterprises, which was created in 1969 to help train and advise SMEs. Both were closed down at the end of the 1980s, after the policy reforms were introduced.

Discussion

In the various question periods, the prevailing view of participants was that the early stages of a structural adjustment program pose serious problems for formal SSEs. Devaluations and higher interest rates are especially difficult for those dependent on imported raw materials and bank loans. Deregulation is usually slower in coming. Participants from Cameroon, Ghana, Kenya, and Zimbabwe claimed that even when legislation is introduced to reform regulations and ease restrictions, implementation is slow, often because reluctant government officials are left with discretionary powers. Such bureaucrats fear a loss of power.

Consequently, the conclusions of Donald Mead (Part III, this volume) were not accepted by many in the audience. Mead contended that small-business growth is significant and that registration formalities are relatively unimportant as a constraint; others countered that this only applies to informal microbusinesses, many of which do not survive long. When microenterprises try to grow and move into the formal sector, regulations can become a problem.

There was a sense that informal microbusinesses are less affected by structural adjustment, foreign exchange devaluations, or the relaxation of price controls and labour regulations. Because these enterprises are usually unable to obtain bank credit, they are not bothered much by higher interest rates. In some cases, the informal sector seems to benefit in the short term from being able to offer cheaper goods and services to consumers in a period of rising prices.

In any event, both governments and the business community now appear to recognize that in the long term there is a need for more market freedom and deregulation for the private sector to cope with prices, labour costs, financial costs, and other restrictions. There have been positive moves by governments in various African countries, even if they are still at an early stage in their implementation.

Financial services

The paper by Gaston Suarez, of the Development Bank of Chile, drew lessons from the Latin American experience in promoting microenterprise. Various policy changes facilitate the emergence of such firms. There has been a change in mentality such that microenterprise is no longer considered a marginal issue. In Bolivia, the President himself played a key role in the creation of Bancosol, a private bank that deals exclusively with microenterprise. Regulations have been simplified in what the speaker called the modernization of the state. More appropriate regulations have been adopted; for example, illiterate clients can give their fingerprints instead of their signatures at the Bancosol.

A more complete range of services has been offered, but no one institution is expected to provide them all. One particularly important innovation in Chile is the Fund for Solidarity and Social Investment (FOSIS). FOSIS acts as an intermediary: it subsidizes the transaction costs of bank lending to SSEs but does not interfere in the lending decision or absorb the risks involved. A subsidiary of the Development Bank of Chile has a leasing program to reduce the up-front cost of machinery and to remove the need for collateral.

International NGOs and other donors were much appreciated for such activities as promoting research and independent evaluations that prompt a rethinking of approaches. However, several cautionary observations were also made. The leading organizations supporting microenterprises usually started from a base of local support. Until recently, the efficiency of local partners has been neglected by foreign partners, on the false premise that efficiency and solidarity are contradictory objectives.

South–south collaboration often provides the most useful form of technical assistance; the inspiration of the Grameen Bank in Bangladesh is one example. Networks of institutions within Latin America are another case in point, provided the participating agencies are willing to be candid about their problems. In the less developed countries of Bolivia and Paraguay, institutions like the Bancosol have clearly benefited from such interaction.

Kodzo Akemakou, from Togo, stressed that SMEs cannot satisfy the stringent requirements or carry out the lengthy procedures imposed by formal commercial banks. Most of these banks are used to dealing with large enterprises and importers and do not appreciate the special situation of these smaller businesses. NGOs can help solve this difficulty. Akemakou described the experience of the Savings and Credit Cooperative, which offers small informal businesses a secure place to deposit their savings and quick access to the funds. The whole organization is based on mutual trust.

Akemakou thought that NGOs must understand the overall needs of small business, the reasons why they face difficulties and so often fail, and the areas where they need assistance. Entrepreneurs are particularly weak at differentiating between their own private expenses and those of the business and at establishing the level of their real costs. Thus, they need to keep records for their own benefit and to convince creditors that they can repay a loan.

Akemakou also thought that NGOs must do more to exchange lessons from their experiences in different countries. He welcomed the creation of APCA, an African association for providers of credit to small businesses that was formed by a group of NGOs meeting in January 1993 in Nairobi. NGOs hope that APCA will give them an opportunity to learn from each other how to control arrears, screen successful enterprises as potential borrowers, reduce dependence on the funds of external donors and train and develop qualified staff. They also need to learn how to determine the right interest rate and reduce administrative costs. Akemakou concluded that Africans must learn more from their own experiences and not rely so much on information from outside the continent.

The next speaker dealt with the challenges facing more formal financial institutions in the Franc Zone. Paul Kammogne Fokam, head of a Cameroonian savings and investment group, the Caisse commune d'épargne et d'investissement, listed various characteristics required by any bank wishing to serve SSES:

- It has to be completely private and avoid all the negative results of political pressures.
- It has to have independent finances and management (it should not belong to any multinational group with a controlling centre outside Africa, where the prime considerations are not likely to be the needs of the African people).
- It has to create new financial instruments and use imagination in linking savings and credit.

With the repatriation of Mauritanians from Senegal in 1989, the Société d'investissement et de développement international (SIDI), a French agency, agreed to launch a program to help create SSES. Mouhamedou Diack described the experience of Investissement–développement en Mauritanie (IDM), of which he is Director. Between 1991 and 1993, IDM had generated 30 new firms and 300 jobs.

The key to IDM's success is its emphasis on the entrepreneur rather than on the process of investment, which tends to preoccupy so many other schemes. IDM offers a variety of financial instruments to meet the particular needs of the promoter.

IDM concentrates on providing technical assistance to the entrepreneur as a means of protecting its financial contribution, rather than requiring the normal collateral. The technical assistance begins at the very earliest stage of a project's design and continues with training in accounting procedures to ensure that appropriate records will be kept. However, supervision continues for at least 3 years, with monthly meetings between the promoter, an enterprise consultant, and an accountant. This intensive support is costly but considered essential to getting new enterprises started. Clearly, it is not possible for the entrepreneur to pay for all these services at the beginning, so a developmental subsidy is necessary.

Diack closed by commenting on the difficulties posed by both the very unstable economic environment and the numerous and time-consuming regulations that confront the aspiring new entrepreneur.

Isaac Lobe Ndoumbe, of the Private Sector Development Unit in the African Development Bank, provided an analysis of the difficulties in financing SSEs in Cameroon. Like so many other countries, Cameroon developed strategies and policies to provide assistance and facilitate access to financing. This country's programs included special tax regimes, subsidized loans, credit guarantee schemes, and management assistance. All these programs were public, and they all failed, mainly owing to poor management, too much state involvement, and lack of support from the formal banking sector.

New approaches must now be found, incorporating lessons learned from past mistakes, creating proper incentives, and involving SSEs and banks in the design and implementation stages. A special effort is needed to bridge the gap between the growing informal economy and the formal financial sector. Private schemes, such as venture capital firms, financial cooperatives, and mutual funds, should be encouraged. An interbank guarantee scheme managed by the banks themselves was recommended. The government should be less involved in program management, concentrating instead on creating a sound macroeconomic, institutional, and legal environment.

Discussion

The sessions on financial services were marked by a general recognition that formal financial institutions, whether commercial or development banks, have failed to respond to the needs of SSEs. Many examples were given of credit programs that failed because loan conditions (for example, requirements for business plans, documentation, feasibility reports, collateral, and a proportion of the promoter's equity) were too stringent for SMEs' compliance. Loan recovery rates were low, and funds were decapitalized. Loan processing was slow, and in many cases the loan conditions generated low demand. Administration costs were too high for cost recovery, so when external funding dried up, the credit lines were unsustainable. Because of all this, efforts were made to channel funding through NGOs.

Most participants thought that in a limited way NGOs have succeeded in bringing small credits to microenterprise in both the rural and urban informal sectors. The Kenya Rural Enterprise Program (K-REP) is a prime example of this

(Aleke-Dondo, this volume). However, some speakers complained that there is too little coordination of the large number of NGOs and (or) of their efforts and those of other SME support programs. Also, many of these efforts and activities confuse credit delivery with welfare activities, tolerating poor loan repayment and waste of funds. Most of the programs work on too small a scale to have a major impact on SME development. Because NGOs alone cannot satisfy the increasing needs of the SME sector, the NGOs should try to help enterprises graduate to the stage of borrowing from formal financial institutions.

New formal financial institutions are appearing, often inspired by the Grameen Bank: rural banks in Ghana (Nikoi, this volume), credit and savings cooperatives in Togo, and the Peoples Bank in Nigeria (Ekpenyong and Kebang, this volume). Often the key is the replacement of material collateral with group security, with each member of the group in effect monitoring the group's use of credit and loan repayment. In addition, these formal institutions tend to combine credit provision with savings mobilization, thereby reducing dependency on donor and government funds and improving the prospects for sustainability. Avoiding any government interference was underlined again and again. To gain a proper understanding of the needs of SMEs and establish a context of mutual trust, institutions should be decentralized and preferably be community based.

Although there was still some debate about charging market interest rates, discussion at the conference suggested that the idea was definitely gaining acceptance. Aleke-Dondo (this volume) even argued that there was a case for charging SMEs higher interest rates than commercial bank rates because the transaction costs are higher and because access to credit at reasonable compliance costs is more important to the borrower than the actual interest rate charged. Commercial interest rates on SME loans foster the sustainability of credit schemes and help ensure that loans are used only for feasible business projects.

Although there was widespread criticism of commercial banks, a number of participants recognized that they are still needed. To improve their record and to promote the graduation of small borrowers to the use of commercial banks, more efforts could be made to develop links between NGOs, formal financial institutions, and group lending schemes. Pressure and inducements should be used to change banking habits. NGOs could function as specialized intermediaries to screen potential borrowers, appraise loan applications, and even help guarantee loans to SMEs. In this way, transaction costs could be lowered for both lenders and borrowers.

The consensus seemed to be that NGO credit schemes are needed for very small loans to microenterprises and that commercial banks are needed for loans to larger SSEs. There is also an urgent need for more innovative formal lending institutions that are community based, such as rural, savings, peoples, popular, or cooperative banks and credit unions. In contrast to NGOs, these institutions would be under legislative control and (or) the supervision of the central banks. Some of these institutions might be developed out of informal networks, such as Rotating Savings and Credit Associations (ROSCAs), *tontines,* or other mutual self-help organizations. In this way, a more complete range of financial services would be available.

Innovations for increasing competitiveness

On the third day, the conference was devoted to nonfinancial innovations that could increase the competitiveness of SMEs in Africa. Presentations covered a wide range of issues, including the role of enterprise networks and business associations, human resource development and its capacity for building technology, export marketing, and small firm–large firm links.

The president of Women's World Banking (WWB), Nancy Barry, led off the plenary session with an exciting presentation on the need for a break from traditional approaches to SME promotion. She insisted that the failure of SMEs to compete stems from their reliance on old products, processes, and practices; their relative isolation; their lack of resources to respond to change; and their failure to exploit the advantages of being small. The solutions she suggested were best-practice training and enterprise networks.

Entrepreneurs do not emerge from classrooms where NGOs or government employees are lecturing. They learn by doing, by being exposed to best practices within their subsector, where other business people are doing the training. The best training takes place through the transfer of practical knowledge in ongoing relationships between buyers and sellers and through subcontracting. Governments can facilitate such transfers of information by making resources available, but private-sector organizations must be the principal channels of delivery.

Enterprise networks can be involved in such activities, as well as input supply, transport, and marketing, wherever there is potential for economies of scale. Networks can contribute by making more competitive bids, obtaining concessions, and improving the eligibility of SMEs for bank funding. These networks evolve in various ways around individual enterprises, business NGOs, producer associations, traders, and exporters.

Barry listed a number of sectors where there is a high potential for new products: lighting fixtures manufacturing and assembly, food products and agro-processing, and services (for example, health, repair, and computer services). New initiatives can be diffused as local best practices through subsector-specific workshops and visual media. Global best practices can be obtained through trips made for gaining exposure and through apprenticeships.

Barry then outlined WWB activities, including a three-part enterprise training program, and gave examples of how WWB's local affiliates have assisted in establishing innovation councils with SMEs. Finally, she proposed that governments and donors create enterprise innovation funds for local action research, local and global best-practice training, and the creation of consortia and enterprise networks. However, these activities must be operated by the private sector, on a self-sustaining basis.

Strive Masiyiwa submitted a case study of how the Indigenous Business Development Centre (IBDC), which he used to direct, acts as a change agent in Zimbabwe. IBDC was created in 1987 to strengthen the voice of black business, which, it was felt, was still prevented from reaching its full potential. IBDC is actually a movement involving a wide range of large and small indigenous organizations and people in every sector of the economy, including farmers, women, miners, contractors, cooperatives, and even veterans of the liberation struggle.

IBDC bases its strategy for SME development on the recognition of four rights:

- the right of people to go into business (without legal and attitudinal barriers);
- the right of SMEs to exist (without the stifling impact of monopoly power and restrictive practices);

- the right of SMEs to close down, (without the social stigma attached to business failure); and
- the rights of the natural environment.

From the start, IBDC realized that it was competition, not protection, that would unleash opportunities for indigenous businesses. As a result, it has become the main lobby group for antitrust legislation and the creation of a competition council. IBDC's most successful campaign against monopolies resulted in liberalization of urban transport, and almost instantaneously several hundred new SSEs sprang up to run minibuses and taxis to provide transport for the public. IBDC also helped convince Zimbabwe's parliament to develop a national policy for SMEs, which was finally adopted in April 1993. IBDC is now campaigning for greater liberalization of financial and capital markets.

Masiyiwa held that an African business organization cannot confine itself to advocacy or lobbying. It must also do something to improve the skills and abilities of its members. Donors do not always understand this well enough, and the assistance that external donor agencies provide to business associations is disappointing. IBDC wants to develop its members' management skills and their ability to adapt technology and to mobilize financial resources. To address management needs, IBDC created the Business Extension and Advisory Services. IBDC has had less success developing its members' ability to adapt technology or to obtain credit, mainly owing to a lack of donor support. IBDC is working to set up an institution called the Business Research and Industrial Development Institute to help manufacturing SSEs obtain technical information and assistance.

The theme of business associations and networks was further developed by two women. Hassania Chalbi, of Tunisia, is the President of the Association for the Advancement of Women Entrepreneurs. She started by emphasizing that women in north Africa have always played an essential role in food production and handicrafts. Now their potential is becoming more visible, particularly with the recent phenomenon of women's involvement in the industrial sector. However, they still face many constraints. Although school attendance among girls in Tunisia has risen dramatically, women's illiteracy remains at 48%, much higher than men's (26%). With such levels of education, most female entrepreneurs remain in low-technology activities that require little innovation but have little potential for growth.

Women have also been disadvantaged in their access to credit. In three credit agencies, the share of resources going to female entrepreneurs varied between a mere 5% and a maximum of only 15%. Nonetheless, women are responsible for 730 of the 9 960 industrial projects launched in the 1980s in Tunisia. Of these, 520 were in the textile sector.

Chalbi felt that the social status of Tunisian women has improved with their new role as economic agents and that young women now realize that they can have a successful career in the private sector, as an alternative to the civil service. Furthermore, some women are now applying their scientific training in truly innovative, modern-sector activities. The Association for the Promotion of Women Entrepreneurs is now working as a regional network for north Africa. The association plans to share experiences and products, encourage joint ventures, and facilitate marketing.

Simone Zoundi is an entrepreneur from Burkina Faso and a leader of the local association of women entrepreneurs, as well as being active at the regional level. In her country, SME growth has been stifled by high taxes, in particular, as well as by unfavourable monetary policies, dumping, and the lack of consultation by government with the private sector on policies affecting it. The political and economic uncertainty discourage new investment.

To improve the investment climate, the private sector must organize and make its voice heard. For this reason, the Enterprise Network was formed. The Network consists of 150 business women and men from eight countries in West Africa; four more countries are planning to join. The Network is based on national networks in each country. The main objectives are to facilitate the organization of the private sector and, through dialogue with policymakers, to establish a favourable environment for SMEs.

In Burkina Faso, the Association of Women Heads of Enterprise plays an important role both within the Enterprise Network and at the national level. This association has developed programs for information and training in marketing and management, a mutual guarantee fund to facilitate access to credit, and a sales network to help unemployed women get started in business.

Generally, there has been a new culture of enterprise in Burkina Faso. The idea is to restore entrepreneurs to their true role as agents of development — wealth creators contributing to community welfare while receiving a fair return on investment. This vision of development has been supported by aid agencies but still requires some changes in attitude at all levels of Burkinabé society.

Godfred Frempong, of the Technology Transfer Centre, discussed the low level of technological capability among SSES in Ghana, with particular focus on the manufacturing of capital goods. A number of institutions were created to assist in this area: the National Board for Small-Scale Industries (NBSSI), the Technology Consultancy Centre (TCC), the Ghana Regional and Appropriate Industrial Service (GRATIS), and the National Vocational Training Institute (NVTI).

NBSSI is a government body that has had some success organizing management and entrepreneurial guidance courses, as well as linking SSES to relevant technical institutes. However, NBSSI's lack of attention to credit has impeded the SMES' adoption of new technology. NBSSI has also missed the opportunity to influence government procurement policy, which could have provided an indirect incentive for technical change.

TCC was established in 1972 to serve as a conduit for research from the University of Science and Technology in Kumasi. An intermediate technology transfer unit was set up, which proved so successful that GRATIS was formed with the mandate to create similar units in all the regions of the country. Many small engineering firms have benefited from such technical training, which leads to the importation of modern machine tools, among other things.

More formal technical and vocational training is provided by NVTI. Unfortunately, it has not been as effective: very few entrepreneurs have enrolled. Frempong cited a survey that found that only 6% of entrepreneurs have technical education of any type.

Frempong concluded with a theoretical overview of the benefits to be derived from subcontracting, local enterprise networks, national associations, and entrepreneurial development programs. He cited one example of a foreign motorbike company that eliminated its imports of gears and sprockets by subcontracting to a local small engineering firm. However, there was no evidence of concerted government initiatives to promote any of these strategies.

Julius S.M. Mburugu, the National Coordinator of the ILO/UNDP Entrepreneurship Education Project in Kenya, described how his program targeted young men and women who had completed formal education. Although the program was particularly interested in young people entering the vocational training institutions, it also worked with university students, male and female operators of informal enterprises, owners of established small businesses, and experienced trainers and administrators. The program is based on the assumption that positive attitudes toward business are best incorporated during the formative years and that many people have latent entrepreneurial talents that could be enhanced through a training program. The focus is on both changing attitudes and motivating trainees to generate business ideas.

By late 1993, the Entrepreneurship Educational Project had reached more than 40 000 trainees, enrolled in 144 institutions throughout the country. The first group of graduates completed the program in July 1993, and each prepared a business plan to determine the prospects for financial assistance in starting their own small business. A number of trainees have already started microenterprises.

Another part of this UNDP project involved the creation of small business centres (SBCs) within technical training institutions. SBCs are designed to facilitate the development of SMEs and to promote an enterprise culture within the institution and the local business community. SBCs encourage students to start microenterprises while training, and they offer advisory services to local SSEs and microenterprises, at reasonable cost. SBCs will also try to link prospective entrepreneurs, both among students and others in the community, to possible sources of finance.

At the time of the conference, 17 training institutions had established SBCs, and the project had earmarked 9 of these for more support so that they could act as models for the others. It is expected that 40 centres will be established. Mburugu acknowledged that the program would be able to make only a limited contribution to the creation of new enterprises, but he felt that the program could act as a change agent by developing positive attitudes toward entrepreneurship among the target groups.

Marketing is an often neglected but critically important constraint to SME growth, so one workshop looked at this question from various perspectives (one paper on this by Masinde and another by Muzamani are in this volume). Ahmed Azirar, of the Business and Trade Institute for Enterprises, explored Morocco's growing success in exporting manufactured products and the problems faced by SMEs taking part.

Azirar first reviewed the general development of industrial exports from Morocco, where the government has emphasized export promotion as the main pillar of its industrial strategy. He admitted that SMEs face many problems developing exports. In particular, he mentioned the low quality of their products, their lack of information on potential markets, and their financial and insurance difficulties. To play a greater role in exporting, Moroccan SMEs need to have better quality products, improved packaging, and access to new technologies. Azirar also noted that SMEs rarely have a sales manager. Usually, the entrepreneur–owner handles all sales, with the result that he or she does not have the time to get to know potential markets or to deal with the administrative complexities of exporting.

Things are beginning to change, according to Azirar. Moroccan businesses are starting to appreciate that a competitive price alone is not enough to compete in export markets. Quality is as important as price, and there is also a need to keep up with the tastes and needs of overseas customers.

Discussion

In the plenary session, some participants were concerned about the critical comments about the government's role and about the perhaps excessive optimism regarding the private sector. Many chambers of commerce are not representative, business associations are weak, and business-oriented NGOs are few. Furthermore, it was not clear to many participants why private companies would share their best practices or why large companies would assist small ones. What is really needed, it was suggested, is a redefinition of roles in a public–private partnership. Public services are still needed, but perhaps they need to be provided by private organizations through performance-based contracts.

When discussion turned to the issue of technology, some participants expressed doubts about the relevance of sophisticated new technology. They pointed out that "just-in-time" processes may not be appropriate when most enterprises operate on a basis of "just-in-case." However, other participants recognized the need to be globally competitive and the role of technology in raising quality standards. Several regretted the limited attention paid to technology at the conference.

The group workshop on human resource development produced a lively discussion and various comments and suggestions from the participants. The need for subregional and regional training programs was underlined by some. Others pointed out that operators of SSEs find it difficult to benefit from training programs designed for larger enterprises. Research into appropriate methods to assess the impact of training programs in Africa was recommended.

Some comments were made about the formal education system (inherited in most African countries from the colonial period), which instills in people a negative attitude toward entrepreneurship. It was argued that the formal education system encouraged students to seek the presumed security of employment in large organizations. The education system needs to incubate an enterprise culture. However, most participants thought that training and education for entrepreneurship should be linked to practical support programs on preparing business plans, obtaining credit, and acquiring the skills and facilities to set up and operate businesses.

Final sessions

The final afternoon was devoted to a review of the conference proceedings by representatives of the private sector, NGOs, government, and donor agencies, and this review was followed by a synthesis of the various reports of the sessions and workshops.

Review of the conference proceedings

Abdoulaye Ndiaye, from the Senegalese private sector, argued for a new approach. Competition could be a positive factor, according to most participants. Ndiaye believed that entrepreneurs can be agents of change but that the image of the private entrepreneur needs to improve. It is the government's task to formulate policies, but this should be done only after full consultation with the private sector. The government isn't the only sector that needs to reform — so does the private sector.

Hassania Chalbi of Tunisia spoke as a representative of NGOs, focusing mainly on ways of supporting female entrepreneurs. She stressed that, in her view, women are more innovative and more ready to collaborate with each other and with business people in general. She thought that women entrepreneurs could express themselves best through NGOs and urged government to take both women in business and NGOs more seriously.

Isaya Onyango, a government official from Kenya, agreed that SMEs need a clear, coherent policy framework. The consensus was that governments should act as facilitators, leaving direct intervention and support to the private sector.

Michael Farbman, of USAID, represented the donor agencies. Donors, he pointed out, play only the role of a catalyst, mainly behind the scenes. They can give support, and they can even provide resources in the process of formulating more appropriate policies and help with implementation, but it is up to the government and the local business community to carry through programs. Of course, donors could generate and help communicate ideas by spreading information on success stories.

Farbman stressed two particular needs of SME development: the need to support women in business and the need to encourage the formal financial sector to provide funds for SMEs. A way has to be found (and has in fact been found in some countries) to involve commercial banks in channeling capital to SMEs. Only this sector has the resources to meet the large needs of a growing SME sector, so innovative approaches must be found.

Discussion

In the discussion that followed, participants stressed the need to distinguish between microenterprises and formal SMEs. Their needs are different, and there must be different approaches and support programs for them. Nor was it necessarily appropriate to expand support to all SMEs. SMEs have to become more competitive and not expect to be protected and subsidized continuously. New types of credit guarantees are required if commercial banks are to be persuaded to do more for SMEs.

The general view of participants seemed to be that all the change agents represented at the conference had to collaborate to build effective policies and programs. These included the public and private sectors, national governments, multilateral and bilateral donor agencies, NGOS, SMES, and a variety of academic, research, support, and financial institutions.

Synthesis of the sessions and workshops

Two experts with a lot of experience to share on the topic of SMES in Africa were invited to summarize the conference. Jacob Levitsky, of the United Kingdom, contrasted the presentations and discussions with those at the last similar gathering in Abidjan organized by the Donor Committee, again in cooperation with the African Development Bank, in 1983. He pointed out that the 1983 meeting had focused on development finance institutions (DFIS) and their role in financing SSES. There was little mention of NGOS; nor was there a great deal of interest in microenterprises or the informal sector. Most papers and discussions at that meeting concentrated on government-assisted programs directly implemented by public, state-supported agencies.

At the 1993 conference, there was little talk of relying on DFIS for financial support. Many of the African DFIS have either disappeared or face major financial difficulties. There has been a recognition of the importance of correct policies and less regulation and an understanding that deregulation alone would be insufficient to ensure the successful development of SMES. Greater access to finance and markets is essential. After years of reform and adjustment, there may be more opportunities for entrepreneurial development, but effective support programs with training, advice, and financial services are needed to make SME development a reality.

The discussions and papers at both conferences emphasized that the informal and microenterprise sectors are still the predominant form of SME in Africa. It was repeated many times during the 1993 conference that most of these enterprises do not grow and graduate into large, formal SMES, so some programs have to be carried out to improve the SMES' performance and output. NGOS have a most important role to play in catering to this large sector.

The reliance on government for implementing programs for SME promotion seems to have diminished, and there is considerable disenchantment with the institutions that governments have set up at great cost to the donors. Many SME promotion agencies have been closed down or restructured to perform a much more limited role. In several African countries, there is now an inclination to see governments as facilitators rather than as implementors of programs. Governments should provide resources, but private-sector organizations, independent bodies, or NGOs should provide support services. More participants (than in previous conferences) accepted the idea that SMEs have to do more to help themselves and not look to government for help and protection all of the time.

SME business associations have developed in several African countries both to encourage governments to consult with the sector on all policy issues and to develop appropriate services that provide information, training, consulting, and other forms of assistance to members. Most of these associations are still weak and at present can offer only very limited services, but there is hope that with outside assistance, they may gradually take on a more supportive role in the SME sector. This could be supplemented by linkage of small firms with larger firms, which are often prepared to help SMEs. The private sector would also need to collaborate with private consulting groups, universities, and research and development institutions.

In his final comments, Levitsky dwelt on the changes that had taken place in the financing of SMEs. Several papers had described innovative efforts to create new financial institutions, such as rural banks, credit and savings cooperatives, credit unions, people's banks, and community banks, that are attuned to the needs of SMEs. Notwithstanding the importance of all these innovations, Levitsky, too, contended that the commercial banks have a key role to play as providers of SME finance. In various parts of the developing world, ways have been found to involve commercial banks through refinancing schemes, credit guarantees, group lending, NGO intermediation, and increased margins to compensate for higher transaction costs. All these approaches need to be explored further.

Georges Hénault rounded out the debate with a more global perspective. After highlighting some of the conclusions of the discussion, he pointed out that the appropriate relationship between the state and the private sector remains the fundamental, underlying question. If the historic role of the state is changing, the state is nevertheless critical to successful development.

Because of the significant change in culture, or mentality, observed in Africa today, which was evident at the conference, Hénault cautioned that there are still some important questions to be answered. The prejudices of the state toward the private sector are now being openly discussed and criticized. Is the same true of the prejudices of the private sector? Everyone agrees on the need for greater cooperation between the two, but it goes without saying that the majority of SMEs are rural, whereas the civil service is invariably urban. Do these two groups speak the same language?

The ethics of development should not be overlooked. Corruption is often a fact of life in this relationship, whether it be related to taxes, import duties, or regulatory authorizations. Social justice should not be sacrificed in the pursuit of economic efficiency.

Finally, the unavoidable challenge of globalization must be addressed. The vibrancy of informal, regional trade is not well managed, which results in negative repercussions and lost opportunities. In the foreign market, African SMEs face a formidable challenge meeting international competition. Should the African SMEs follow the Asian example and rely on large trading houses and multinational corporations to conquer world markets?

Levitsky and Hénault agreed that Africa is passing through a difficult time and that, for most if not all African countries, it is not yet over. The extent of indigenous SME development in Africa may be disappointing, but there are important signs of hope. Numerous SMEs continue to be created every year; the entrepreneurial spirit is not lacking. Lessons are being learned from past failures, and there is a readiness to innovate. Entrepreneurs are putting new emphasis on maintenance, technology transfer, quality control, and consumer satisfaction. Governments are reaching out to the private sector, listening to it and collaborating with it in the implementation of joint programs. The policy framework is gradually improving. One can only be optimistic about the future of Africa. ❊

APPENDIX 1.
CONFERENCE PARTICIPANTS

This appendix lists the names and addresses of all participants at the Abidjan conference. It also indicates which participants acted as chairpersons and rapporteurs during the conference: C, chairperson; R, rapporteur.

Austria

Konstantin F. Huber
Senior Advisor
Small Scale Industry Development
Austrian Federal Chancellery
Department of Development
  Cooperation
Minoritenplatz 9
A-1010 Vienna
Tel: (43) 1 53115 4468
Fax: (43) 1 53115 2960

Leny van Oyen
Industrial Development Officer
UNIDO
PO Box 300
A-1400 Vienna
Tel: (43) 1 21131 5083
Fax: (43) 1 239934

Christian Zimmerman
Senior Industrial Development
  Officer
UNIDO
PO Box 300
A-1400 Vienna
Tel: (43) 1 21131 3424
Fax: (43) 1 237288

Belgium

Paolo Logli
Deputy Head
Industrial Cooperation, Private
  Investment, Enterprise Unit
Directorate-General for Development
European Commission
200, rue de la Loi
1049 Brussels
Tel: (32) 2 299 30 09
Fax: (32) 2 299 25 43

Luis Ritto
Division Head
DG VIII/B/4
European Commission
3, rue de Genève
1140 Brussels
Tel: (32) 2 299 98 50
Fax: (32) 2 299 25 43

Benin

Claude A. Agbemavor
Head
General Inspection Unit
Department of Trade and Tourism
Cotonou
Tel: (229) 31 54 02, 31 52 58
Fax: c/o Denis Baker, USAID/Benin,
(229) 30 12 60

Innocentia Attanaso
Lawyer
Ministry of Justice
BP 1149/032695
Cotonou
Tel: (229) 31 34 04
Fax: (229) 31 34 14

Théophile Capo-Chichi
Director General
Centre for the Promotion of
   Employment and Small and
   Medium Enterprise
BP 2093
Cotonou
Tel: (229) 31 44 47, 31 45 39
Fax: (229) 31 59 50

G. Lucien Glélé
Business Manager
Chambre de commerce et de
l'industrie du Bénin
BP 31 G
Cotonu
Tel: (229) 31 20 81

Houessou Joseph Gnonlofoun
Lawyer/Counsellor
National Assembly
BP 171
Cotonou
Tel: (229) 31 39 03, 31 52 12
Fax: c/o Denis Baker, USAID/Benin,
   (229) 30 12 60

Botswana

Elias Dewah
Deputy Director
Botswana Confederation of
   Commerce, Industry and
   Manpower
Debswana House, The Mall
PO Box 432
Gaborone
Tel: (267) 353 459
Fax: (267) 373 142

Burkina Faso

Rosine Coulibaly
Officer
Cellule d'appui à la petite entreprise
   de Ouagadougou
01 BP 6443
Ouagadougou
Tel: (226) 31 37 62
Fax: (226) 31 37 64

Fabrice Coupel
Professor
Business Management and
   Creation Interstate School —
   Rural Equipment
BP 7023
Ouagadougou
Tel: (226) 30 71 47
Fax: (226) 31 27 24

Michel Fréchette
Training adviser and support
   consultant
Support Group to the small
   entreprise in Ouagadougou
01 BP 6443
Ouagadougou
Tel: (226) 31 37 62
Fax: (226) 31 37 64

Robert Ouedraogo
GTZ — Project Handicraft Master Plan
BP 1910
Ouagadougou
Tel: (226) 31 30 77

Jürgen Schrôder
Senior Advisor
GTZ
01 BP 1910
Ouagadougou
Tel: (226) 31 30 77
Fax: (226) 31 08 73

Y. Joseph Zoromé
Direction de l'artisanat
01 BP 1910
Ouagadougou
Tel: (226) 31 30 77

Simone Zoundi
President and Director General
SODEPAL
BP 1749
Ouagadougou
Tel: (226) 30 01 50
Fax: (226) 31 37 64

Cameroon

André Delchef
Director
Centre de création d'entreprise
  de Yaoundé
BP 572
Yaoundé
Tel: (237) 20 34 35
Fax: (237) 21 37 79

Marguerite Etock Nengue
Sub-Director
Small and Medium-Sized Enterprises
Ministry of Industrial and
Commercial Development
Youndé
Tel: (237) 23 07 75

Paul K. Fokam (C)
Director General
Caisse commune d'épargne et
  d'investissements
BP 11824
Yaoundé
Tel: (237) 23 60 41
Fax: (237) 22 17 85

Louise Minville
First Secretary (Cooperation)
  Private Sector
Canadian Embassy
BP 572
Yaoundé
Tel: (237) 22 19 36
Fax: (237) 22 10 90

Clement N. Ngwasiri
Vice Dean
University of Buea
PO Box 170
Buea
Tel: (237) 32 26 90
Fax: (237) 43 08 13

Jean-Pierre Ndy
General Manager
Partenaires, entreprise de
  communication
BP 6290
Yaoundé
Tel: (237) 20 70 52

Georges Tchokokam
Director General
Winstel Research & Consulting
BP 2937
Douala
Tel: (237) 42-90-41
Fax: (237) 43-24-38

Canada

Alain Berranger
Vice President
Coginter Group Inc.
48 Cours le Royer Ouest
Montreal, Québec
Tel: (514) 849-1710
Fax: (514) 849-2822

Ghislain Dussault
Program Officer
CIDA
200 Promenade du Portage
Hull, Québec
Tel: (819) 997-6380
Fax: (819) 953-9454

Philip English (C)
Social Sciences Division
IDRC
PO Box 8500
Ottawa, Ontario
Tel: (613) 236-6163 (ext. 2313)
Fax: (613) 567-7748

Catherine Gold
Director of Programs
Foundation for International Training
200 – 1262 Don Mills Road
Toronto, Ontario
Tel: (416) 449-8838
Fax: (416) 449-8547

Georges Hénault (R)
Professor
University of Ottawa
136, Jean-Jacques Lussier
Ottawa, Ontario
Tel: (613) 564-7027
Fax: (613) 564-6518

Gilles Lessard (C)
Senior Advisor
Small Enterprise Development,
   Policy Branch
CIDA
200 Promenade du Portage
Hull, Québec
Tel: (819) 997-6607
Fax: (819) 953-3348

Jean-Claude Lorin
CIDA
200 Promenade du Portage
Hull, Québec
Tel: (819) 997-1515

Chile

Gaston G. Suarez Crothers
Managing Director
Microenterprises Credit Program
Development Bank of Chile
Alameda 1486
Santiago
Tel: (562) 698 5155, 695 1766
Fax: (562) 698 4944

Congo

Clémence Bakonma
Handicraft Promotion Service,
   Small Enterprise
Chambre de commerce du Kouilou
BP 665
Pointe-Noire
Tel: (242) 94 12 80
Fax: (242) 94 36 38

Jurgen Koch
Economist
GTZ/FGU
BP 796
Pointe-Noire
Tel: (242) 94 36 38
Fax: (242) 94 36 38

Jean-Baptiste Moukissi
Head, Small and Medium-Sized
   Enterprise
Project Handicraft and Small
   Enterprise
BP 796
Pointe-Noire
Tel: (242) 94 36 38
Fax: (242) 94 36 38

Alphonse Oko
Assistant professor
Université Marien Ngouabi
BP 5722 Ouenze
Brazzaville

Marguerite Tomb
Director
Formation et promotion des
   PME-PMI, artisanat
Chambre nationale de commerce,
   industrie et agriculture
BP 1119
Brazzaville
Tel: (242) 83 29 56
Fax: (242) 83 61 99

Côte d'Ivoire

Augustin Zilma Badiez
Director
ARSAT
04 BP 1827
Abidjan
Tel: (225) 21 12 27
Fax: (225) 22 45 03

Amparo Ballivian
Economist
World Bank
PO Box 1850
Abidjan
Tel: (225) 44 22 27

Dieneba Bamba
Secretary General
ONG/GONOSI
03 BP 1059
Abidjan
Tel: (225) 21 12 27
Fax: (225) 22 45 03

Alain Bambara
President
Cosmivoire
Abidjan

Denis Bélisle (C)
Canadian Ambassador
Immeuble Trade Center
23, avenue Nogues, Le Plateau
01 BP 4104
Abidjan
Tel: (225) 21 20 09
Fax: (225) 22 05 29

André Bogui
Director
ETAM
06 BP 18
Abidjan
Tel: (225) 41 34 24

Arnoult Boissau
Côte d'Ivoire Fund for Development
and Investment
10th floor, CCIA Tower
04 BP 2237
Abidjan
Tel: (225) 22 42 93
Fax: (225) 22 41 74

Mamadou Diodandé
Director
Agence nationale de la formation
professionnelle
15 BP 95
Abidjan
Tel: (225) 22 20 30
Fax: (225) 25 24 99

Koffi Maxime Houdénou
Director
Geste International
06 BP 545
Abidjan
Tel: (225) 41 18 52
Fax: (225) 41 06 38

Ginette Johnson
Management Consultant
Geste International
06 BP 645
Abidjan
Tel: (225) 41 18 52
Fax: (225) 41 06 38

Théodora Komaclo
Geste International
06 BP 645
Abidjan
Tel: (225) 41 18 52
Fax: (225) 41 06 38

Mongo N'Da Komenan
Consultant in Industrial Economy
Department of Industry and
Commerce
01 BP 4536
Abidjan
Tel: (225) 21 65 27

Kouaho Boniface Kouaho
S/D of Promotion of Small and
Medium-Sized Enterprise
Department of Industry
and Commerce
BP V65
Abidjan
Tel: (225) 22 78 94

Guy Mercier
Canadian Embassy
Immeuble Trade Center
23, avenue Nogues, Le Plateau
01 BP 4104
Abidjan
Tel: (225) 21 20 09
Fax: (225) 22 05 29

Brou Gaston N'Chu
Head of Studies
Department of Trade and Commerce
09 BP 110
Abidjan
Tel: (225) 46 06 36

Isaac Lobe Ndoumbe
Senior Investment Officer
Private Sector Development Unit
African Development Bank
01 BP 1387
Abidjan

Louis B. Ngassa Batonga
Investment Officer
APDF
01 BP 8669
Abidjan
Tel: (225) 21 96 97
Fax: (225) 21 61 51

Jean-Pierre Ouya
President
African NGO Collective
03 BP 1059
Abidjan
Tel: (225) 21 12 27
Fax: (225) 22 45 03

Mariam S. Pal
Senior Social Policy Officer
African Development Bank
01 BP V316
Abidjan
Tel: (225) 20 59 82
Fax: (225) 20 49 07

Peter G. Rwelamira (C)
Principal Economist
Private Sector Development Unit
African Development Bank
01 BP 1387
Abidjan
Tel: (225) 20 41 68, 20 48 68
Fax: (225) 20 49 64, 20 49 00

Ulla Salonoja
Commercial attaché
Embassy of Finland
Deux Plateaux-vallons
01 BP 1835
Abidjan
Tel: (225) 41 50 01
Fax: (225) 41 50 62

Ousmane Somali
Business Department
Canadiam Embassy
Abidjan
Tel: (225) 21 20 09
Fax: (225) 21 77 28

Alimata Soumahoro
Secretary General
Réseau mutualiste entreprise
09 BP 109
Abidjan
Tel: (225) 44 96 43
Fax: (225) 44 75 72

Karim Sory Traore
Head of Service
Handicraft and Small and
    Medium-Sized Enterprise
Department of Trade and Commerce
20 BP 1385
Abidjan
Tel: (225) 21 12 85

Oren E. Whyche
Regional Coordinator, Private Sector
USAID
01 BP 1712
Abidjan
Tel: (225) 41 45 28
Fax: (225) 41 35 44

Pierre d'Alcantara Zocli
President
Centre international de gestion
    pour les établissements
    scientifiques, techniques et
    entreprises
06 BP 545
Abidjan
Tel: (225) 411 852
Fax: (225) 410 638

France

Guy Dupasquier
President
Association épargne sans frontière
35/37 Boissy d'Anglas 8ᵉ
Paris 75008
Tel: (33 1) 42 66 22 83
Fax: (33 1) 47 42 75 14

Raundi Halvorson-Quevedo
Administrator
Financial Policies and Private
    Sector Division
Development Co-operative
    Directorate
OECD
2, rue André-Pascal
Paris 75116
Tel: (33 1) 45 24 91 59
Fax: (33 1) 45 24 16 50

Pierre Traimond
29, rue des Mathurins
Paris 75008
Tel: (33 1) 42 65 30 81
Fax: (33 1) 46 34 99 83

Gabon

Bengono-B'Eyele Lambert
Technical Adviser to the Minister
Department of Small and Medium-
    Sized Entreprise and of Handicraft
BP 3848
Libreville
Tel: (241) 74 87 36
Fax: (241) 74 87 37

Bruno Pindi
Director General
Concept International
BP 3848
Libreville
Tel: (241) 74 87 36
Fax: (241) 74 87 37

Germany

Régine Frechen
Economist
Kreditanstalt Für Wiederaufbau
Palmengartenstr
60325 Frankfurt
Tel: (49) 69 7431 2739
Fax: (49) 69 7431 2944

Wilhelm Hankel (C)
University Frankfurt/GTZ
D-53639 Konigswinter
Tel: (49) 2244 7447
Fax: (49) 2244 82034

Léon Houdret
Planning Officer
Small Enterprise Development
GTZ
Dag-Hammarskjöld-Weg 1-5
65760 Eschborn
Tel: (49) 6196 791441
Fax: (49) 6196 796146

Christian Pollak
Head of Division
Industrial Consulting and Private
    Sector Promotion
GTZ
Dag-Hammarskjöld-Weg 1-5
65760 Eschborn
Tel: (49) 6196 791445
Fax: (49) 6196 797181

Dieter Reuter
Project Manager
Carl Duisberg Gesellschaft EV
Hohenstaufenring 30-32
D-50674 Cologne
Tel: (49) 221 2098331
Fax: (49) 221 2098111

Wolfgang Schneider-Barthold
Senior Research Fellow
IFO Institute for Economic Research
Poschingerstr. 10
D-81679 Munich
Tel: (89) 922 4301
Fax: (89) 922 4462

Brigitte Spath
Consultant
GTZ
Dag-Hammarskjöld-Weg 1-5
65760 Eschborn
Tel: (49) 6196 791441
Fax: (49) 6196 796146

Gabriele Trah
Planning Officer
Small Enterprise Development
GTZ
Dag-Hammarskjöld-Weg 1-5
65760 Eschborn
Tel: (49) 6196 791414
Fax: (49) 6196 796146

Ghana

Kofitse Ahadzi
President
Association of Small Scale Industries
PO Box 15578
Accra
Tel: (233) 21 227 028

Daniel Baffour-Awuah
Senior Technical Officer
Gratis Project
PO Box 151
Tema
Tel: (233) 221 42 43

Robert Buatsi
Head
SECOM Division
Gratis Project
PO Box 151
Tema
Tel: (233) 221 42 43

Godfred K. Frempong
Research Officer
Policy Research and Strategic
    Planning Institute
PO Box C 519
Accra
Tel: (233) 21 773 856
Fax: (233) 21 773 068

Carol Kerfoot
Canadian High Commission
Accra
Tel: (233) 21 228 555, 21 228 566
Fax: (233) 21 773 792

Alan Kyerematen (C)
Director
Empretec Ghana
Private Mail Bag
Accra
Tel: (233) 21 668 571, 21 668 572
Fax: (233) 21 665 574

Gloria Nikoi
Chair
AKUPEM Rural Bank
41 Sir Arku Korsah Road
PO Box 9874, Airport
Accra
Tel: (233) 21 775 919
Fax: (233) 21 669 913

George Prah
c/o Ken Ofori-Atta
Databank Ghana Ltd
Ministries Post Office
SSNIT Tower Block, 5th floor
Private Mail Bag
Accra
Tel: (233) 21 225 676
Fax: (233) 21 225 664

Bert Wesselink
Associate Expert
ILO
PO Box 1423
Accra

Guinea

Sylla Alseny
Director
Division of Small and Medium-Sized
  Enterprise
Ministry of Industry and Small and
  Medium-Sized Enterprise
Conakry
Tel: (874) 44 49 20

Douda Bangoura
Associate Director, Loans
Banque centrale de Guinée
Bd du Commerce
Conakry
Tel: (874) 151 7436
Fax: (874) 151 7437

Himi Yansane
Adviser to the Minister
Ministry of Industry and Small and
  Medium-Sized Enterprise
Près Immeuble CBG
Conakry
Tel: (874) 151 7436
Fax: (874) 151 7437

Hungary

Eva Bakonyi
Managing Director
B'nai B'rith Foundation
1126 Roszormenyi ut 8 J.12
Budapest
Tel: (361) 1562 357, 2014 601
Fax: (361) 1562 357

Kenya

Deepal Adhiraky
Training Advisor, GTZ
Kenya Institute of Management
PO Box 43706
Nairobi
Tel: (254) 2 332 507
Fax: (254) 2 333 255

C. Aleke-Dondo
Kenya Rural Enterprise Programme
PO Box 39312
Nairobi
Tel: (254) 2 718301, 2 718302,
  2 720173
Fax: (254) 2 711645

Situah Anyamba
Training and Project Officer
Kenya Management Assistance
  Programme
PO Box 59400
Nairobi
Tel: (254) 2 220883, 2 22090
Fax: (254) 2 216396

Alfreda Brewer
Deputy Chief
Private Enterprise Office, USAID
Box 30261
Nairobi
Tel: (254) 2 331160
Fax: (254) 2 337304

Ellen Brown
Ford Foundation
PO Box 41081
Nairobi
Tel: (254) 2 338123
Fax: (254) 2 338565

Anthony Chan
Economist
USAID/REDSO/ESA
PO Box 30261
Nairobi
Tel: (254) 2 331160
Fax: (254) 2 330945

Ralph Heinz Engelmann
Project Manager
Kenya Institute of Management
PO Box 47996
Nairobi
Tel: (254) 2 337406
Fax: (254) 2 562671

Almaz Gebru
Assistant Resident Representative
UNDP
PO Box 30218
Nairobi
Tel: (254) 2 228776, 2 228779
Fax: (254) 2 331897

Joseph Mwariri Karau
Divisional Manager
Kenya Industrial Estates
PO Box 78029
Nairobi
Tel: (254) 2 542127, 2 542138
Fax: (254) 2 542070

Maria Kitiabi R.M.K.
Consultant
University of Nairobi
Box 70051
Nairobi
Tel: (254) 2 714749

Micheal Klesh
Regional Private Sector Advisor
USAID/REDSO
PO Box 30261
Nairobi
Tel: (254) 2 331160
Fax: (254) 2 330945

Catherine K.M. Masinde (C)
Faculty of Commerce
University of Nairobi
PO Box 30197
Nairobi
Tel: (254) 2 726361
Fax: (254) 2 741251

Julius B.M. Mburugu
National Coordinator
ILO/UNDP Entrepreneurship
    Education Project
PO Box 44600
Nairobi
Tel: (254) 2 520635, 2 521920
Fax: (254) 2 331897

Mary McVay
Monitoring and Evaluation Officer
Private Enterprise Office
USAID
PO Box 30261
Nairobi
Tel: (254) 2 331160
Fax: (254) 2 337304

Andrew K. Mullei
Director
Africa Program
International Center for
    Economic Growth
PO Box 55237
Nairobi
Tel: (254) 2 215295
Fax: (254) 2 223220

Jospiiat Murage
Manager
Small Business Unit
Barclay's Bank of Kenya Ltd
PO Box 30120
Nairobi
Tel: (254) 2 332230
Fax: (254) 2 337201

Albert Kimanthi Mutua (C)
Kenya Rural Enterprise Programme
PO Box 39312
Nairobi
Tel: (254) 2 718301, 2 718302
Fax: (254) 2 711645

Mwangi Ngumo
Associate Director for Enterprise
  Development
Kenya Institute of Management
PO Box 47996
Nairobi
Tel: (254) 2 337406
Fax: (254) 2 562671

Isaya Onyango
Head
Strategy and Policy Analysis Division
Office of the Vice-President and
Ministry of Planning and National
  Development
PO Box 30007
Nairobi
Tel: (254) 2 230501
Fax: (254) 2 230501

Tom Owuor
Executive Director
Federation of Kenya Employees
PO Box 48311
Nairobi

Zachariah Ratemo
Project Officer
USAID KENYA
PO Box 30261
Nairobi
Tel: (254) 2 331160
Fax: (254) 2 337304

Ernest C.A. Saina
Deputy Managing Director
Industrial Development Bank Ltd
PO Box 44036
Nairobi
Tel: (254) 2 337079
Fax: (254) 2 334594

Hugh Scott (R)
Coordination Office
British Aid to Small Enterprise
Small Enterprise Development
  Programme
PO Box 30465
Nairobi
Tel: (254) 2 212172
Fax: (254) 2 336907

Pius Amaasi Singora
Program Officer
Federation of Kenya Employers
PO Box 48311
Nairobi
Tel: (254) 2 713684
Fax: (254) 2 721990

James Tomecko
GTZ Team Leader
Kenya Industrial Estates
Informal Sector Programme
PO Box 78832
Nairobi
Tel: (254) 2 542127
Fax: (254) 2 542070

Leon Tomensen
SED Advisor, East Africa
Netherlands Government
PO Box 41537
Nairobi
Tel: (254) 2 227111
Fax: (254) 2 339155

Madagascar

Jean-Claude Bikiny
Expert Equivalent
GTZ
BP 118
207 Nosy-Be
Tel: (261) 40495
Fax: (261) 41407

Wolfgang Hannig
Project Team Leader
GTZ
GTZ-SAP BP 869, Nanisana
Antananarivo
Tel: (261) 2 40495
Fax: (261) 2 41407

Francis Rakoto
Director General
Société d'oxygène et d'acétulène
  de Madagascar
BP 53
Antananarivo 101
Tel: (261) 2 22506
Fax: (261) 2 20909

Wilson Rakotoarivelo
Director of Industrial Affairs
Department of Industry and
    Tourism promotion
Ambohidahy
Anatananarivo 101
Tel: (261) 2 25515
Fax: (261) 2 27790

Edmond Razafimandimby
President and Director General
Vintana
Lot VB 5 ter Ambatoroka
Antananarivo
Tel: (261) 2 25489
Fax: (261) 2 34883

Malawi

Mary Nyandovi-Kerr
Chairperson
Women's World Banking — Malawi
PO Box 1648
Blantyre
Tel: (265) 622 702
Fax: (265) 671 686, 677 013

Sosten M.C. Nyoni
Principal
Malawian Entrepreneurs
Development Institute
Private Bag 2
Mponela
Tel: (265) 286 244
Fax: (265) 286 412

Volker Wittmann
General Manager
INDEFUND Ltd
PO Box 2339
Blantyre
Tel: (265) 620 244
Fax: (265) 628 680

Mali

Mariam Konaté
Technical Adviser
Department of Trade, Industry
    and Transport
Bamako
Tel: (223) 22 92 08

Morocco

Ahmed Azirar
Business and Trade Institute
    for Enterprises
Km 9, 500 Route de Nouasseur
BP 8.114
CASA — OASIS
Tel: (212) 33-54-82, 33-54-85
Fax: (212) 33-54-96

Driss Eskalli
Treasurer
Projet DYNA-PME
rue Misk Allail, Secteur 229b
Hay Ryad, Rabat
Tel: (212) 7 71-12-24, 7 71-15-86
Fax: (212) 7 71-15-85

Mauritania

Mouhamedou L. Diack
Director
SIDI/Investissement-développement
    en Mauritanie
BP 5004 ILOT K 120
RC No 715
Nouakchott
Tel: (222) 2 56121, 2 56122
Fax: (222) 2 56122

Mauritius

Jairaz Pochun (R)
Chief Executive and Acting Director
Small and Medium Industries
    Development Organization
Ministry of Industry and Industrial
    Technology
Royal Road
Coromandel
Tel: (230) 233 5030
Fax: (230) 233 5545

Farzana Nahaboo
Chairperson
SMIDO
9A, Willoughby Street
Curepipe
Tel: (230) 676 3420
Fax: (230) 233 5545

Netherlands

Pieter de Lange
Ministry of Foreign Affairs
PO Box 20061
2500 EB, The Hague
Tel: (31) 70 348-6539
Fax: (31) 70 348-5956

Albertus Helmsing (R)
Associate Professor
Institute of Social Studies
PO Box 29776
2502 LT, The Hague
Tel: (31) 70 426-0460

Frans van Rijn
Advisor
Financial Services and Enterprise
    Development
Directorate General for International
    Cooperation
Ministry of Foreign Affairs
Bezuidenhutseweg 67, PO Box 20061
2500 EB, The Hague
Tel: (31) 70 348-6539
Fax: (31) 70 348-5956

Meine Pieter van Dijk (R)
Associate Professor, Economics
Economics Faculty
Erasmus University
PO Box 1738 H6-10
3000 DR, Rotterdam
Tel: (31) 10 408-2174
Fax: (31) 10 452-3660

Teun van Dijk
Ministry of Foreign Affairs
PO Box 20061
2500 EB, The Hague
Tel: (31) 70 348-6539
Fax: (31) 70 348-5956

Niger

Winfried Muziol
Coordinator
Programme d'appui à l'artisanat
BP 209
Niamey
Tel: (227) 735 988
Fax: (261) 734 067

Nigeria

Olatunji Daodu
Executive Secretary
WAMDEVIN
c/o Ascon, PMB 1004, Topo-Badagry
Lagos
Tel: (234) 1 73 24 15
Fax: (234) 1 66 61 00

David B. Ekpenyong
Department of Economics
University of Ibadan
Ibadan

Senegal

J.J. Kojo Asiedu
Postharvest Expert
African Regional Centre for
    Technology
BP 2435
Immeuble Fahd Ben Abdel Aziz
Ave Djily Mbaye
Dakar
Tel: (221) 237 712, 237 710
Fax: (221) 237 713

Olivier Baldi
Consultant
SMEC Support Program
ILO
BP 414
Dakar
Tel: (221) 231 042 (ext. 4799)

Roger Kouessi
Department Head
Small and Medium-Sized Enterprises
African Centre for Advanced
    Management Studies
BP 3 802
Dakar

Youssou Ndiaye
Project Director
Fondation excellence/Institut
    supérieur de management
BP 5018, Rue 1 Pointe
Dakar
Tel: (221) 259 374

Abdoulaye Ndiaye
Director General
Institut supérieur africain pour le
développement de l'entreprise
BP 3827
Dakar
Tel: (221) 222 266
Fax: (221) 218 010

Mamadou Mademba Ndiaye (R)
Director
Cellule d'appui à l'environnement
de l'entreprise
Dakar
Tel: (221) 222 752
Fax: (221) 222 773

Khoudia Kholle Ndiaye (C)
Director General
Domaine industriel de Dakar (SODIDA)
rue 14 angle Borguiba Prolongée
Dakar
Tel: (221) 241 432, 241 339
Fax: (221) 241 433

Singapore

Anton Balasuriya (C)
Executive Director
Technonet Asia
291 Serangoon Road,
#05-00 Serangoon Building
Singapore 0821
Tel: 291 2372
Fax: 292 2372

Heiko Gustav Wasch
Regional Coordinator
ZDH-TA Programme
ZDH-Technonet Asia
291 Serangoon Road,
#05-00 Serangoon Building
Singapore 0821
Tel: 291 2372
Fax: 292 2372

South Africa

Chris Darroll
Executive Director
Sunnyside Group
PO Box 1198
Johannesburg 2000
Tel: (27) 11 403-5500
Fax: (27) 11 339-3909

Claudia Manning (R)
Researcher
Industrial Strategy Project
4, Crown Street, Observatory
Cape Town
Cape Town
Tel: (27) 21 476033, 21 448-3288
Fax: (27) 21 476079

David Moshapalo
Sunnyside Group
PO Box 1198
Johannesburg 2000
Tel: (27) 11 403-5500
Fax: (27) 11 339-3909

Teddy Mtshali
Director
Entrepreneurial Development
(Southern Africa)
Private Box 38140
Booysens 2016
Tel: (27) 11 496-1638
Fax: (27) 11 496-1270

Louise Tager
Executive Director
Law Review Project
PO Box 47390
Parklands 2121
Johannesburg
Tel: (27) 11 728 4954
Fax: (27) 11 484 3396

Sweden

Lars Berggren
Deputy Director
Africa Department
SWEDECORP, Box 3144
S-10362 Stockholm
Tel: (46) 8 677 6600
Fax: (46) 8 249 290

Switzerland

Bernd Balkenhol
Programme Coordinator
Enterprise and Cooperative
Development Department
ILO
4, route des Morillons
1211 Geneva 22
Tel: (41) 22 799-8171
Fax: (41) 22 799-7691

Peter Kunzi
Head
Industry, Vocational Education, and
  Urban Development Service
Swiss Development Cooperation
Eigerstrasse 73
CH-3003 Bern
Tel: (41) 31 322-3571
Fax: (41) 31 371-4767

Jurgen von Muralt (C)
Director
Enterprise and Cooperative
  Development Department   ✱
ILO
4, route des Morillons
1211 Geneva 22
Tel: (41) 22 799-8171
Fax: (41) 22 799-7691

Tanzania

Andrea Iffland
Programme Development Advisor
GTZ
c/o GTZ PO Box 1519
Dar es Salaam
Tel: (255) 51 31481
Fax: (255) 51 46454

Benjamin Mutagwaba
Project Officer
Royal Netherland Embassy
PO Box 9534
Dar es Salaam
Tel: (255) 51 30428, 51 46391,
  51 46394
Fax: (255) 51 46198

Thailand

Peng Lim Chee
Economic Affairs Officer
Development Planning Division
Economic Commission for Asia
  and the Pacific
ESCAP/UNCTC/UN Building
Rajadamnern Ave
Bangkok 10200
Tel: (66) 2 282 9161
Fax: (66) 2 282 9602

Togo

Kodzo Akemakou
Director
FUCEC — Togo
BP 3541
Lomé
Tel: (228) 22 25 74
Fax: (228) 21 78 25

Efia Assignon (R)
Faculty of Economic and
  Management Sciences
Centre for Business Administration
Benin University
BP 1515
Lomé
Tel: (228) 22 04 49
Fax: (228) 21 85 95, 25 87 84

Douato Adjémida Soedjede
Faculty of Economic and
  Management Sciences
Benin University
BP 1515
Lomé
Tel: (228) 22 04 49
Fax: (228) 21 85 95, 25 87 84

Tunisia

Hassania Chalbi
President
Association for the Advancement
  of Women Entrepreneurs
6, rue Ali Ibn Tabeb. El Menzah VI
1004 Tunis
Tel: (216) 1 238 954
Fax: (216) 1 750 658

Salah Brik Hannachi (C)
Secretary of State for International
  Cooperation and Foreign
  Investment
149, avenue de la Liberté
Tunis
Tel: (216) 1 791 366
Fax: (216) 1 799 069

United Kingdom

Richard Boulter (R)
Small Enterprise Adviser
Overseas Development
  Administration
96 Victoria Street
London
Tel: (44) 71 917-0010
Fax: (44) 71 917-0797

Mark Havers (R)
Director
Overseas Development Group
Durham University Business School
Mill Hill Lane
Durham City
Tel: (44) 91 374-2209
Fax: (44) 91 374-4765

Jacob Levitsky (R)
Independant Consultant
37 Arkwright Road
London
Tel: (44) 71 435-0816, 49 481-2219
Fax: (44) 49 481-2446

United States of America

Nancy Barry
President
Women's World Banking
8 West 40th Street
New York, NY
Tel: (212) 768-8513
Fax: (212) 768-8519

Michael Farbman
Director
Office of Small, Micro and
  Informal Enterprise
USAID
Room 214 New State
Washington, DC
Tel: (202) 663-2360
Fax: (202) 663-2708

Henry Jackelen
Deputy Manager
Private Sector Development
  Programme
UNDP
821 United Nations Plaza,
  Room TM-0905
New York, NY
Tel: (212) 697-9692
Fax: (212) 697-5058

Phyllis Kibui (R)
Regional Coordinator, Africa
Women's World Banking
8 West 40th Street 10th Floor
New York, NY
Tel: (212) 768-8513
Fax: (212) 768-8519

Donald C. Mead (R)
Professor of Agricultural Economics
Department of Economics
Michigan State University
East Lansing, MI
Tel: (517) 353-7167
Fax: (517) 336-1068

Glen Rogers
Regional Program Economist
USAID
Abidjan/Redso/WCA State
  Department
Washington, DC
Tel: (225) 41 45 28
Fax: (225) 41 35 44

Berta Romero
World Bank
Room S-4121, 1818 H Street, NW
Washington, DC
Tel: (202) 473-1070
Fax: (202) 522-3103

William F. Steel
Principal Industrial Economist
Africa Technical Department
World Bank
1818 H Street, NW
Washington, DC
Tel: (202) 473-4831
Fax: (202) 477-2978

Leila Webster (C)
Industrial Specialist
Private Sector Development Division
World Bank
Room S-4121, 1818 H Street, NW
Washington, DC
Tel: (202) 473 1070
Fax: (202) 522 3183

Robert Young
Advisor
USAID and US Department of Labor
USAID/AFR/ARTS/GA (2744 NS)
Washington, DC
Tel: (703) 235-4451
Fax: (703) 235-4466, 235-5058,
235-5454

Uganda

Ephraim Kamuntu (C)
Chairman/Managing Director
Nile Bank
PO Box 2834
Kampala
Tel: (256) 41 231 904
Fax: (256) 41 257 779

Mary Maitum (C)
Vice Chairperson
Uganda Women's Finance
and Credit Trust
PO Box 6972
Kampala
Tel: (256) 41 241 275
Fax: (256) 41 233 956

Justin Zake (R)
Commissioner for Management
Services
Uganda Revenue Authority
PO Box 7279
Kampala
Tel: (256) 41 221 730
Fax: (256) 41 221 778

Zimbabwe

Edgar Chigudu (C)
National Economic Planning
Commission
Office of the President and Cabinet
Private Bag 7700
Causeway, Harare

Strive Masiyiwa
Chief Executive Officer
RETROFIT
Suite 22 East Wing
1 Union Ave PO Box 1348
Harare
Tel: (263) 4 794 716, 4 726 764
Fax: (263) 4 794 718

Enoch Moyo
Economist
Friedrich Naumann Foundation
1 Phillips Avenue
Belgravia, Harare
Tel: (263) 4 793 445
Fax: (263) 4 793 446

J.T. Muzamani
Dean
Faculty of Commerce
University of Zimbabwe
Harare

APPENDIX 2.
THE COMMITTEE OF DONOR AGENCIES FOR SMALL ENTERPRISE DEVELOPMENT

Established in 1979, the objective of the Committee of Donor Agencies for Small Enterprise Development is to promote small enterprise in developing countries by exchanging information on programs of participating agencies, by sharing experience and lessons learned in the implementation of projects, and by coordinating efforts in these fields. The members of the Committee are listed below (those agencies indicated with an asterisk [*] provided funding for the conference presented in this book).

African Development Bank*

Asian Development Bank

Austrian Federal Chancellery, Department of Development Cooperation

Belgian Administration for Development Cooperation

Caisse française de développement

Canadian International Development Agency*

Danish International Development Agency

European Bank for Reconstruction and Development

European Commission*

Export–Import Bank of Japan

Federal Ministry for Economic Cooperation and Development, Germany*

Finnish International Development Agency*

Food and Agriculture Organization of the United Nations

Ford Foundation*

German Agency for Technical Cooperation*

Inter-American Development Bank*

International Development Research Centre*

International Fund for Agricultural Development

International Labour Office*

Japan International Cooperation Agency

Kreditanstalt fur Wiederaufbau, Germany

Ministry of Foreign Affairs, Italy

Ministry of Foreign Affairs, Netherlands*

Norwegian Agency for Development Cooperation*

Organisation for Economic Co-operation and Development
(OECD)

Overseas Development Administration, United Kingdom*

Overseas Economic Cooperation Fund, Japan

SWEDECORP, Sweden*

Swiss Development Cooperation*

United Nations Conference on Trade and Development

United Nations Development Fund for Women*

United Nations Development Programme

United Nations Industrial Development Organization*

United Nations Secretariat

United States Agency for International Development*

World Bank*

APPENDIX 3.
ACRONYMS AND ABBREVIATIONS

ADB African Development Bank

AFVP Association française des vonlontaires du progrès [French Association of Volunteers for Progress]

ASCE Association sénégalaise des créateurs d'entreprises [Senegalese Association of Enterprise Creators]

AUPELF–UREF Association des universités partiellement ou entière-ment de langue française – Université des réseaux d'expression française [Association of Partially or Entirely French Language Universities – University of Francophone Networks]

BAT British American Tobacco Co. Ltd

BCEAO Banque central des États de l'Afrique de l'Ouest [Central Bank of the West African States]

BCFA Bauchi Cooperative Financing Agency

BESO British Executive Service Overseas

B-MAP Botswana Management Assistance Programme

BOCCIM Botswana Confederation of Commerce, Industry and Manpower

BOG Bank of Ghana

CAPEN Centre d'assistance à la promotion de l'entreprise nationale [National Enterprise Promotion Assistance Centre]

CCAI Chambre de commerce d'agriculture et d'industrie de Dakar [Chamber of Commerce for Agriculture and Industry of Dakar]

CCCE Caisse centrale de co-opération économique [Central Bank for Economic Cooperation]

CCFD	Comité catholique contre la faim et pour le développement [Catholic Committee Against Hunger and for Development]
CEDEAO	Communauté économique des États d'Afrique de l'Ouest [Economic Community of West African States]
CENTRE	Creation of Enterprise and Promotion of Entrepreneurship
CEPE	Création d'entreprises et développement de la petite entreprise [Program for Enterprise Creation and Small Business Development]
CEPEPE	Centre for the Promotion of Employment and Small and Medium Enterprise
CESAG	Centre africain d'études supérieures en gestion [African Centre for Advanced Management Studies]
CIDA	Canadian International Development Agency
CKD	completely knocked down
CNP	Conseil national du patronat [National Employers' Council]
CZI	Confederation of Zimbabwean Industries
DFI	development finance institution
DUBS	Durham University Business School
EDSA	Entrepreneurial Development (Southern Africa)
EEC	European Economic Community
EPF	Economic Promotion Fund
FES	Friedrich Ebert Stiftung
FGCEI	Fonds de garantie des crédits aux entreprises ivoiriennes [Credit Guarantee Fund for Côte d'Ivoire Enterprises]
FGCET	Fonds de garantie des crédits aux entreprises togolaises [Credit Guarantee Fund for Togolese Enterprises]
FIDI	Fonds ivoirien de développement et d'investissement [Côte d'Ivoire Fund for Development and Investment]
FNI	Fonds national d'investissement [National Investment Fund]
FOSIS	Fund for Solidarity and Social Investment

FPPS	Fonds de participation aux prestations de services [Equity Fund for Loan Services]
FUSMED	Fund for Small and Medium Enterprises Development
GDP	gross domestic product
GEMINI	Growth and Equity through Microenterprise Investments and Institutions
GMK	General Motors Kenya Ltd
GRATIS	Ghana Regional and Appropriate Industrial Service
GTZ	German Agency for Technical Cooperation
HPC	Horticultural Promotion Council
IBDC	Indigenous Business Development Centre
ICDC	Industrial and Commercial Development Corporation
IDA	International Development Association
IDM	Investissement–Développement en Mauritainie [Investment–Development in Mauritania]
IDRC	International Development Research Centre
IDS	Institute of Development Studies
ILO	International Labour Office
IMF	International Monetary Fund
JLBS	Joint Loan Boards Scheme
KCB	Kenya Commercial Bank
Kfw	Kreditanstalt für Wiederaufbau
KIE	Kenya Industrial Estates
KIE/ISP	Kenya Industrial Estates/Informal Sector Project
KIST	Korea Institute of Science and Technology
K-MAP	Kenya Management Assistance Programme
K-REP	Kenya Rural Enterprise Program
KSPX	Kenya Sub-Contracting and Partnership Exchange
KWFT	Kenya Women's Finance Trust
LRTF	legal, regulatory, and tax framework
LSE	large-scale enterprise

MASU	Mutual Assistance Susu Ltd
MBA	Master's Degree in Business Administration
MCGS	Mutualist Credit Guarantee Scheme
MEDI	Malawian Entrepreneurs Development Institute
MGA	mutualist guarantee association
MSME	micro-, small-, and medium-scale enterprises
MTTAT	Ministry of Technical Training and Applied Technology
MUSOTAL	Mutuelle de solidarité des tontiniers ambulants de Lomé [Lomé Itinerant Bankers' Mutual Solidarity Fund]
NBSSI	National Board for Small-Scale Industries
NCCK	National Council of Churches of Kenya
NEF	National Economic Forum
NERFUND	National Economic Reconstruction Fund
NGO	nongovernmental organization
NIF	National Investment Fund
NSBAG	National Small Business Advisory Group
NVTI	National Vocational Training Institute
ODA	Overseas Development Administration
OECD	Organisation for Economic Co-operation and Development
OPEI	Office de promotion de l'enterprise ivorienne [Office for the Promotion of Côte d'Ivoire Enterprise]
PAMSCAD	Programme of Action for Mitigating the Social Costs of Adjustment
PAYE	pay as you earn
PBN	People's Bank of Nigeria
PEDP	Private Entreprise Development Project
PNCI	Programme national d'assistance aux commerçants ivoriens [National Assistance Program for Côte d'Ivoire Merchants]
PPEP	Projet de promotion de l'entreprise privée [Private Enterprise Promotion Project]
PVO	private voluntary organization
R&D	research and development

ROSCA	rotating savings and credit association
RPE	Rural Private Enterprise
RPED	Regional Program on Enterprise Development
SA	société anonyme [public company]
SBC	small business centre
SECA	Small Enterprise Credit Association
SED	small-enterprise development
SEDCO	Small Enterprise Development Corporation
SEFCO	Small Enterprise Finance Company
SIDI	Société d'investissement et de développement international [International Investment and Development Corporation]
SIDO	Small Industries Development Organization
S&L	savings and loans
SME	small and medium-size enterprise
SMI	small and medium-size industry
SMIDO	Small and Medium Industries Development Organization
SNI	Société nationale d'investissement [National Investment Corporation]
SSE	small-scale enterprise
SSG	Sunnyside Group
S&T	science and technology
TCC	Technology Consultancy Centre
TIN	taxpayer identification number
TNC	transnational corporation
UMA	Uganda Manufacturers Association
UNCCI	Uganda National Chamber of Commerce and Industry
UNDP	United Nations Development Programme
UNIDO	United Nations Industrial Development Organization
UNIFEM	United Nations Development Fund for Women
UREF	Université des réseaux d'expression française
USAID	United States Agency for International Development

USSIA   Uganda Small Scale Industries Association

VAT   value-added tax
VTI   Vocational Training Institute

WADB   West African Development Bank
WAMU   West African Monetary Union
WWB   Women's World Banking
WWBG   Women's World Banking (Ghana)

ZANU   Zimbabwe African People's Union
ZNCC   Zimbabwe National Chambers of Commerce
ZOPP   aim-oriented project planning

BIBLIOGRAPHY

ADB (African Development Bank). 1993. The Networker, Enterprise Network Bulletin, 1(4).

BCEAO (Banque centrale des États de l'Afrique de l'Ouest). 1989. La nouvelle politique de la monnaie et de crédit. BCEAO, Dakar, Senegal.

───── 1992. L'Avenir des banques de développement et le financement du développement. Paper presented at a seminar of the Union africaine de management des banques pour le développement, 22–23 October 1992, Brazzaville, Congo. BCEAO, Dakar, Senegal.

Becattini, G. 1990. The Marshallian industrial district as a social economic notion. In Pyke F.; Becattini, G.; Sengenberger, W., ed., Industrial districts and inter-firm cooperation in Italy. International Institute for Labour Studies, Geneva, Switzerland.

Bekolo-Ebe, B.; Bilongo, R. 1988. Comportement des gains et structure des taux d'intérêt dans les tontines : étude de quelques cas. In Hénault, G.; M'Rabet, R., ed., L'entrepreneuriat en Afrique francophone : culture, financement et développement. Université francophone, Paris, France. pp. 107–113.

Berg, E., coord. 1981. Accelerated development in sub-Saharan Africa: indicative action plan. World Bank, Washington, DC, USA.

Biermann, W.; Reinhart, K. 1980. The settler mode of production: the Rhodesian case. Review of African Political Economy, 18, 106–116.

Brasch, J.J. 1978. Export management companies. Journal of International Business Studies, 1978 (Spring/Summer), 59–71.

Brusco, S. 1986. Small firms and industrial districts: the experience of Italy. In Keeble, D.; Wever, E., ed., New firms and regional development in Europe. Croom Helm, London, UK.

CCAI-Dakar (Chambre de commerce d'agriculture et d'industrie de Dakar). 1992. Conditions d'accès au financement du Fonds de promotion économique/BAD. CCAI-Dakar, Dakar, Senegal. Publication No. 10 (Apr.).

Chambre de commerce. 1990. Annuaire des entreprises. Chambre de commerce, d'industrie et d'artisanat du Burkina Faso, Ouagadougou, Burkina Faso.

Chidzawo, W. 1990. The markets for Zimbabwe floriculture products in the Netherlands and the Federal Republic of Germany. Prodec, Market Research Report, 1/90.

Chusimir, L.H. 1988. Entrepreneurship and MBA degrees: how well do they know each other? Journal of Small Business Management, 1988, 71–74.

Cloutier, A.G. 1973. Profil sélectif d'entrepreneurs exploitant des entreprises à succès au Québec. Faculty of Administration, Université Laval, Sainte-Foy, QC, Canada. MA thesis.

CNP (Conseil national du patronat). 1991. Mémorandum du secteur privé. CNP, Lomé, Togo.

Commonwealth Secretariat. 1991. Entrepreneurship and small enterprise development: policies and strategies. Commonwealth Secretariat, London, UK.

Daniels, L.; Ngwira, A. 1993. Results of a nationwide survey on micro, small, and medium enterprises in Malawi. GEMINI Technical Report, No. 53.

de Soto, H. 1989. The other path: the invisible revolution in the Third World. Harper & Row, New York, NY, USA.

Deeks, J. 1976. The small firm owner–manager. Praeger, New York, NY, USA.

Dijkman, H.; van Dijk, M.P. 1993. Female entrepreneurs in the informal sector of Ouagadougou. Development Policy Review, 11(3), 273–288.

EEC (European Economic Community). 1991. Étude et propositions pour le développement de l'initiative privée au Togo et pour l'émergence de nouveaux entrepreneurs. A study carried for the EEC by Eurexcel Associés, a private enterprise of Donnet, McKenzie, Sene, Assignon and Badohou (Lomé, Togo). EEC, Brussels, Belgium.

Ekpenyong, D.B. 1991. Small and medium-scale enterprises development in Nigeria: their characteristics, problems and sources of finance. AERC, Nairobi, Kenya. Research Paper.

―――― 1992. Relevance of Bangladesh Grameen Bank experience for Nigerian small business financing: a case study of the People's Bank of Nigeria. Journal of Financial Management and Analysis (Bombay, India), 1992.

Gaidzanwa, R. 1992. The ideology of domesticity and the struggle of women workers: the case of Zimbabwe. Institute of Social Studies, The Hague, Netherlands. Working Paper No. 16.

Gasse, Y.; Bouchard, M.; d'Amours, A.; Ndiaye, A. 1992. Création d'entreprises en Afrique. Fisher Presses, Québec, QC, Canada.

Ghana, Republic of. 1984. 1984 Population census of Ghana: demographic and economic characteristics. Total country. Ghana Publishing Corporation, Accra, Ghana.

Gibb, A.A.; Manu, G. 1989. Design of extension and related support services for small scale enterprise development. International Small Business Journal, 8(3).

GTZ (German Agency for Technical Cooperation). 1992. ZOPP in brief. GTZ, Eschborn, Germany.

Helmsing, A.H.J.; Kolstee, T., ed. 1993. Small enterprise and changing policies: structural adjustment, financial policy and assistance programmes in Africa. Intermediate Technology Publications, London, UK.

Hénault, G.; M'Rabet, R., ed. 1990. L'entrepreneuriat en Afrique francophone : culture, financement et développement. Universités francophones, Paris, France.

Henri, A.; Tchente, G.H.; Guillerme-Dreumegard, P. 1991. Tontines et banques au Cameroun. Éditions Karthala, Paris, France.

Hirsch, R.D.; Candida, G.B. 1985. The woman entrepreneur: starting, financing and managing a successful new business. Lexington Books, Lexington, MA, USA.

ILO (International Labour Office). 1972. Employment, incomes and equality: a strategy for increasing productive employment in Kenya. ILO, Geneva, Switzerland.

——— 1993. Entrepreneurship and small enterprise development in urban and rural sectors. Director General's Report to the 8th Regional African Conference. ILO, Geneva, Switzerland.

Imani Development (Pvt) Ltd. 1993. Government regulations and the cost of compliance for small food processing industries in Zimbabwe. Environment and Development Activities, Harare, Zimbabwe.

Jackelen, H.; Rhyne, E. 1991. Toward a more market- oriented approach to credit and savings and for the poor. Small Enterprise Development, 2(4), 4–20.

Joumard, I.; Liedholm, C.; Mead, D. 1992. The impact of laws and regulations on micro and small enterprises in Niger and Swaziland. OECD Development Centre, Paris, France. Technical Paper No. 77.

Kaplinsky, R. 1991. From mass production to flexible specialization: a case study from a semi-industrialized economy. IDS Publications, Sussex, UK. Discussion Paper No. 295.

Kenya, Government of. 1986. Economic management for renewed growth. Economic Survey of Kenya, Nairobi, Kenya. Sessional Paper No. 1/1986.

——— 1989a. National development plan for the period 1989 to 1993. Government Printers, Nairobi, Kenya.

——— 1989b. A strategy for small enterprise development in Kenya: towards the year 2000. Government Printers, Nairobi, Kenya.

———— 1992. Small-scale and *jua kali* enterprise development in Kenya. Economic Survey of Kenya, Nairobi, Kenya. Sessional Paper No. 2/1992.

Kilby, P. 1988. Breaking the entrepreneurial bottleneck in late-developing countries: is there a useful role for government? Journal of Development Planning, 18, 221–249.

Kirkpatrick, D.L. 1979. Techniques for evaluating training programs. Training and Development Journal, 32(6), 78–92.

———— 1984. Techniques for evaluating training programs. Training and Development Journal, 32(9), 6–9.

Kogut, B. 1988. Joint ventures: theoretical and empirical perspectives. Strategic Management Journal, 9(d), 319–332.

Lelart, M. 1993. Tontine, innovation et développement. *In* Ponson, B.; Schaan, J.L., ed., L'esprit d'entreprises UREF : aspects manageriaux dans le monde francophone. Éditions AUPELF–UREF, John Libbey Eurotext, Paris, France.

Lelart, M.; Gnassounou, S. 1990. Tontines et tontiniers sur les marchés béninois : le marché Saint Michel de Cotonou. *In* Lelart, M., La tontine. Éditions John Libbey Eurotext, Paris, France.

Liedholm, C.; McPherson, M. 1991. Small-scale enterprises in Mamelodi and Kwazakhele townships, South Africa: survey findings. GEMINI Technical Report 16.

Liedholm, C.; Mead, D. 1993. The structure and growth of microenterprises in southern and eastern Africa: evidence from recent surveys. GEMINI Working Paper 36.

Malkamaki, M.; Aleke-Dondo, C.; Muriithia, N. 1991. Small Enterprise Development Policy Project and Creation of Enterprise and Promotion of Entrepreneurship (CENTRE) Project: report of the evaluation mission. United Nations Development Programme, New York, NY, USA.

McLelland, D. 1961. The achieving society. The Free Press, New York, NY, USA.

Mead, D.C.; Mukwenha, H.; Reed, L. 1993. Growth and transformation among small enterprises in Zimbabwe. GEMINI Working Paper.

Mensah, S., ed. 1994. African capital markets conference: conference report. School of Management, University of Michigan–Flint, Flint, MI, USA.

Mutua, A.K. 1992. The change from a traditional integrated method to a financial systems approach. Kenya Rural Enterprise Programme, Nairobi, Kenya. Occasional Paper 19.

Mutua, A.K.; Aleke-Dondo, C. 1991. Informal financial markets in Kenya. Kenya Rural Enterprise Programme, Nairobi, Kenya. Research Paper 4.

OAU (Organization of African Unity). 1980. Action plan for implementation of the Monrovia strategy for African economic development, adopted by the second extraordinary session of the Summit Conference of Heads of State and Governments, dedicated to economic issues and meeting in Lagos, Nigeria, 28–29 April 1980. OAU, Addis Ababa, Ethiopia.

OECD (Organisation for Economic Co-operation and Development). 1964. Export marketing groups for small and medium-sized firms. OECD, Paris, France.

―――― 1990. Promouvoir le secteur privé dans les pays en développment. OECD, Paris, France.

―――― 1994. The private sector in West Africa: facing the challenge. Proceedings of the Regional Conference at Accra, Ghana, 12–15 Nov. 1993. OECD-Sahel Club, Paris, France.

Osoba, A.M. 1986. Towards the development of small-scale industries in Nigeria. Nigeria Institute of Social and Economic Research, Ibadan, Nigeria.

Pate, J.L. 1969. JV Activity, 1960–1968. Federal Reserve Bank of Cleveland, Cleveland, OH, USA. Economic Review 16–23.

Poire, M.J.; Sabel, C. 1984. The second industrial divide. Basic Books, New York, NY, USA.

Ponson, B.; Schaan, J.L., ed. 1992. L'esprit d'entreprise : aspects managériaux dans le monde francophone. Universités francophones, Paris, France.

Rabino, S. 1983. Webb-Pomerene and the construction industry. California Management Review, 25(2), 21–33.

Robidoux, J.; Garnier, G. 1973. Facteurs de succès et faiblesses des PME manufacturières au Québec, spécialement des entreprises utilisant des techniques de production avancées. Faculty of Administration, Université de Sherbrooke, Sherbrooke, QC, Canada.

Ronsdadt, R.C. 1984. Entrepreneurship. Lord Publishing Co., Dover, MA, USA.

Rosson, P.; Blunden, R. 1985. Northumberland Seafoods Limited: case study. Centre for International Business Studies, Dalhousie University, Halifax, NS, Canada.

Sato, Y. 1989. Small business in Japan: a historical perspective. Small Business Economics, 1, 121–129.

Savitt, R. 1977. Consortium marketing for small business: Canada and eastern Europe. Journal of the Academy of Marketing Science, 5 (special issue), 115–118.

Sexton, D.L.; Bowman, N.B. 1984. Entrepreneurship education: suggestions for increasing effectiveness. Journal of Small Business Management, 22(2), 18–25.

SNI (Société nationale d'investissement). 1980. Fonds de garantie des crédits aux entreprises : règlement intérieur. SNI, Lomé, Togo.

Soedjede, D. 1987. Étude sur les possibilités d'utilisation du crédit en milieu rural au Togo. Financement ADF–USA, Lomé, Togo.

———— 1990a. L'épargne et le crédit non structurés au Togo. *In* Lelart, M., La tontine. Éditions John Libbey Eurotext, Paris, France. pp. 203–237.

———— 1990b. Politique de financement de l'entrepreneuriat au Togo. *In* Hénault, G., M'Rabet, R. L'entrepreneuriat en Afrique francophone : culture, financement et développement. Universités francophones, Paris, France.

———— 1990c. L'épargne et le crédit informels au Togo: la tontine financière sans enchères. Financement de l'entrepreneuriat et mobilisation de l'épargne, AUPELF–UREF, Paris, France. Note de recherche No. 90-10.

———— 1992. Mécanisme de collecte de l'épargne et de financement de l'entrepreneuriat informel et formel par les banquiers ambulants au Togo. Pour le compte de l'IRAM avec la participation de SAFECO, Lomé, Togo. 119 pp.

———— 1993a. L'Initiative privée et le financement des activités des femmes du grand marché de Lomé. *In* Ponson, B.; Schaan, J.L. L'esprit d'entreprises : aspects manageriaux dans le monde francophone. Éditions AUPELF–UREF, John Libbey Eurotext, Paris, France. pp. 293–304.

———— 1993b. Initiative privée et expériences des femmes banquiers ambulants au Togo. Paper presented at the 3rd Scientific Days of the AUPELF–UREF Network, Cotonou, Benin, 31 March–2 April 1993. Éditions AUPELF–UREF, John Libbey Eurotext, Paris, France.

———— 1994. Étude de faisabilité pour le renforcement du mécanisme de collecte de l'épargne et de crédit d'une coopérative de banquiers ambulants de Cotonou: cas de convergence 2000. Financement ADF–USA, Lomé, Togo.

———— 1995a. Le rôle du banquier ambulant dans la collecte de l'épargne et dans le financement de l'entrepreneuriat au Togo. Paper presented at the 2nd Scientific Days of the AUPELF–UREF Network, Ottawa, ON, 19–20 September 1991. Épargne sans frontière, Paris, France. In press.

———— 1995b. Les Banquiers ambulants de Lomé et leurs activités financières. L'annale de l'Université du Bénin, Lomé, Togo. In press.

Stearns, K.; Otero, M., ed. 1990. The critical connection: governments, private institutions and the informal sector. Accion International, Washington, DC, USA. Monograph Series No. 5.

Stenburg, T. 1982. System co-operation: a possibility for Swedish industry. Department of Business Administration, University of Göteborg, Göteborg, Sweden.

Sverrisson, A. 1992. Flexible specialization and woodworking enterprises in Kenya and Zimbabwe. Institute of Development Studies, University of Sussex, Falmer, Brighton, UK. IDS Bulletin, 23(3).

Tager, L. 1993. Deregulation of the economy. Paper presented at the Seminar on Small Business, Bulawayo, Zimbabwe, 2 November 1993. National Small Business Advisory Group, Harare, Zimbabwe.

Togo, Goverment of. 1989. Code des investissements du Togo. Government Printers, Lomé, Togo.

Togo Ministry of Economy and Finance. 1983. Loi 83/22 portant Code des impôts du Togo. Ministry of Economy and Finance, Lomé, Togo.

Togo Ministry of Planning and Land Development. 1991. Direction de la statistique : annuaire des entreprises du Togo, année 1990/91. Ministry of Planning and Land Development, Lomé, Togo.

Tomecko, J.; Aleke-Dondo, C. 1992. Improving the growth potential of the small scale and informal sector. Kenya Rural Enterprise Programme, Nairobi, Kenya.

Uganda Minister of Finance and Economic Planning. 1993a. Budget speech delivered at the meeting of the National Resistance Council at the International Conference Centre on Friday, 25th June 1993. The Uganda Printing and Publishing Corporation, Entebbe, Uganda.

———— 1993b. Background to the budget 1993–1994: economic performance 1992–93 and prospects for 1993–94. The Uganda Printing and Publishing Corporation, Entebbe, Uganda.

UNIDO (United Nations Industrial Development Organization). 1989. Burkina Faso: industrial profile. UNIDO, Vienna, Austria.

UNDP (United Nations Development Programme). 1992. Human development report. Oxford University Press, New York, NY, USA.

USAID (United States Agency for International Development). 1990. Possibilités et contraintes d'implantation d'une entreprise au Togo. USAID, Lomé, Togo.

USSIA (Uganda Small Scale Industries Association) and the Friedrich Ebert Foundation. 1992. Policy statement on taxation. USSIA, Kampala, Uganda.

van de Ven, A.H. 1976. On the nature, formation and maintenance of relations among organizations. Academy of Management Review, 7 (October), 24–36.

van Dijk, M.P. 1986. Burkina Faso; le secteur informel de Ouagadougou. L'Harmattan, Paris, France.

——— 1991. Institutional constraints for micro-enterprise development. *In* H. Elsenhans, H.; Fuhr, H., ed., Administrations and
industrial development. National Book Organisation, New
Delhi, India.

——— 1992a. How relevant is flexible specialisation in Burkina Faso's
informal sector and the formal manufacturing sector? Institute of Development Studies, University of Sussex, Falmer,
Brighton, UK. IDS Bulletin, 23(3).

——— 1992b. Methodological problems of informal sector research,
with results of a follow-up study in Ouagadougou, Burkina
Faso. *In* Reichert, C.; Scheuch, E.K.; Seibel, H.D., ed.,
Empirische sozialforschung uber entwicklungslander, metho-
denprobleme und praxisbezug. Breitenbach, Saarbrucken,
Germany.

——— 1992c. Strengthening the private sector: World Bank's experience with informal sector development in Burkina Faso,
1976–91. *In* The practice of institutional development. Euro-
consult, Arnhem, Netherlands.

——— 1992d. The importance of flexible specialisation, new competi-
tion and industrial districts for the modern industrial sector in
Burkina. Paper presented at a workshop of the EADI Working
Group on Industrialization in the Third World. European
Association of Development Research and Training Institutes,
Lund, Sweden.

——— 1993. Lessons from changes in the informal sector in
Ouagadougou, 1976 to 1991. Goethe University, Frankfurt,
Germany.

Vesper, K.H. 1982. Research on education for entrepreneurship. *In*
Encyclopedia of entrepreneurship. Prentice-Hall, New York,
NY, USA. pp. 321–343.

Welch, L.S.; Joynt, P. 1984. Grouping for export: an effective solution?
In Rosson, P.J.; Reid, S.D., ed., Managing export entry and
expansion: concepts and practices. Praeger, New York, NY,
USA. pp. 55–70.

——— 1987. International small enterprise review: Scandinavia: developments in the promotion of small business internationalisa-
tion. Management Forum, 10 (June), 52–59.

World Bank. 1989a. Sub-Saharan Africa: from crisis to sustainable
development. World Bank, Washington, DC, USA. Long-Term
Prospective Study.

——— 1989b. Burkina Faso. World Bank, Washington, DC, USA. Economic memorandum.

——— 1992. Development and the environment: world development
report 1992. Oxford University Press, New York, NY, USA.

——— 1993. Africa can compete. Presented at Regional Program on Enterprise Developmant (RPED) Seminar, November 1993. World Bank, New York, NY, USA.

Young, R.C. 1993. Policy biases, small enterprises and development. Small Enterprise Development, 4(1), 4–15.

Zeral, D. 1990. Les restructurations bancaires en zone franc. *In* La recherche d'une meilleure productivité pour les banques africaines. ITB/CIFPB, Paris, France.

Zimbabwe, Government of. 1989. Zimbabwe: a framework for investment 1990–1995. Government Printers, Harare, Zimbabwe.